America 3.0

James C. Bennett · Michael J. Lotus

# AMERICA 3.0

Rebooting American Prosperity in the 21st Century – Why America's Greatest Days Are Yet to Come

ENCOUNTER BOOKS

NEW YORK · LONDON

First American edition published in 2013 by Encounter Books, an activity of Encounter for Culture and Education, Inc., a nonprofit, tax exempt corporation.

Encounter Books website address: *www.encounterbooks.com*

Manufactured in the United States and printed on acid-free paper. The paper used in this publication meets the minimum requirements of ANSI/NISO Z39.48–1992 (R 1997) (*Permanence of Paper*).

FIRST AMERICAN EDITION


LIBRARY OF CONGRESS CATALOGING-IN-PUBLICATION DATA

Bennett, James C., 1948–
America 3.0 : rebooting American prosperity in the 21st century : why America's greatest days are yet to come / James C. Bennett, Michael J. Lotus.
pages    cm
Includes bibliographical references and index.
ISBN 978-1-59403-643-9 (hardcover : alk. paper)
ISBN 978-1-59403-656-9 (ebook)
1. United States—Economic conditions—20th century. 2. United States—Economic conditions—21st century. 3. United States—Economic policy—21st century. 4. Families—United States—History. I. Lotus, Michael J., 1963– II. Title.
HC106.82.B46 2013
330.973—dc23
2012048969

# CONTENTS

To our children

*Nobody knows*
*what kind of trouble we're in.*
*Nobody seems to think*
*it all might happen again.*

GRAM PARSONS
"One Hundred Years From Now" (1968)

# Foreword
## America Reinvents Itself, Again

Back in the 1980s, everyone was scared of Japan, the fearsome economic competitor that was going to eat America's economic lunch. Hundreds (thousands?) of books were published on the theme of America's inevitable decline at the hands of Japanese mercantile wiles. But there was also one book, Joel Kotkin's *The Third Century: America's Resurgence in the Asian Era*, that took a different position. America, according to Kotkin, had an underappreciated advantage: Its ability to reinvent itself when presented with new challenges. (The Japanese word used by Kotkin and his coauthor, Yoriko Kishimoto, to describe this condition is "sokojikara.")

Now we're undergoing another round of fashionable doomsaying, though now China is the big foreign threat that's invoked. On the domestic front, worries revolve around excessive debt, dysfunctional educational systems, and, more generally, what Walter Russell Mead calls the failures of the "Blue Model" of centralized big-government, big-business entities shored up by high taxes and heavy regulation.

Bennett and Lotus call the Blue Model America 2.0. Built up from the early days of the past century, and hitting its peak in the postwar, post-New Deal 1950s, America 2.0 was based on centralization, technocratic/ bureaucratic oversight, and economies of scale. For those still recovering from the stress of the Depression and World War II (once, talking about the 1950s' emphasis on comfy domesticity, my grandmother said, "You have to understand – we were all just so tired by then.") this centralized model also promised stability and safety. You didn't have to be afraid. There were Top Men on the job, and there were Big Institutions ranging from the FHA to Social Security to serve as shock absorbers against the vicissitudes of the greater world.

It worked for a while. But in time, the Top Men in charge looked more like the bureaucratic wasteland referenced at the end of *Raiders of the Lost Ark*, while the Big Institutions became not only "too big to fail," but also too big – and too hidebound – to succeed, or to deliver on the promises made on their behalf by politicians. Not only are they no longer the path to the future, their failures are such that we must address them if we are even to have a future.

My favorite reference for the current decade is Stein's Law, coined by the late economist Herbert Stein: *Something that can't go on forever, won't.* The America 2.0 approach, which delivered stability and prosperity to many for decades, is now more problem than solution, as banks fail, bureaucrats flounder, and the economy fails to deliver the jobs – or the tax revenues – needed to keep the whole enterprise going. Something that can't go on forever, won't.

The old America 2.0/Blue Model is certainly failing, and there is plenty of reason to believe that the transition to something different will have plenty of bumps along the way. But as Bennett and Lotus note here, the problems of the Blue Model are all solvable – and, in what they call America 3.0, they will be solved.

I'll add just one further observation. The changes that Bennett and Lotus describe are important, but they are never total. The Jeffersonian individualism that was embodied in America 1.0 never really went away: It exists even now as a layer in our society, one that was overlaid by the America 2.0 structure but that still wields considerable power, both in national mythology and – as the constant entrepreneurial breakthroughs coming out of America's garages demonstrate – in reality as well.

Likewise, the replacement of America 2.0 with America 3.0 won't mean that all the bureaucrats will suddenly be begging in the streets, however much some Americans might wish for such an outcome. There will still be big institutions doing things that only big institutions can do. But they won't be as big, or as pervasive, or as important as they used to be.

Something that can't go on forever, won't. Because even a casual look around the American scene reveals a lot of things that can't go on forever – ranging from Social Security schemes premised on rising, not falling population; to tuition at colleges and universities that grows faster than family incomes; to government deficits that increase faster than the tax base is likely to; to a criminal justice system that has produced so many criminal laws that even judges and prosecutors can't understand them all – it's obvious that we're in for change in all sorts of areas. Bennett and Lotus's *America 3.0* provides an excellent – and hopeful – look at what's likely to come next.

GLENN HARLAN REYNOLDS
*Knoxville, Tennessee*
*March, 2013*

# Introduction
# Hope and Continuity

## REGARDING HOPE

We are optimistic about the long-term prospects for American freedom and prosperity. You should be, too.

We believe that positive change is coming, based on the historical record, and on developments underway today. We do not hold to the "doom and gloom" purveyed in much conservative and even libertarian thinking. Yes, there were good things in the past. Yes, liberty is under attack. And, yes, the current situation is dire. But, no, we are not on an inevitable road to tyranny and poverty. Predictions of the end of America are deeply mistaken.

The current politico-economic regime is falling apart. Yet the underlying strengths we enjoy are also apparent, if you look for them. The short and medium terms, maybe a decade, maybe more, are likely to be difficult. This book explains why we are confident about the future. It also offers some proposals to help get us to a better, freer, more productive life, at least for our children and grandchildren.

## REGARDING CONTINUITY AND CHANGE

To understand America's past, and more importantly its present and future, we need to impose some organizing principle on a very large mass of information and create a simplified model. In so doing we inevitably sacrifice details to try to capture the big picture. We are necessarily imposing an almost brutal oversimplification on a very complex history. But we trust our readers will indulge us, and look at the big picture we are sketching.

We have adopted the current parlance of software development, to describe by analogy the three phases of American life, as America 1.0, 2.0, and 3.0. This terminology should not be taken literally. It is merely a metaphorical shorthand.

America 1.0 was the combination of America's English cultural and institutional roots with American frontier conditions. These English roots go very deep, back to the settlement of England by Germanic tribes, who displaced the Romans, starting roughly fifteen centuries ago.

Note that the use of the word "Germanic" for these barbarian tribesmen is the accepted scholarly term. It should not be confused with the German-speaking peoples of Europe. They went down a different cultural path from the English-speaking peoples. Nor should the word "Germanic" be confused with any modern German political regime.

These Germanic conquerors, Angles, Saxons, Jutes, brought with them a particular type of family structure, which was the ultimate foundation of England's later culture, politics, law, and economic life. This type of family, in its main elements, continued on for centuries in England, and made its way with English settlers to America.

What we call America 1.0 developed during the colonial period, took off during and after the Founding, reached its peak in the early Republic, and began to fade away during the mid-nineteenth century. America 1.0 predominated from roughly 1603–1860, fought a rearguard action for another generation or two, and went into a long decline thereafter.

The Declaration of Independence and the Constitution, as well as other critically important documents of the Founding, were products of America 1.0. It was a world of individual and family-scale farms and businesses, with limited market participation, and a high degree of family and local autonomy. Travel and transport were difficult, and markets were typically local rather than regional, though there were lucrative export markets in certain commodities such as tobacco. Government power was mainly face-to-face and local, with power above that level limited both by law and plain practicability. As Alexis de Tocqueville observed in 1837, by European standards, America seemed not to have any government at all during this period.

The power sources for America 1.0 were human and animal muscle power, and some wind and water power. The breakthrough to fossil fuels and engine power had not yet happened in America 1.0.

America 1.0, the world of farms and small towns and frontier settlement, has never entirely gone away. There are still bits of it here and there. And it has never lost its grip on the American imagination. It will always be part of what we are. Many people who want to define what makes America unique think of this phase of our history as the "real America."

America 2.0 arose from the transformation of American life by adding fossil fuels and power machinery to the preexisting culture, institutions, and geography. This created an explosion of productivity, and new and widely disseminated wealth. The earliest stirrings of America 2.0 could be seen in New England towns by the early nineteenth century, where the first American factories appeared, with mills powered by water. But the major agent of change was the steam engine, powered by coal, which was later replaced by electric power and transmission. Transport was no longer by foot, horseback, or horse-drawn wagon but by coal-fired railroads, followed by street cars, and by automobiles. In a few generations, revolutionary change swept through every part of American life.

In America 2.0 we experienced a steady shift toward wage labor, increasingly for large and remote corporations, and away from individual and family self-sufficiency. This meant insecurity for families in economic downturns, which were frequent and severe in the century between the Crash of 1837 and the Crash of 1929. Even though wealth was rapidly increasing overall, the ordinary citizens of this era were at the mercy of events beyond their control, and the old methods and attitudes seemed not to be working. As a result Americans demanded help from their government, to a degree they had not needed or wanted in the past.

At the same time that more Americans were turning to government for security, the nature of government was changing. The face-to-face government of small towns and rural communities was replaced by an increasingly distant and unaccountable state. This period also saw the amazingly rapid rise of huge cities. The enormous city of Chicago was a wonder of the world, which seemed to spring out of the ground overnight. These industrial-age cities were difficult to govern, to supply, and to keep safe or clean. Nothing drawn from America's past seemed to work, and the governance of large cities remains a challenge to this day.

A negative feature of the more powerful state sector in America 2.0 was the increasing entanglement of government power and private business, and the corruption that inevitably resulted. This is another seemingly insoluble problem that we have never overcome and that haunts us to this day. In fact, this problem has become pathological in our day, and it is getting worse and worse.

The change from America 1.0 to America 2.0 was far from painless, and there were many political and economic crises throughout the transition period, roughly 1860 to 1920. Americans created a new political and economic order characterized by "big units," like big cities, big corporations, increasingly big government, and eventually big labor unions.

The political features of America 2.0 were firmly in place by the end of Franklin Roosevelt's New Deal, 1932–1940. It was also on FDR's watch that America 2.0 had its greatest success and its moment of glory: America's victory in World War II. America did not contribute the most brilliant field commanders, or the most troops under arms, or even the best quality weapons in most categories. American instead made an immense productive effort that created thousands of ships and tanks, tens of thousands of warplanes and trucks, all good enough to do the job. America fed and armed not only its own armies but those of our allies as well. Josef Stalin, no friend of American capitalism, nonetheless raised a toast at the Tehran conference in 1943 to American production, which made victory possible in the greatest of all wars.

America 2.0 institutions had immense prestige in the two decades or so following World War II. The big units, Big Government, Big Labor, and Big Business had earned the trust and respect of the American people to a degree they would never enjoy again. Nonetheless, the "big unit" approach was starting to become less effective as the postwar economy boomed. America 2.0 finally reached beyond its grasp with Lyndon Johnson's ambitious Great Society programs. Medicare, which is popular and relied on by millions of Americans, nonetheless began to face spiraling costs with no end in sight from the very beginning.

Throughout America 2.0, the expanding state periodically ran up against the grain of much of our underlying individualistic culture. Those who wanted to build a state capable of providing a communal guarantee of economic security had to adapt their programs, or at least frame their proposals, to our individualistic way of thinking. Otherwise they would not have been politically feasible. America never turned into a European-style social democracy, despite the power and the eminence of the people promoting this course, to their perpetual frustration. Presidential candidate Michael Dukakis brought a book about Swedish land-use controls to the beach on vacation. He was mocked, but he was almost certainly sincere in thinking that making America more like Europe would be good for us. But trying to make America more like Sweden, the terrestrial nirvana of Progressives, never caught on. It was always a bad fit and it was repeatedly rejected. We never wanted to go that far.

Throughout the 2.0 era America experienced a haphazard and episodic, but nonetheless continuous, expansion of government power. The ever-increasing promises of security provided by government came at ever-increasing cost. But the costs and burdens of our ever-more powerful state are outrunning their utility. New and broader promises of economic security are unsustainable from the moment they are made. Even Progressive think tanks, and some politicians, have begun to admit as much.

In recent years we have seen an increasingly dysfunctional government sector, which is crushingly expensive yet failing at many of its basic obligations. It is increasingly nosy and intrusive. It has incarcerated a huge portion of the American population, while it failed to prevent or to prosecute a fraud on a continental scale that has financially ruined millions of people. Its unfunded liabilities exceed what can ever be extracted from the economy. These ongoing failures show that our current set of institutional arrangements has run its course. Many who directly benefit from the old model will, reasonably enough, try to keep it going. Promises that something better will happen tomorrow are rarely convincing in the face of a tangible benefit today. Nonetheless, we are living in a period of crisis as the failure and ineffectiveness of the government sector of America 2.0, also known as the "Welfare State" or the "Blue Model," becomes so glaring that even its champions and current beneficiaries cannot ignore them.

America 2.0 was, in many ways, great in its day. But it is over. The technological and economic changes we foresee are already happening, or about to happen. The government sector is in a state of decay reminiscent of the Brezhnev period in the Soviet Union, with apparatchiks with no new ideas repeating the same cliches and the same failed policies, seemingly unaware that their system was doomed. The government that

Americans built to meet the needs and fears of an earlier age is now the chief impediment to our progress and to our transformation into something better.

We have a long way to go before we replace the twentieth century state and economy with their successors. It is far too early to pick an end date for America 2.0, which will only become apparent in hindsight, and probably in distant hindsight. And, much like America 1.0, some aspects of America 2.0 will linger on far into the future. Nonetheless, we are currently in the midst of a profound transition period.

The institutional "iterations" of America have each been long in developing and very slow to fade away. The lingering remnants of America 1.0 can still be found here and there. The first seeds of America 2.0 existed well over a century before it reached its peak, and it is still predominant to this day.

America 3.0 is the name we have assigned to the emerging set of institutional arrangements, political and economic, which are now coming into being to replace our currently failing legacy institutions. The beginnings of America 3.0 quietly arrived, but are not yet recognized for what they are. As the science fiction writer William Gibson wrote, "[t]he future is already here – it's just not very evenly distributed." Nonetheless, the rise of America 3.0 has been a long time in coming, and such deep trends are almost impossible to reverse.

The emerging America 3.0 will require us to refit our institutions for the post-industrial, networked, decentralized America. This new, more individualistic, more voluntarist, antibureaucratic culture will also be consistent with our deeply rooted underlying culture. We will provide a description of what this future may be like in Chapter 1.

In the meantime, we need to wrap up the 2.0 legacy state. That is the task immediately before us. Only then can we build new institutions that will serve us better in the future.

A novel feature of this book is our identification of the defining cultural element that makes us different from the rest of the world. That element is the unique American style of family life that has an unbroken history going back at least a thousand years and possibly for fifteen centuries or more. A feature of our lives we take for granted has made us what we are, and has been the continuous thread linking each of the three "versions" of America.

and what the future holds. We do not ask you to love the English of bygone centuries, but to join us in trying to understand them, to see as clearly as possible what they gave to us, to assess what the impact of that inheritance has been, and to try to look into the mists ahead, to make a guess at how our past will shape our future.

## REGARDING SOURCES

The Bibliographic Commentary appended to this book, lengthy as it is, cannot possibly be complete or conclusive. The authors have been engaged in a dialogue, almost daily, for well over ten years, regarding the topics covered in this book. Many books, many blog posts, both read by and written by the authors, many email or discussion board conversations, all contributed to the thinking, analysis, and conclusions in this book. Our cited references are generally the most important ones, but there are certainly many others.

We can truthfully say that we have not found anything that has caused us to doubt the major points made in this book. To the contrary, we have been continually astonished to find that the more facts we learn, the more coherently they all seem to fit together, and to support our model.

## REGARDING CONTEMPORARY POLITICS

The authors are extraordinarily opinionated people. They have been known to pour forth torrents of words regarding current politics, whether in person or telephone, by email or on blogs, from podiums, or barstools. However, the focus of this book is on the longer term, centuries into the past and decades into the future. Over such a large span of time our current political struggles, as engrossing as they are now, will mostly sink into history as mere noise around a discernible signal. Only the passage of time will confirm what that signal is, and whether our hopeful predictions were well grounded.

Therefore, this is the only sentence in this book that will contain the name Barack Obama.

\*　\*　\*

## REGARDING AUTHORSHIP OF THIS BOOK

None of the writers whom we reference in this book had any hand what-soever in its preparation. None of them were consulted, and none of them commented on any draft of this book prior to publication. None of them are in any way responsible for the use we make of their work, nor for any conclusions we draw, predictions we make, or proposals we offer.

# Chapter 1
# America in 2040

## AMERICA'S BEST DAYS ARE YET TO COME

We are living through a period of transformation. The last change on this scale was from the rural and agrarian society of America 1.0 to the urban and industrial society of America 2.0. We survived that earlier transition, painful though it was, and America became the wonder of the world in the industrial age. Today's political and economic regime was built for that earlier world. That world is now dying and the transition from America 2.0 to 3.0 is accelerating. Although a new world is forming, we can only make educated guesses about what it will be like. Meanwhile, institutions that once looked permanent are cracking at the foundations. It feels like a crisis because it is.

But America is more resilient than most people realize. Our culture has roots going back over many centuries of slow evolution and tenacious continuity. We have inherited an individualist culture that embraces change, and a "can do" spirit that does not give in to despondency but instead plans, works, and tries again. We have inherited from our cultural ancestors exceptional notions of freedom, work, enterprise, cooperation, association, competitiveness, and neighborliness, which we are barely aware of, but that underlie everything distinctively American. We are better equipped than most of us know to take advantage of the changes that are already underway, to turn them to our advantage, and to once again astonish the world. We will reform and rebuild our political and economic institutions to suit the free and prosperous America that is coming. The sooner we become aware of the need to reform and rebuild, and get started on that task, the better off we all will be.

## NEW MORNING

It is 2040. The oldest of the Baby Boomers have turned ninety, and there are more of them still around than anybody had expected a quarter-century before. The Social Payments Resolution Fund was still making income-maintenance payments to some of them, but most had accepted the lump-sum termination payment of 2028 during the Third Fiscal Reform, as the returns from the reviving stock markets were too good to pass up the option. A surprising number still work a bit, as antiaging medicine had kept their memories and eyesight sharper than previous generations had expected. The youngest of the Boomers, those born in 1964, were approaching their mid-seventies, and most of them were still working at something or other, although few were working full-time. However, their defined-contribution accounts, also prospering with the rising markets, had made work supplementary, rather than obligatory.

Meanwhile, the Millennials are in full stride in their fifties. They suffered unemployment and underemployment in their twenties, and now that opportunity is opening up again they are making the most of it. Tempered by hardship and enduring frustration, some have retreated into immersive virtual entertainment, which is the synthetic nirvana of the time, replacing drugs for many. But most have grasped with gusto for delayed dreams in the real world. In some ways, their frustrating young adulthood, spent with a patchwork of part-time jobs and self-employment, has trained them well for the current era. Having never known the security of a regular paycheck and the benefits of a long-term position, they never became accustomed to it, and were not traumatized as the great bulk of such positions disappeared.

Memories of the old type of employment are of no importance to the young generation born in the 2010s, as they approach their mid-twenties. Not only have they never experienced the idea of a lifetime salaried job as a normal expectation, they have not even experienced the expectation of university as a distinct phase of life before starting such a job. Of course many have attended universities, and some have actually set aside a year or two to devote primarily to taking classes and living on a university campus – some, swept up in the nostalgic revival of university-themed films, actually took classes at the campus where they resided. For most, however, learning and earning a living have been woven together from their teen years, if not earlier. Some have been earning money producing fan-based content or participating in immersive role-playing universes for cash since childhood. Without income or capital gains taxes, even small sums put away in earlier years, when their needs for market-produced goods and services were few, have added up to a lot.

The new manufacturing revolution has been instrumental in keeping material wants cheap. Additive manufacturing, computer-aided small-run subtractive manufacturing, and, recently, nanotechnology have made large classes of goods available for close to the cost of the raw materials or "feedstock" needed to produce it. A large class of peer-to-peer produced free production-control software exists, and is constantly proliferating. All one has to do is download a design to an additive manufacturing machine, pay for the feedstock, and push the button. As a result, a wide variety of goods can be made on the spot. Of course, these new techniques compete with a wide variety of for-profit produced items, usually superior in some way, or at least more fashionable. Consumer choices are virtually unlimited: antique patterns and styles reappear all the time, and new trends arise – in decoration, dinnerware, dresses, and all variety of con-sumer goods – and disappear again on a rapid cycle.

At the same time, there is a large class of handcrafters, who turn out unique, custom-designed and custom-produced clothes, furniture, and other items. With a much lower cost of living, many people are free to make things they want, and find others who want to buy them, in every possible category. Traditionally-made items are of course more costly, and are typically luxury goods, jewelry, art objects and decorations, gifts or hobby items. So many people do some kind of craft or "old style" work that everyone has some such items. Some traditional-type niche manu-facturers even survived through the transition. You can still get handmade leather biker jackets or wrought-iron coffee tables from long-established businesses.

Of course, the new production modes have not entirely banished the old ones even for purely practical uses. Many items cannot be made, or made well, by the new processes, and subtractive manufacturing is still competitive for large items, from ships down to cars. The rich wear hand-woven cloth and bespoke suits. Whoever can make a jet engine fan blade that won't disintegrate using the new production techniques will make a fortune, but no one has succeeded yet.

Beyond the few remaining old-style factories, islands of the old way of life can still be found all across America. Many of the remaining government employees still work in nine-to-five regular employment, although without the lifetime security they once enjoyed, except in a few states. Likewise, many government defense contractors still work in traditional settings, at least those that turn out warships and large aircraft. Even there only the big hulls and airframes are put together in traditional fashion, while many of the small systems are made on the spot in very high-capacity additive manufacturing machines. Even in traditional plants, almost every workstation has a machine at hand to turn out unique parts, allowing production lines to easily modify and customize products. Yet procurement reform has made it much easier for defense contractors to use small subcontractors for many functions without the large amounts of paperwork that once was involved.

A large part of the workforce is devoted to repair and maintenance of infrastructure, and they still pull up in a truck where the work needs to be done.

Large businesses still exist, including many well-known names from the days of America 2.0. Very few of these businesses have permanent workforces on the scale they once did. Instead, they are aggregations of capital and intellectual property such as patents, brands, and specialized skills. Many tasks are performed on a project basis by a network of contractors and consultants, much as movies were back in the 2010s. Some universities have survived as brands, with campuses, quads, and classes being only one product in a portfolio. Universities and businesses and government continue to collaborate on scientific research, although they have been joined by crowdsourced networks operating over the NewNet.

Surprisingly to some, the political structure in place in America by 2040 has proven to be friendly to this mosaic of old and new ways. The three successive Fiscal Reforms of 2017 through 2028 have made substantial changes to the political and financial structure of the United States. These reforms actually required fewer constitutional amendments than the Progressive era a century or more earlier. Fiscally, the Reforms stripped most of the social programs from the federal level and handed them back to the states or to multistate compacts, among the states that chose to band together and form them.

New England (minus, of course, New Hampshire) was the first to set up a multistate authority to take over their portion of federal health care system. This proved satisfactory enough to them that they ended up taking over almost the whole set of devolved federal social programs. In the end New England effectively set up a confederation within the United States, taking care of most issues once handled at the state level, and most domestic ones formerly federal. The Chairman of the New England Conference of Governors soon became an important figure in US politics. New England has chosen to continue to have an income tax, permitted under each state's traditional "police powers," as did several other East and West Coast states and multistate compacts. The federal income tax was abolished by constitutional amendment during the Reforms, reserving only a maximum 20 percent surcharge on incomes over $10 million. Competition from foreign and private currencies, including gold-backed and commodity-backed currencies, keeps the post-Reform US dollar from inflating.

The Fiscal Reforms required that any bankrupt American state needing federal assistance in reorganizing and refinancing its underfunded pension systems had to offer a referendum on dividing the state into two or (if large enough) three new states. California is one of the first to take advantage of this reform; the new states of Northern, Southern, and Eastern California each has more responsive and responsible politics than the old super-sized state.

Greater New York City (minus Staten Island) is now separate from New York State. New Yorkers' long-standing attitude of superiority is thriving along with their economy as they enthusiastically leave financial ruin in the past. The new towers arising on Manhattan celebrate the rebirth of a world-class city-state, which is once again a magnet for the young and ambitious from around the Anglosphere and beyond.

As a result of the Reforms, the United States now has 71 states, none of which has more than eight million inhabitants. These have arranged themselves into a series of state compacts, and special-purpose agreements between compacts, so that the Northeast and Great Lakes areas form a network with relatively high taxes and levels of government-supplied social services, albeit mostly at the community level. The Pacific Coastal areas comprise a similar network. The Southeast has a separate series of networks, choosing lower taxes and levels of service (but with strong church-based social service networks) and state and local ordinances reflecting religious and social conservative values.

The Plains States also have a network of compacts, although the social-values ordinances cover somewhat different topics, in different manners, and somewhat higher tax levels exist there. This area is sometimes referred to as the "Lutheran Republic," although in fact Catholics and Baptists are almost as numerous. Meanwhile the Rocky Mountain States have chosen in general a mix of low taxes and relatively permissive social values, although with a strong emphasis on personal responsibility and self-reliance. Utah, as always, is an outlier in this respect.

The Texases, as they are called now since they exercised their right to divide into five states, form their own compact. Rivalry and boasting continues about which of them is "the most Texas." The Texases still share some of their more popular features, such as their state universities.

The Southwestern states have partnered with the Texases on a massive public works project. The same super-filters, including molecular-scale sieves, that have revolutionized water purification and sewage disposal, are also capable of cheap desalination. Now that the bugs in scaling up the sieves have been worked out, it is economically feasible to desalinate virtually limitless quantities of ocean water. The Gulf Aqueduct and Desalination Authority (GADA) is constructing giant intake stations far offshore, pipeways to bring it onto land, and aqueducts to pump it to large-scale "green estates" in desert areas now being developed for housing. The project will be completed and people will be moving in within five years, and GADA should turn a profit.

Some states, like New Hampshire, remain apart and have only very limited agreements with other states on particular topics.

Cities, counties, and townships have also taken on more responsibility. The Fiscal Reforms typically forced the state governments to cut back some services, as unfunded state mandates on local governments, beyond the original functions of their charters, were declared unconstitutional in state after state. Some jurisdictions have renewed the old New England custom of allowing a portion of local taxes to be paid in personal service. Part-time township constables join volunteer firemen and auxiliary militia as means of meeting public needs. Local government is more important and responsive than it has been in centuries.

The movement of population to the far exurban fringes of metropolitan areas, and beyond, continues to accelerate. This trend was observed as early as the 1970s, when the first wave of the Time of Troubles (1963–2020) began. During that period, governments raised taxes, degraded the quality of services, and allowed public safety to decline. The migration of peoples accelerated again in the 2010s as the old institutions struggled to maintain services in the wake of the fiscal instability of the old model of government.

In addition, technological and social trends are further reshaping the American landscape. Additive manufacturing and other decentralized production techniques are ending the need for families to be near shopping malls and centralized workplaces alike. Education has been revolutionized with the growth of on-line and home learning, contract tutoring, and the proliferation of independent schools. As a result, there is now little need for families to determine the location of their home by the availability of a good public school district.

Persistent environmental and internal medical monitoring is networked to health care providers and insurance carriers. You often get a retinal text notice from monitors in your bloodstream saying you are sick before you actually feel the symptoms. Masses of depersonalized data are constantly scanned to identify medical trends and disease vectors. New flu viruses are detected, analyzed, and neutralized within hours or days of their appearance. Customized antibiotics for mutant pathogens similarly are also developed quickly. Self-administered medical care and home diagnostic and pharmaceutical systems allow home care, with advice usually via network. Medicine customized to each person's DNA and current health conditions is compiled in a machine on the bathroom counter. Strokes and heart attacks only rarely occur "out of the blue" anymore. The urgency of being near medical facilities is therefore greatly reduced with fewer surprise events.

Persistent medical monitoring has virtually eliminated the long-standing political conflict over abortion. It is now almost impossible to have an unwanted pregnancy. Morning-after pills have been superseded by "minutes-after" devices that are active in a woman's body until she deactivates them. There are no longer any abortion clinics. With viability pushed back almost to the moment of conception, social pressure to employ very early abortion methods, if any, has privatized the matter almost entirely. Surgical abortions are now considered barbaric by all but a shrinking minority of aging Boomers. Some jurisdictions still attempt to legally limit access to abortive products, but hacks are easily available and abortifacients can be made on a home medicine compiler. The moral and theological issues remain the same, and are still hotly disputed; but as a political issue, abortion has fallen off the table.

With families self-sorting by community and religion you can quickly tell by driving through an area what the cultural trend is, either by the absence of children, or by lots of them running around through the yards and leaving their toys and bicycles on the lawn, chalk drawings on the sidewalk, and self-driving cars slowing down as they become aware of children and soccer balls up ahead.

The emergence of self-driving cars as a standard means of transportation is lengthening the distance people are willing to locate from city centers, airports, and hospitals. Self-drivers controlled by networked computers are faster, encounter fewer traffic jams, and allow more productive use of the time en route. Most people no longer need to travel to a central work location every day, so the acceptable radius from home to work has increased significantly, and the total square mileage of land that is acceptable for exurban settlement has multiplied. Thus the price of raw land has dropped, making exurban migration yet more attractive. Much of America has gone from suburban to exurban, or from to exurban to semi-rural, with interspersed town centers for face-to-face activities, restaurants, sports, night clubs as well as regional airports, repair shops, craft stores, and churches.

Additive manufacturing is also transforming house construction, radically reducing construction costs. The viability of these types of homes was demonstrated as early as the late 2010s, using relatively small footprint houses and poured concrete as the additive material. Typically this process is supplemented by modularized house components, most often a mechanical service core module. During the 2020s larger and more elaborate houses were made, and a wider variety of construction materials were adapted to additive deposition. Although some hand-finishing is required in home-building, most labor is no longer spent on the bulk aspects of construction, but on custom detailing and decoration. Various green technologies, which were too expensive for retrofitting to urban or suburban houses in the 2010s, proved to be useful for bringing heat, power, and sanitation to exurban houses in the 2020s.

The big suburban houses of the pre-2007 Housing Bubble – the "McMansions" – wasted their space on pretentious features like Great Rooms intended to impress neighbors rather than provide functional space. By contrast, the houses of the Exurban Boom are designed to accommodate nuclear families that run several money-making activities from their home, with practical office and workshop space in outbuildings or wings, like the America 1.0 farms of old.

Seniors are able to stay at home, both with mechanical assistance and with many people specializing in providing elder care, or they move into modularized units easily attached to their adult children's homes. Retirement communities in Cuba, the Central Highlands of Mexico, and the Mexican border zone are becoming popular. Hypersonic intercontinental aerospace travel, until recently used only by the very wealthy or government officials, is slowly coming down in price, as aerospacelines compete for business. Low-drag supersonic flight has made medium-length journeys, such as transcontinental flights, quicker, thus making visits back and forth to visit grandma far easier.

Homes are comfortable and often attractive as the owners use imagination and creativity in adapting the basic modular and additive housing techniques. In fact, numerous shareware programs are available for the standard house-printing machines, and if you want a structure that mimics Monticello, it's readily available. Many disparate styles of house have appeared, reflecting local and individual tastes. With large lots, frequently surrounded by trees and hedges, neighbors are less likely to take offense at idiosyncratic or flamboyant houses that might jar with the generally accepted local style. An Indo-Saracenic house can sit comfortably as a neighbor to a Deco-Gothic one, because you can only see the towers or spires from the street.

Although physical privacy is easily achieved by large house lots, other kinds of privacy are at perpetual risk. With everyone living in a networked web recording everything they do, the prospect of an ultra-intrusive, all-seeing Big Brother is a perpetual hazard. The proliferation of small electric smart drones for police work, small parcel delivery, and freelance private use has greatly complicated both law enforcement and private privacy, and remains an unresolved issue. Early attempts to limit the state by specifically outlawing various intrusive actions consistently failed in practice, as the "creepy state" found workarounds. The solution came with mandatory, radical transparency of all levels of government operations, required by amendment to the US Constitution. Government petitions to keep information secret are typically refused by elected transparency boards. Federal government "black-boxing" is subject to legal challenge by state government as well as citizen petition. Volunteer networks, media, and interested businesses constantly monitor published operations of all levels of government for irregularities or abuses, and for signs of "opaque" activities. Penalties for violation include not only injunctions but criminal sentences to government personnel or others who violate transparency or privacy provisions. So far the "radical transparency" reforms appear to be working.

A major change in relations between citizen and government came about as the Reforms stripped away much of the sovereign immunity previously enjoyed by persons working for government agencies. With public officials and security personnel liable for unauthorized invasion of privacy, and SWAT teams prosecuted for negligent homicide when they break down the door to the wrong house and shoot its inhabitants, government agents became more careful. Local control of law enforcement lives on, with greater citizen involvement.

The decentralizing reforms made an originalist reading of the Second Amendment more topical again, not only by strengthening the individual right to bear arms, but in stressing the "well-regulated" part of "Well-regulated militia." As local security started to incorporate more part-time and volunteer constables and militia members, local sheriffs resumed their historical role of ensuring that these volunteers were well-trained and held closely accountable when acting in their public role. The chaotic experience of the 2010s left scars that are still not entirely healed, and the individual right to possess firearms for personal and home defense is no longer seriously questioned.

The war on drugs is long over. Effective antiaddiction vaccines have helped curb the demand side, as did the shift to a medical rather than criminal approach to serious drug abuse problems. There are still people who ruin their lives with drugs, but there is a lot less law enforcement devoted to stopping them from doing so. Drug users are penalized only when they present a public menace. America is no longer the world leader in per capita imprisonment. Prisoners are required to take educational courses via the NewNet, and are encouraged to take advantage of individualized tutoring opportunities. The results of this forced education have been mixed, at best. But at least there are fewer prisoners than their used to be.

Political decentralization and the technological drivers of the exurban expansion are reinforcing each other in an accelerating feedback cycle. Decentralization encourages the "Big Sort" as families seek out the kind of communities they want to live in, leading to greatly expanded options in work and education. This creates more demand for new housing as families shift. In parallel, new technologies and settlement patterns reduce the price of available housing. The various "sorted" communities take on a unique community flavor. Visiting relatives in other areas can sometimes cause culture shock. Downtown Chicago, booming again after its decade-long brush with Detroit-level desolation, is full of young, edgy, and childless couples living a high-tempo life. Many of them have never met anyone who has gone to church. Exurban Salt Lake City looks like stock footage of mid-twentieth century America, with a strong family focus, a child-centric community life, and religion woven into daily life as a matter of course. Some people decry this fragmenting of the culture by region and by community. But with a minimized federal government, the need for national consensus on most issues is nonexistent. Free trade and travel and investment across the country, and military security, are areas of general agreement, and other matters are left to local preference.

Food purchases dropped throughout the twentieth century as a percentage of the average family's budget. Basic clothing prices dropped dramatically in the 1990s and 2000s because of aggressive Asian production and big-box stores. By 2040 the price of decent, comfortable housing in safe neighborhoods is dropping dramatically as these revolutions continue. Between low-cost manufacturing for houses and most materials of everyday life, it is now possible to live a safe and comfortable life on a much smaller income. Middle-class respectability is more widely available than ever before. Status spending is now focused on things like handmade goods, hand-sewn clothing, verified antiques, and legacy homes built out of bricks and wood in older, closer-in suburban neighborhoods, where prices are still kept high by scarcity.

The conservative Southern and Great Plains states, and the libertarian

Mountain States, have been the first to feel the full force of these changes in housing, as they have put the fewest obstacles in their path. Unions haven't been able to stop the spread of new technology for home construction in these regions. In addition, land-use planning in the exurban belt was always weak or nonexistent. Much land is now in state hands after the federal government turned over much of the Bureau of Land Management's holdings back during the Fiscal Reform. The states in these regions were readily pressured by the public into selling it or giving it out in new, nonagricultural homestead programs. Taxation was also traditionally low in these states, enabling families to afford to move and buy sooner than elsewhere. However, as the red states demonstrated the effectiveness of these solutions, pressure also built up in the blue states, where many of the techniques have now been adopted. Eventually blue state politicians have realized that making the cost of living generally lower for ordinary people makes high taxes more tolerable, allowing the higher level of social spending their constituents demand.

Even in the red states, the drop in new housing prices has been useful in regard to taxation. True, states have faced a double whammy: decentralized livelihoods have undercut income taxation as a main source of revenue for government at the same time as decentralized manufacturing and public-domain design software for additive-manufacturing machines have undercut sales taxation. Goods and services taxes deliver a nice revenue stream on the status- and luxury-driven purchases of the richer strata, but it is now possible for people to have a perfectly comfortable and pleasant life in an additive-manufactured house on cheap land in a far exurban area, mostly using public-domain additive-manufactured products, home-gardened food, and local bartered goods (often mediated by sophisticated on-line barter matching services). Such a lifestyle actually requires very little cash expenditure on a day-to-day basis, and thus allows voluntary family and individual withdrawal from the cash economy and the tax system. The ultimate consequence is that local government now has to rely more on land taxation. But even in the case of land, which cannot be hidden from the taxing authority, the drop in land and housing cost at the exurban fringes has cushioned this blow for the self-reliant. Assessed house prices are moderate. The possibility of substituting voluntary personal services for cash taxes, where it was adopted, is now often used by such people.

America has always been a mosaic of many very different lifestyles. The America 3.0 of 2040 is no less so. For example, in many respects a government official in Boston effectively still lives in America 2.0, commuting daily by train from an inner suburb (where he owns a traditional suburban house) to his office in the city center, reading a crisp paper version of the Boston daily paper (albeit a special luxury item run off a wide-format printer at a kiosk at the station), and sending his child to good private schools where they sit in rows facing their teachers (although several of those schools had been public schools before the follow-the-child funding had become the general practice). But the same official's sister in Colorado runs several small businesses with her husband from their additive-manufactured house, located about 90 minutes from Denver International Airport by self-driven car. She is a product designer who established her early reputation with several public-domain designs. He is a crafter of handmade iron fixtures for upscale houses. He is also a local police volunteer, receiving a small salary and a substantial tax offset, but is thinking of taking the firefighter's course or becoming a medical first-responder. Their three children have chosen different school solutions: one goes to a school run by a neighborhood church which is highly traditional in method, one is enrolled in an online learning system run by the local school board, and the third a combination of high school and university courses supervised by her personal online tutors, who happen to be based in India, Mindanao, Australia, and Cincinnati.

With the switch to a points-based, national-need-driven immigration system on the Canadian and Australian model, immigration has changed substantially. After the Fiscal Reforms, welfare on the old model became less available to undocumented immigrants, while limited amnesties converted the better-assimilated among them to citizenship over time. The abolition of federal-level drug prohibition, and its replacement with a variety of state-based control systems, has severely cut back the profitability of the Latin American narco-cartels, and the Mexican state has regained effective control of the northern regions. Spurred by the successful decentralization in El Norte, the northern states of Mexico now have greater autonomy from Mexico City and are quite prosperous, drawing many Mexicans back to their homeland through the lure of greater opportunity in their own language and culture. However, their familiarity with the United States has enabled them to maintain ties in the country, and cross-border economic integration continues to accelerate, particularly in the new "free zones" along the border, which have provided a shield against Mexican government corruption while mixing American capital and Mexican labor and local knowledge.

The rest of the world is experiencing some of the same massive changes as the United States. In particular, China – once the great economic threat to American dominance – has experienced a shock as new manufacturing techniques have hollowed out many of their previous export markets. Of course China can and does install its own machines, but where is the cost advantage of having a Chinese employee push the "print" button rather than having the American consumer do so? The product still had to be shipped, and the cost of the product manufactured in the United States is lower than the cost of shipping. The initial reaction of the Chinese government was to stir up nationalistic claims against Japan and Taiwan and the disputed islands of the South China Sea in order to distract the Chinese public, but the leadership soon began to fear that the public protests would get out of hand and turn against the government. Over time the Chinese government has pursued a combination of providing more goods to the Chinese public, and concentration on export of those goods in which it has a genuine comparative advantage. This policy change has stabilized China, where experts had been predicting a complete collapse as recently as ten years ago. However, because of technological, economic, and demographic factors the rapid growth figures of China's past are long gone, leaving China faced with the question of why the Communist government, which is no longer bringing dramatic and visible success, should be tolerated. This domestic Chinese issue is still unresolved, and it appears that the country will be facing "interesting times" for the next few decades.

In 2040, the United States is still the strongest single economic and military power in the world, and several attempts to create a global coalition to replace the United States have fallen apart as the members could not maintain their unity for very long. However, the United States no longer projects its power as forcefully into every corner of the world as it did before. A light touch with a few Special Forces and advisers is often the most effective thing the US military can do; if that doesn't do the trick, usually a best available solution is then negotiated. When the heavy hammer does have to fall, for example on terrorist havens implicated in attacks on Americans, the action is substantial, memorable, and brief, with images broadcast to the world. Americans make an effort not to stay where they will be shot at regularly. They prefer to work with local governments, maintaining contacts and providing training. We also rely on clandestine observers, sometimes human but mostly machines, to monitor potential trouble spots.

NATO remains in existence, and in fact has expanded its reach into a global alliance with the addition of Japan, Australia, and others. It is now focused on global maritime patrol and protecting the freedom of the seas, a task in which the US Navy is still the lead player. However, the United States maintains only a skeleton force in Europe, with facilities for rapid reinforcement if NATO ever has to repel an invasion (although that does not seem likely given the demographic implosion in Russia).

With the rapid development of new energy resources in North America, Europe, Australia, and Latin America, the Mideast is much less important to the West than it used to be. Middle Eastern regimes are mostly left to their own problems, as many of the states established after the First World War by the victorious powers have finally fallen apart into smaller statelets based on sect and tribe. Israel, rendered more independent by its new energy resources, and its rapid and avid grasp of new technology, is booming, but is still not at peace with its neighbors. However, it is not seriously at war either, as the three would-be claimants to the title of Palestinian state merely joined the collection of occasionally warring statelets that now fill the void between the four actual nations in the area (Israel, Egypt, Turkey, and Iran).

The European Union staggers on in a vestigial form, now effectively neutralized by the terminal consequences of its demographic decline. Distributed manufacturing and other new technologies, combined with cheap local energy supplies from Poland, Britain, and Ireland, have allowed the local economies to make do with a series of economic patch-fixes. But the more ambitious, future-oriented young people on the Continent tend to choose emigration to English-speaking nations, where it is easier to establish a business and to raise a family. Although the euro was abandoned years ago as a truly common currency, its namesake remains as the highly inflated currency for the Mediterranean countries, while the northern nations, still economically more robust, use the revived "Nordmark" these days.

Britain left the European Union in 2020, choosing to establish a closer union with Canada, Australia, and New Zealand. All of the English-speaking countries are now increasingly integrated with the USA as members of NAFTA, and sharing in the new prosperity of the revived North America. In fact, other English-speaking countries have often taken the initiative in lowering taxes, balancing their economies, and decentralizing power. This has helped put pressure on the United States to follow suit, as millions of Americans began to find places like Alberta and Western Australia attractive alternatives to the terminal America 2.0 and its moribund institutions. The Commonwealth Union composed of the UK, Canada, Australia, and New Zealand has closely integrated its member militaries. Although still a close ally of the United States, the CU is possibly the second greatest military power with global reach on the planet, and if India continues to grow, and to deepen its defense ties with the CU, that alliance may one day surpass even the United States.

Demographically, the United States is also feeling the effects of the global fertility decline, although it is not as extreme here as in Western Europe, Japan, or China. The decentralization of power and the continued sorting of population by cultural values has resulted in an even lower fertility rate for the blue areas, approaching European rates of hardly more than one child per couple. Meanwhile the red states have drawn the more religious populations that tended toward higher fertility, giving these areas an average natural increase rate well over replacement, almost uniquely so for the developed world. Combined with the positive effects of continued immigration, America as a whole has population growth above replacement rates, again almost uniquely so, although other English-speaking nations came close. By 2040, religious communities with high reproduction rates have begun to visibly increase in size and influence; the selection of a new president for the Mormon church, for example, was a nationally discussed news event recently.

The Social Settlement of the Reform Era, which decentralized power and accelerated the different paths of the red and blue states, has been (as Marshall Foch had characterized the Versailles Treaty) not a peace but an armistice for twenty years. Only the substantial differences within and among each side of the "Social Issues" prevent them from appearing to be two separate nations within one federal framework. But the truth is more complicated than any simple binary depiction.

For example, some of the states that divided had been ones with sub-stantial African-American populations in one side of the split, and this has resulted in the creation of several black-majority states. This actually had a good effect: because leading Democratic politicians had been ada-mantly opposed to the division, correctly fearing the loss of a key constit-uency, independent parties emerged in such states to push for separation. Even after the division of several states, these separatist parties remain viable, their leaders were founders, and they created a genuine two-party system in the black community for the first time in decades, and one in which traditional community leaders did not control both sides. The Senate and congressional Black Caucuses are divided into two factions as a result.

The governments of these new black-majority states, often led by retired African-American military officers with strong leadership and administrative skills, have moved effectively to reform welfare, educa-tion, and social services under the pressure of fiscal reform, an area in which there had been much low-hanging fruit to pick. African Americans have also been aided by the end of federal drug prohibition and the general amnesty for those convicted of nonviolent, victimless crimes, conditional on future good behavior. This has greatly reduced prison populations and removed barriers to participation for many already out of the penal system. New educational models have broken the monopoly provision of primary and secondary education. Black children, even from disadvantaged backgrounds, are showing steady academic progress. Most African Americans now have access to the most dynamic part of the economy, and many are popular designers of consumer products and fashion items for local production throughout the country and the world. Always a hothouse of new styles, especially in music and clothing, the Black community has been able to cut out the middle man and sell directly to the whole world with the new technology, for the first time capturing most of the economic fruits of its own creative energy.

The red-blue divisions in America have not disappeared. In some ways decentralization has sharpened the divisions, with politically like-minded people self-sorting into different communities, states, and regions. However, dispersion and local governance have complicated the matter by replacing a two-sided game with a complex multiplayer game. In some corners of the country, extremes on either side of the political spectrum (often highly publicized) have given rise to perceptions that the other side has gone crazy. Yet the majority of Americans still live by and hold to values that are close to the middle of the road in our culture. On the other hand, the old "middlebrow" media and culture that reflected the middle of the road back in the twentieth century is long gone. Multiple generations of "new media" dominate the flow of information; in fact, many people these days have no idea what "old media" was, even though many of the brand names still exist. And most of today's media is still politically polarized, although perhaps no more than it was at the Founding, or in the age of Lincoln.

By contrast, art and culture are less politically polarized than they used to be during "culture wars." Part of the Fiscal Reforms included the end of a great deal of federal discretionary spending, including support of the arts, and of the academic arts and literature world via federal aid to universities. Some of this was picked up by state spending, but of course the states were under fiscal pressure as well.

Nonetheless, in a world of cheap material plenty, the arts are thriving, even without much government funding. Individuals and small groups can inexpensively make high-quality films and music, not to mention emerging art forms that were completely unknown in the past. Additive manufacturing cannot make a hand-painted portrait in oils, put on a four-piece chamber music performance, stage *La Bohème,* or bash out a crowd-pleasing heavy metal show at the local tavern. People seeking authentic experiences are able to find them, or to make them independently. Educational innovation is having a tremendous impact on the availability of skill, knowledge, and training in the various arts. Music lessons from the greatest teachers, using artificial intelligence programs to tutor, are cheap and easily available. Financing for a wide range of cultural endeavors is provided by public subscription, crowdfunding, local community support, and even renewed models of patronage.

The copyright and digital media aspects of the Reform Era have greatly shortened the copyright periods and degrees of protection of original works, taking the arts out of the hands of the big motion picture and recording studio systems. These reforms have made almost all sound and visual media independent. Most art, music, and literature nowadays has to appeal to audiences or crowdfunding donors to gain support. Thus "superstars" in film and music can no longer command multimillion dollar fees, celebrities have stopped being a sort of nobility, and entertainment products tend to reflect the actual tastes and values of the audience, rather than dictating them. As a result, the different sectors of America have begun to communicate on a much more level playing field. Paradoxically, this is lessening the distance between the cultural camps. The effects of these changes, however, have yet to fully play out.

Private space development has expanded dramatically in the last two decades. Access to orbit is getting cheaper all the time. Lunar and asteroid resource extraction are operating profitably, though these are still high-risk ventures, and the principal markets for those resources are still the space-based research stations and tourist destinations. Space tourism is booming, but it is still a luxury good for the wealthy. Manned Mars missions have led to a renewed excitement about space exploration, and plans for permanent extraterrestrial settlements are in development. Dreams of even bigger things are inching toward practical possibility.

America in 2040 is not perfect, but nothing human ever is. Nonetheless, overall, this is an era of freedom and excitement, and of material well-being with reasonable security for America's citizens. Technology, science, and medicine are progressing on all fronts, at a rapid pace. The new institutions of local and regional government are infused with the energy of their recent founders, and the solidarity of having passed through wrenching changes, and hard and dangerous times that are now truly over. And the Constitution of the United States of America, with its new amendments, is still the law of the land. Indeed, the vision of the Founders does not seem outdated at all, but almost futuristic.

## THE OTHER PATH

Many other possible scenarios exist for the year 2040. We believe the most likely alternative scenario is that the narrow stalemate between the main political forces in America will not be resolved, no major reforms will be made, and no social settlement will be achieved. The positive scenario we have just described required over 5,000 words to outline briefly. The results of the stalemate scenario can be summarized much more briefly: we will get more of the same, on and on, as conditions get worse and the reforms we describe in this book become more and more necessary, but are also more and more painful when they finally happen.

We originally subtitled this section "Gradual Reform or Systemic Crash." After undertaking much research and discussion, we concluded that an actual systemic crash is improbable. More likely is a bad scenario consisting of gradual stagnation and deterioration, until either the laws of political chance bring up a sufficiently bold reformer to finally break the logjam. Of course, some unpredictable internal or external event could destabilize America or the world sufficiently that we experience some form of catastrophic system-wide breakdown. We hope that does not happen.

The demise of the Austro-Hungarian Empire is a useful analogy. The ancient empire of the Habsburgs occupied the area currently governed by Austria, the Czech Republic, Slovakia, Hungary, Croatia, Slovenia, Bosnia-Hezegovina, and pieces of Italy, Poland, Serbia, Ukraine, and Romania. Its rulers had kept this patchwork of disparate peoples together over the centuries by dynastic marriages and by preserving many antique practices, which seemed out of place in the modern age.

In its last decades the Habsburg Empire was in dire need of reform, and everyone knew it. It was stagnant to the point of absurdity. Its stasis was the subject of comic novels; it was almost defined by its bureaucratic immobility. But the political forces were so stalemated that reform was difficult to achieve. Nevertheless, the Empire was reformable, and a ruler with very realistic ideas and the will and authority to implement them was about to come to power – the Heir to the Throne, Archduke Franz Ferdinand. His idea of transforming the Empire into a federation of self-governing nationalities, while preserving federal armed forces, a free trade area, and a common currency, would have been by far the best solution to the many problems besetting the Empire. Political reforms would have provided a secure basis for exploiting the work of the brilliant technical pioneers in automotive engineering, aviation, and medicine who were working in the Empire of that time.

Unfortunately, before the old Emperor Franz Joseph died in 1916, Franz Ferdinand was murdered by a terrorist in Sarajevo. Those pistol shots brought on the First World War. The War was such a disaster for the unreformed Empire that it finally broke under the strain. The last

Emperor, Franz Ferdinand's brother Karl, tried to implement similar reforms and bring the war to an end by a negotiated peace, but he was far too late, and the Empire was too weak to influence the German Kaiser and his war party. Hyperinflation, political chaos, a hostile break-up of the regions, a bloody Communist revolution bloodily suppressed, street violence and attacks on minorities, especially Jews – all these ensued. The chaos in Central Europe caused by the collapse of the Empire was a proximate cause of the rise of the Nazis and all that followed from it.

We look back and think the breakdown was inevitable. But it wasn't. The Empire had muddled through many disasters. It seemed oppressive in its day, but the decades of bloodshed and tyranny and genocide that followed it showed how good it had actually been. Had it not been for the shock of the war, the Empire might have lived on into our own times.

Without some sort of major shock, external or self-inflicted, an unreformed USA might drift on for quite a while, certainly another twenty-five or thirty years, without facing and tackling the fundamental problems facing it. The institutions of America 2.0 can survive a while longer by borrowing irresponsibly, defaulting silently on their creditors through inflation, squeezing the taxpayers with more thorough intrusion and coercion, confiscating the private savings of Americans in the guise of "rescuing" them, eating our seed corn by confiscating medical facilities and running them down without proper reinvestment, and in general stripping and looting the country. The problem will be characterized as old people of the wrong sort who are living too long and eating up resources. Once they are effectively euthanized by medical rationing, the managers of the current system will waste the money saved, and find someone else to target.

Every one of these actions has precedents in foreign countries in decline: Britain, Europe, Argentina, and Zimbabwe. It is going on right now, and it went on under past American administrations (Republican and Democrat alike). America 2.0 will also receive an undeserved cash infusion from the new energy discoveries that promise to slash domestic energy costs and give us continental self-sufficiency in energy.

Sooner or later, however, even all of these tricks will prove inadequate. The political and economic model we now live under cannot go on forever. Some shock may force reform, and may God preserve us from a disaster that knocks down the rickety system before we can replace it and rebuild. Or the American people will at some point get fed up and find the will and the leadership to demand something better. And then the sort of reform program we describe, decentralizing power and unleashing the creative powers of the American people, will happen.

We are betting on the positive scenario.

There are compelling reasons to bet on the American people.

In the rest of the book, we will tell what they are.

# Chapter 2
# The American Family

## AMERICAN EXCEPTIONALISM IS A FACT

The American way of life is based on freedom and individualism. Compared to people elsewhere, and even compared to our cousins in the other English-speaking nations, Americans tend to value liberty over equality of outcome, to be enterprising and competitive, to move far and often for work and housing, to be suspicious or hostile toward government power, to engage in voluntary rather than coerced collective action.

These features of the American character, despite many exceptions and variations, and some erosion in recent generations, are not myths. The individualistic, liberty-loving, enterprising, competitive, mobile, voluntaristic culture of America – as compared to the rest of the world – is demonstrated by countless historical and contemporary facts, some of which we will discuss in this book. This is how we really are, especially compared to the rest of the world, and everyone who is paying attention knows it. As we will show, Americans have been like this since the beginning. In fact, we have been like this since long before the beginning.

Because there is indeed a unique and distinctive character to American life, political and economic arrangements that work well in other places work less well in America. Conversely, what works for Americans does not necessarily work for people elsewhere. Some of the things Americans value highly are not even considered to be good things in many other world cultures. Other people are often appalled by the degree of insecurity and inequality Americans accept as the price of our freedom of action, by the "wastefulness" and hard work we accept as the price of our single-family houses, by our reluctance to grant or claim benefits from the government as a matter of right, by our acceptance of a large role for religion in private life, by our personal possession of lethal force to protect ourselves, our homes and our families, and by our reliance on and recourse to armed force for defense against foreign threats to our lives, freedom, and economic well-being.

Most people in the world have distinctly different beliefs. For instance, the countries of continental Europe have consistently voted for quite different political and economic arrangements whenever they had the chance. When American politicians tell us to be more like Sweden, or France, let alone China, they are making a fundamental mistake. For example, after a century of universal suffrage most Americans have rejected European-style social democracy, or accepted it grudgingly and in bits and pieces. This is true even though Western Europe is more like America than almost any place on earth.

The reverse is also true. America's unique character means that some political and economic arrangements that work well here cannot be successfully exported to foreign locales. For example, American politicians are likely to be wrong when they tell us that we can successfully export democracy, or make other countries look and act more like the United States. We may as well celebrate this diversity among the various cultural families of mankind. There is every reason to believe that this genuine diversity will continue, probably forever.

When we say that America is different from the rest of the world, we are necessarily saying that America is exceptional. We are not embarrassed to say this. Observing and stating the reality of American exceptionalism requires no more than recognizing facts. America has a unique culture that has played a key role in making us a uniquely wealthy, powerful, and influential country. America's impact on the rest of the world has been exceptionally large. Whether you think that impact has been good or evil, it is undeniable that it has been big. American exceptionalism is therefore not an opinion, nor is it a sentiment, but rather an observable fact. Recognizing American exceptionalism is not necessarily to make any claim of American moral superiority. American exceptionalism is real whether you love America or hate America.

As it also happens, sometimes people who see and understand our culture very clearly, or have penetrating insights about it, are people who do not love America, or even people who hate America. Sayyid Qutb, the father of modern jihad, hated America. Yet he correctly understood that a distinguishing feature of American life was the unusual degree of freedom enjoyed by women. Alexis de Tocqueville had mixed emotions about the USA. He saw the rise of American-style democracy as something to be dreaded. He reconciled himself to the loss of the older, aristocratic world by seeing God's providential hand in the rise of democracy. Yet, despite his misgivings, Tocqueville understood us better than any other foreign observer.

The authors of this book both love America and consider our way of life, for all its many and sometimes grave imperfections, to be good and valuable and worth preserving. But we base the arguments in this book on history, facts, and evidence, not on sentiments. We are ready, willing, and able to argue about the history, facts, and evidence without regard to what we like or dislike about America.

Why does it matter that America has a unique and exceptional culture?

It matters because America is in urgent need of reform at a fundamental level. If we want to know what will work for us, in terms of political and economic reforms, we need to understand ourselves. That means we need to know what we are and how we got to be like this. When we know that, we will be able to think intelligently about what we are today, and what our realistic prospects and options are.

The first question we must ask is: Why are Americans like this? Many great thinkers and writers have offered answers to this question. We are bold enough to say that all of those prior answers have fallen short because they did not delve deeply enough or look back far enough, in part because they did not have all of the information available to us today. No one will disagree when we say that we are not keener observers or better thinkers than Alexis de Tocqueville, for example. Very few people ever have been. But we do have 180 years of accumulated data that Tocqueville did not have. And we have attempted to put together some of this large mass of new information in ways that no one else apparently has done.

What we have found in our research is that our distinctive and exceptional American culture has extremely deep roots, stretching back over a thousand years, long before our own national Founding and our Constitution, long before the the first English settlements in North America.

Our culture has developed and adapted and evolved and changed over that great stretch of time, certainly. It is not quite the same thing from age to age. Nonetheless, despite many changes in politics, law, economics, and technology, our culture has remained recognizably continuous over all that time. Our American culture today is part of a living and evolving organism, spanning centuries and continents.

The word "culture" may seem amorphous, something you would know by intuition but cannot necessarily pin down. Even professional anthropologists, whose job it is to study and understand culture, seem to have trouble pinning down exactly what they mean by it. For our purposes, we define culture as the distinctive patterns of behavior within a specified group of people that are transmitted from one generation to the next and are not genetic in origin.

It is very important to understand that culture is not genetic. Adopted children and immigrants may come from entirely different genetic backgrounds, but they adopt artifacts of culture such as language, values, and customs as readily as do biological children of parents within that culture. It is indisputable that the culture we describe in this book can be and has been adopted by people of every possible ethnic background. The view held a century or more ago, that there was something special about the "Anglo-Saxon blood" that led to the culture of English-speaking peoples, has by now been rebutted by an overwhelming mass of evidence. We discuss this in greater detail later in this book.

What then is the core of our American culture, its unique feature, the thing that makes us what we are? Can we pin it down to something clear and simple and tangible? Yes, we can. It is not some mysterious "x factor." In fact, the answer is right under our noses, something we take for granted, because it seems so normal to us.

The continuous core of our distinct American culture is *the American nuclear family.*

The fundamental importance of the American nuclear family to our culture is not an opinion, but a historical and contemporary fact, as we will explain. Observing and stating this fact is not a moral judgment about the importance of family life. Just as you don't have to love America to follow our argument, you don't have to love the traditional American family, either. As discussed in this book, the American family operates on principles that shape individual expectations, even if one lives in a non-traditional family, or alone. Our American type of family, as it has developed over the centuries, has shaped us and continues to shape us, and it makes us different from the rest of the world. Furthermore, we continue to live in a culture that is still intricately linked with the peculiar nature of the American nuclear family. This remains so, despite the significant, even radical changes in American family life that have occurred in the last few generations, and which are likely to continue.

## THE AMERICAN NUCLEAR FAMILY

What is this American nuclear family? The following features distinguish the American nuclear family from families in other cultures.

- Individuals freely select their own spouses. Once people reach adulthood, they are expected to make their own choices about whom they will marry. A marriage between two people who have reached the age of consent is valid without the consent of anyone else, including parents. Families can try to influence these decisions, but parents and extended families cannot tell adult children whom they can marry. Their families cannot compel them to marry, or not to marry, any particular person, or to get married at all. There are no arranged marriages.

- There are no limitations on whom a person can marry, except that marriage to close relatives, including first cousins, is forbidden. This causes family members to disperse and seek marriage partners outside the group they come from. Moving far from home in adulthood is commonplace.

- Women enjoy a high degree of freedom and autonomy compared to other cultures. Women have a free choice about whom they will marry. There is a high degree of equality between the sexes in family decision making, and in other aspects of life, again, in comparison to other cultures.

- Parents are free to give more or less financial assistance to different children, as they see fit. Parents are also free to leave as much or as little, including nothing at all, to their children at the time of death, by means of a will. There is no requirement or expectation that children will be treated equally. Children have no legal right to demand any particular support or inheritance from their parents. Adult children have no legal right to any support from their parents while their parents are living. Similarly, parents have no legal right to demand support from their children.

+ Grown children leave their parents' homes and form their own households. They do not stay in their parents home, or under the parents' control, as adults. They are instead expected to go out and make their own way in the world. It is unusual, and it is considered a sign of failure, for adult children to remain in their parents' homes, especially if they are married. Adult children are supposed to marry and form new households and new nuclear families of their own. They are expected and required to become independent adults, and to form independent and self-sustaining families.

+ Extended families are weak. People have no right to expect or demand help from relatives. Members of extended families may choose to help relatives, but they typically do not do so in any significant way. Members of extended families will suffer no legal or social penalty if they do not assist and care for relatives.

All of these things sound "normal" to Americans. They are too ordinary for most Americans to notice or to mention. But the American nuclear family and its "rules of the game" are anything but normal across the world or over the centuries. They are "the ocean we swim in" and just as fish do not know they are wet, we do not know that we have family arrangements that are different from most people in the world, historically and today. In fact, the American type of nuclear family is shared almost exclusively with other English-speaking peoples. But this broader "Anglospheric Exceptionalism" is a large topic that lies mostly beyond the scope of this book.

In many cultures, and for most of history, individuals have had little control over who their spouse will be. That decision is made by their parents and relatives. In many cultures, strict equality is required in the treatment of all children by their parents, particularly in terms of inheritance. In many cultures, grown sons are expected to live with their parents, and the wives who come into their homes would then be subject to the authority of their mothers in law. In many cultures, the extended family acts as a protective network, and all members of it have a strong duty of loyalty and assistance to each other, and a competitive or hostile attitude to other extended family networks. On the other hand, people seeking to live autonomously and not be dependent on, or be depended on, by an extended family network, do not have that option.

There are large consequences to these cultural variations, and the family types they arise from. America developed as it did in terms of culture, law, politics, economics, and technology because it was built on a culture that had as its bedrock this distinctive type of nuclear family. The extraordinary level of individual choice, of personal freedom, and personal responsibility that are at the heart of our traditional family life are the basis of all the other freedoms we enjoy.

The impact of marriage and family practices on our American life and our history have been overwhelming. It has caused Americans to have a uniquely strong concept of each person as an individual self, with an identity that is not bound by family or tribal or social ties. Most cultures historically and around the world today have nothing like this American spirit of individualism. Our distinctive type American nuclear family has made us what we are.

## CONSEQUENCES OF THE AMERICAN TYPE OF NUCLEAR FAMILY

The following are some of the consequences of the American type of family life, and of the culture that developed along with those families. We try to accurately depict these traits, without suggesting that all of them are necessarily admirable. We are what we are, warts and all.

The portrait we paint below does not describe all Americans, and is even something of a caricature. Nonetheless, it is a generally accurate depiction of life and attitudes among suburban, middle- class people who make up the largest group in the American population.

There are over 300 million Americans and the variations between and among them are limitless. As Tom Wolfe called it, America is a "billion-footed beast" and any generalization will have literally millions of exceptions. Further, there are many people who actively dislike or oppose some or all of the features we describe below, or due to historical circumstances, or recent immigration, retain significantly different attitudes. Also, many individuals, and some communities, have a less individualistic and more collectivist mindset than others. For example, Minnesota was settled by Germans and Scandinavians who had a more communal attitude toward politics. It has been a notably progressive state for well over a century. Nonetheless, a large plurality, if not a majority of Americans accept and live in accord with some or most of the features described below.

**Americans Are Individualistic.** Americans have a uniquely strong concept of each person as an individual self, with an identity that is not bound by family or tribal or social ties. Most cultures, historically and around the world today, have nothing like this American spirit of individualism. As a general matter, Americans have always been psychologically more independent and less willing to place themselves under the control of others, to a degree that sometimes bewilders foreigners. The American nuclear family pushes Americans to be autonomous, self-reliant, and freedom-loving.

Americans see themselves as free, independent individuals, who take responsibility for themselves and their families. They make their own choices about the major decisions in life, and they reap the rewards or suffer the consequences of those decisions. Although there are any number of exceptions and qualifications in reality, the belief in individualism is a starting point most Americans share.

These same features could be negatively characterized as being selfish, uncooperative, and lacking public spirit. But as we will see, this negative spin would leave out a lot of the picture.

One graphic example of our unique individualism is the American attitude toward guns. To the consternation of the rest of the world, and to many Americans, majorities of our fellow citizens consistently demand their right to possess lethal force to defend their homes, their property, their families, and themselves. Despite predictions that this attitude would eventually die out, the political trend in recent years has been toward strengthening gun rights, and increasing resistance to limiting them.

**Americans Are Liberty Loving.** Americans expect to be on their own, choosing their own spouses, forming their own nuclear families, establishing their own homes, making their own way in the world, and generally running their own affairs. They have always wanted and demanded the freedom to do these things, which in turn leads to demands for political freedom as well.

Surveys prove that Americans have a uniquely powerful commitment to individual liberty, which they share only with other English-speaking peoples. Most Americans, however they describe themselves politically, are libertarian compared to the rest of the world. Americans are generally committed to their own version of freedom, and believe it to be their birthright, as something they want to preserve. As Gunnar Myrdal wrote, Americans are "conservative in fundamental principles . . . but the principles conserved are liberal and some, indeed, are radical." No explicitly authoritarian ideology has ever enjoyed mass popularity in the United States.

A love of freedom for its own sake is far less of a universal value than many Americans realize, and far less than many Americans currently wish it was. Other people simply don't care about it as much as we do, and no amount of preaching or even coercion is likely to change that. This commitment to personal freedom is rooted in our type of family life, and our historical experience built on that family life, as we will show below.

President George W. Bush, in his second inaugural address, stated that all peoples of the world loved freedom and aspired to it. But this is true only in a very narrow sense and is not true in the way he seems to have meant it. Most people around the world seek to carry out their obligations to their family, their community, and their faith as they understand those obligations. To the extent that external forces get in the way of those obligations, they resent such forces and wish for their removal. Often that removal is all they mean by "freedom." And sometimes Americans have been the very external force these foreign people sought to remove, however good our intentions may have been. So in foreign policy, it is important to remember that our idea of freedom may differ radically from that of other people. We discuss this in detail in Chapter 8. We may not like the fact that others place a different value on personal freedom, but it is beyond our capacity to change and it is at best a waste of time to try.

**Americans Are Nonegalitarian.** The flip-side of American liberty-mindedness is a comparatively low interest in equality, specifically in economic equality. Compared to most of the world, we don't care about equality very much. In fact, most Americans are willing to tolerate a degree of material inequality that people in many other countries cannot fathom and are sometimes shocked by. As a result Americans typically apply a different standard of fairness in economic affairs than do people in most other countries. This comparative American indifference to economic equality works its way into many aspects of our culture.

Americans do profess to believe in a "level playing field," which means equality of opportunity, but not outcomes. The level playing field is at least an aspirational goal. But, as we know, in practice the level playing field barely exists. We all know that the wealthy, the powerful, and the well-connected all too often write their own rules. Most Americans struggle to gain wealth and status, and to hold on to them, and sometimes they do not play fairly in that struggle. Most American parents strive to find ways to give their children advantages over others in the hardball game of life. Every American starts out holding a certain hand of cards, and it is very hard to play your way up the social and enconomic scale, though some, heroically, manage to do so. Many opportunities for advancement exist, but seeing those opportunities and seizing them is uncommon. It is often recent immigrants, who may come from truly oppressive and unequal societies, who clearly see the many opportunities America offers to get ahead and even to become wealthy.

Whatever reality there may actually be in the ideal of equality of opportunity, it is certain that Americans have, on a global scale, little interest in equality of results. For example, in certain other cultures parents are required to treat their male children with absolute material equality. This equality is embedded in their family life, and thus became part of the foundation of their culture. As a result, equality becomes, for these foreign communities, an ideology, and a political mandate. France is the classic case. This demand for equality is very strong in parts of France, particularly the Seine basin, where Paris is located, and which has long been the political and cultural heart of France. French egalitarianism is embodied in their national motto, "Liberté, Egalité, Fraternité" – "Liberty, *Equality*, Brotherhood."

The French political ideal is in stark contrast to the key phrase in our own Declaration of Independence: "Life, Liberty and the Pursuit of Happiness." These are considered to be sacred words by many Americans. Although the immediate derivation of this phrase is from the political philosopher John Locke, he was drawing on the English culture around him and preceding him. America's sacred political words do not contain any reference to equality, nor to the communal rather than individualistic idea of brotherhood. Instead, Americans hold that God Himself has allowed each of us to participate in a "pursuit" with no promise that we will capture the happiness we strive for, or even capture anything at all. We are simply all allowed, and in practice required, to try.

Although we are nonegalitarian, it is also true that we are not *inegalitarian*, as certain other communities have been historically, for instance the modern Germans. We do not feel the need to have a hierarchy where everyone knows exactly who is superior and who is inferior. Germans are uncomfortable when this is unclear, and they want it to be sorted out when it is not clear. This inegalitarianism also carries an expectation that the elder brother has an obligation to look out for the younger siblings, provided they are obedient and helpful. This explains, for example, why the German policy of "co-determination," in which the labor unions have a minority of seats on corporate boards, succeeds there but would be a disaster in America: the unions take the role of younger brother, almost always act for the overall well-being of the company, and expect to be taken care of in return. American unions, on the contrary, have historically used any power they could get to extract better wages and benefits from the company, even if this presented a threat to the long-term health of the company. The individual well-being of their members was the driver. The relationship has always been confrontational and usually zero-sum.

Americans indifference to equality and inequality is very important to our political reactions, and goes a long way to explaining why neither communism nor fascism ever developed a mass following in any English-speaking country. Americans have always done it this way. Our style of family life has always pushed us to be independent but not equal.

The alert reader will at this point be wondering, quite possibly angrily, about a major contradiction to our depiction of a nonegalitarian, but not inegalitarian America. Of course, the exception is slavery and the status of African Americans over the centuries. An additional, significant outlier has been the treatment of Native Americans, who lost a continent and got very little in return. Black people and Indians were not included in the world of nonegalitarian relations where most Caucasian Americans spent their lives. Instead they were excluded and marginalized and treated as subordinate categories. This is of course a tragic tale, and the gap between our professed ideology and this history requires an explanation, which we will take up later.

In one sense, a noneconomic one, Americans are often egalitarian. Generally they do not believe that one individual has greater moral worth or greater dignity than any other. They do not consider anyone to be their "betters" and resent any such pretensions. They don't think there is anything special about rich people, nor have they traditionally treated them as any kind of aristocracy. Americans firmly believe that rich people should be subject to the same rules as everybody else and resent it when they are not.

Americans have a similar attitude in the work place. We have bosses, not masters or lords. Most Americans are themselves some kind of boss at some stage in their working lives. A boss is only a boss at work, not at home, or to neighbors or to other citizens. There is nothing special about it. Being a boss is limited to the workplace and does not give you any special status in society. Bosses do not constitute an aristocracy with any special priviliges.

Americans, at least in theory, believe the poor have the same human dignity as the rich. However, there is a dark side to this attitude. We generally think there is nothing so permanently wrong with most poor people that they cannot take advantage of opportunities to better themselves. In practice this often means that we hold the poor to be morally responsible for their own predicament, as unjust as this often is.

**Americans Are Competitive.** Someone once quipped, with some accuracy, that everything in American life that is not actually football is merely the continuation of football by other means. Although American life is in theory a level playing field, it is always, in practice, a playing field, level or not. American life is a competition, in almost every area, and it always has winners and losers. Americans generally consider an economy with winners and losers to be fair, and to be the best way to get the best work out of everybody. This view of life as relentless competition gives a hard edge to American life, and a feeling of isolation, that many foreigners and not a few Americans, find repellant. But this feature is built-in and is unlikely to ever change.

No less an authority than Gen. George S. Patton, Jr. taught us that "America loves a winner. America will not tolerate a loser." The revered teachings of Vince Lombardi are of a similar flavor. As a result of the sports-like, competitive spirit that permeates much of our life, being personally or professionally unsuccessful in American life is hard, harder than in most cultures. Americans like and respect winners, they admire success, and typically shun and avoid losers.

The stress of struggling to succeed has been a perpetual theme in American literature. Many people crack under the strain, or give up and drop out, or turn to one sort of addiction or another, if they find they are not succeeding. For example, in large organizations all but a small number of workers in early middle age will not be suited for further promotion. There is not much room at the top. Yet to falter at this stage is felt by many, and all too often perceived by others, as a personal failure. On reaching this stage in life, many Americans need to re-create themselves professionally, and this can be a painful and even humiliating process. Yet, even though millions of people have gone through this process, few have called it unfair, or tried to bring about any basic change in our society or economy, despite their own personal hardships.

On the other hand, Americans do not want people who fall short of seizing the prizes of life, or their children, to starve. Americans have long supported some kind of safety net, especially for the middle class. Government unemployment insurance, for example, has long been accepted, and the notion that government help should be a "hand-up not a hand-out" is a commonly accepted idea.

Relatedly, America has a remarkably open and forgiving process for personal and business bankruptcy. We recognize that failure is possible, especially if you engage in any new or risky venture, and we want people to take risks. We also do not want people to be ruined for life for bad judgment, or bad luck with a business. Americans know the game is hard and usually believe in giving people second chances. F. Scott Fitzgerald said "there are no second acts in American lives," and he was absolutely wrong. There are second, third, and fourth acts in the American drama. Many of the greatest fortunes, and countless ordinary successes, have come only after repeated failure, even disaster. Some undergo repeated cycles of failure and success through their careers. America's sporting spirit toward life includes the expectation that people who have been knocked flat many yards short of the goal line will get up, shake it off, play through the pain, and keep on trying.

The spirit of competitiveness that permeates much of American life may not be, on its face, our most admirable characteristic. But it has made us what we are, and probably, mostly, for the better. It has made us work hard. It has rewarded people who push themselves to excel. It has driven people to create new and "insanely great" things against all odds and be rewarded for it. Just as in sports, business competitiveness makes us face objective standards we would never impose on our selves, and to gain the rewards or suffer the consequences. It gives us earned success, which is the most satisfying kind, when we do enjoy some professional success or achieve a hard-sought goal. And it permits respect among competitors who play the game well, or in earnest, or with heart, even though not everyone can win.

Competitive capitalism is a game Americans have been willing to play, but, recognizing that it is not always fair, with some safeguards built in. Americans generally expect people to pursue happiness by working. They expect others to work and earn what they get, and to be paid what they have earned. They think that the rewards of life should be granted to those who have earned them in an open, competitive process, while recognizing that there is a certain amount of luck involved.

Crony capitalism, where the winners routinely get picked based on political clout, is a system that contradicts and degrades all of these values, and seeing it in operation angers many Americans. The "Chicago way," where clout and connections determine all the important outcomes, has not been America's way in most places, and we don't want it to be. When Americans perceive that the game is rigged, or that they have played by the rules but have not been treated fairly, they are angered by it and they want it corrected. The perception of a rigged game, and a lack of fairness, is a large part of what caused the rise of the American welfare state, as we will discuss later on, when we talk about America 2.0.

The growing awareness that American life is indeed more and more a rigged game offends our "inegalitarian" spirit. Success is seen, all too often correctly, as unfair and not based on adding anything of value. As we will discuss, much of the corruption of our current system is the perverse result of the regulatory state we have built. Started with good intentions, this machinery has grown ever more powerful, and has at the same time been captured by private interests to create monopolistic and anti-competitive sources of wealth. Any discussion of "more" or "less" regulation is meaningless. Instead, we need to get into the weeds and ask "which" regulation and "who" benefits from it and "what" its cost will be. Unfortunately, this is hard work and few people have the incentive to do it unless they have a large financial interest in shaping the rules of the game. The devil is in the details, and the details are hard to discover. As a result, powerful and wealthy and well-connected people who did not earn what they have in a fair and open way will get little respect, no deference, and increasingly angry opposition from the American people – once the American people take notice of them.

**Americans Are Enterprising.** As noted, Americans have traditionally respected hard work. But more than that, Americans have encouraged and respected entrepreneurship, which combines hard work with personal autonomy and creativity. American families, when they are working for their own well-being, work harder, and work longer hours, and take more risks, and make more sacrifices, than they would ever do as someone else's employee. This intense effort is referred to as "self-exploitation" by some economists. But the term is not really accurate. So long as a family has ownership of the property they are improving or the business they are building with their labor, they are not exploiting themselves, but investing in themselves with sweat equity. They may lose the value of their investment due to disaster, mistakes, economic cycles, or plain bad luck. But that is a risk they knowingly accept, so it is not "exploitation." This was true of family farms on the frontier four centuries ago, and it is true of start-up businesses today.

There is nothing wrong with America's work ethic. Americans are eager to start new businesses, large and small, to provide for themselves and their families. This attitude continues to live on in America, despite increasing disincentives and burdens to starting a business. As we will describe below, the primary obstacle to new business formation, and an economic boom greater than any we have ever known, is the taxation and regulation imposed by our own overgrown government, which mainly serves the interests of its allies and stakeholders and cronies.

Americans want and even need to have economic autonomy. Americans, as individuals and as nuclear families, do not live as part of an extended family group, as people in many other countries do. As a result we have always been "on our own" to a far greater degree than people in many other cultures. This is, in a way, the dark side of the American nuclear family, the lack of security and warmth that a strong, extended family provides. Americans living in nuclear families know that no one has an obligation to take care of them, no one has a duty to leave them an inheritance, no one has a duty to take them in if they fail. As a result, American families have always coped with a deeper sense of insecurity, and a heavier burden of personal responsibility, than many people have had to live with. But there is a silver lining to even this dark cloud. Americans always knew that they had to work hard and make a go of things, and so they very often did. This very insecurity has helped to make our people ambitious and entrepreneurial, and our society dynamic.

Societies based on extended families discourage people from being enterprising because any success you achieve personally necessarily "belongs" to your extended family. As a result, the trade-off for security in other societies has been stagnation. In contrast, if a nuclear family is successful, there is no extended family that can claim a right to the wealth it has generated. People may help out their relatives out of love or kindness or loyalty, but they do not have a legal or even social obligation to do so. This accumulated personal wealth has been the source of investment capital, which has in turn made per capital income growth possible.

In short, American family life has made our country, at its most fundamental level, a high-risk, high-return culture. You are on your own, but you can keep what you get in the struggles of life. This combination of sticks and carrots faced by an American nuclear family is different and more powerful than what people in most other cultures have faced. This has led to our well-known "go-getting" and "hustling" spirit, which is admired by some and despised by many of our global neighbors. The upside is a powerful work-ethic and a willingness to take risks to get ahead. Thus the nuclear family has been the hidden but fundamental engine of economic development and economic progress in America.

**Americans Are Mobile.** Because Americans expect, and are expected, to acquire their own home for their families, they have always been willing to move to wherever they could get themselves a house of their own. As a result, Americans do not have much sentimental attachment to any particular plot of land or any particular building. Although Americans treat Thanksgiving with their family as almost sacred, even if inconvenient travel is required, it is the people not the building who matter.

Other cultures are very different. In some peasant cultures land, especially farm land, is sacred and bound up with the family with deep emotional ties. But to Americans land is a commodity and always has been. Land and buildings are to be invested in and used. American houses, even mansions, have numbers, not names.

The absence of strong extended families also makes us mobile. Because Americans do not rely for their well-being on access to extended family networks, so they are not compelled to live near their relatives. They are almost always willing to "up stakes" and move away from their current home to wherever there are opportunities. The young couple leaving for another state or even traveling over the ocean, may be sad when they leave their parents and the old home town, but they pretty much always do leave. This was true in the days when leaving town meant you would likely never see the other person again. In the age of telephones, skype, and jet travel it is even easier to do. Nuclear families spin off other nuclear families, and the new ones go wherever they need to go.

As a result, Americans want and expect the freedom to come and go as they please. This leads to yet another feature of American life that foreigners, and many here, find irritating, which is our commitment to personalized transportation: We love our cars. This is a big continent, still largely empty, and you need motor transport to get around in it. Henry Ford meant to provide mobility for the masses, and he succeeded. Technology, culture, and geography converged to create our car culture. America and Americans were made for the automobile. And most of us are in no hurry to give them up. The fact that Tesla, a California corporate start-up has taken the lead in creating a beautiful, affordable mass-market all-electric car is a perfect convergence of American appetites and characteristics.

**Americans Are Voluntaristic.** Although Americans do not have extended family networks, they are not "loners," either. Instead Americans, as families and as individuals, have usually been "joiners" who form an incomprehensibly dense network of voluntary associations. This is the basis of our civil society, which fills a need that our smaller families cannot fill.

Voluntary association is also the foundation of our economy, which is composed mainly of organizations that are not based on extended families or nepotism but on personal decisions to contract with each other. Americans believe in individualism, but they also have a remarkable aptitude for cooperating freely in larger institutions.

A society based on free and voluntary association requires a high degree of trust among people who are not blood relatives. This high degree of nonfamilial interpersonal trust is unusual in the world, and is far beyond what most people in most other countries would consider normal. Americans rely on voluntary organizations and networks to accomplish many collective tasks that in other countries would either not be done at all, or which would be handled by extended families, or by the government. Most businesses in America, most of the time, hire people based on experience, credentials, apparent competence, and referrals, but not routinely or primarily based on family ties. American businesses, like the rest of American life, are not based mainly on family networks, but on a basis of trust and voluntary agreements, on contracts. This high degree of interpersonal trust has allowed us to assemble the necessary talents and skills to make all kinds of organizations work effectively, to have the flexibility to assemble teams for jobs based on the demands of the task rather than on other considerations.

In economic terms, trust reduces transaction costs. Societies with a "low radius of trust" tend to stay poor. In a society where people are always watching their backs and playing a zero-sum game, it is impossible to undertake large or long-term projects, or to create large businesses that benefit from economies of scale. Americans, somewhat paradoxically for an individualistic people, have also been good at large-scale cooperative effort, and have traditionally been well known for being able to do "big things in a big way."

The American openness to non–kin-based cooperation has made America uniquely able to assimilate immigrants and foreigners. Again, this is not a friction-free process. But, by comparison to the rest of the world, the United States has been notably able to accept and assimilate immigrants, to successfully extend trustworthy behavior and to demand it in return.

An important element in America's trust-based society is religion. Much of our American civil society has historically been built on participation in church communities, and this still remains true for many people. Compared to the rest of the developed world, very many Americans are religious, and not embarrassed to be religious, or to talk about their faith. But they also believe in keeping the peace and not coming to blows, let alone killing each other, over their religious differences, including with nonbelievers. This combination of religious seriousness combined with tolerance is unique to America. It is the only way hundreds of millions of people can get along with each other and work together. This high degree of religious tolerance is an underappreciated achievement and it is a big part of the American way of life. The intolerance, contempt, and dehumanizing epithets directed against American religious believers by some of their fellow citizens in recent years may foreshadow a much more confrontational future. But, hopefully, the general tolerance we have shared will continue.

Despite is historical and current importance, it is indisputable that civil society and voluntary association have been in decline in America in recent decades. Part of the problem is that government at all levels has become a nanny-leviathan, squeezing out civil society. One plain fact is that there must be significant limits on what civil society can accomplish when the government takes half of all the money out of society. Another factor has been female participation in the workforce, because much of the activity of civil society had been handled in the past by women who were not engaged in the cash economy. Even if you consider the movement of women from homemakers to employees a triumph, everything is a trade-off and success is never costless. Long commute times and job demands are another source of decline in civil society.

Nonetheless, a revival of civil society appears to be in store. New technology, which allows people to connect in new ways, is likely to lead to a revival of civil society in new forms. We expect this process to continue and to evolve rapidly. What we now refer to as "social media" are only early and primitive versions of the civil society-enabling technology we will be seeing in the years ahead. Nonetheless it is too early to say exactly how, and how much, new technology will revive and strengthen civil society.

**Americans Have Middle-Class Values.** Most Americans describe themselves as middle class, including many people who would be objectively considered either rich or poor. But most Americans think of themselves as middle class by their attitudes, particularly the need and desire to acquire a home and to care for a family, at least as much as their wealth. Americans have remarkably consistent values and preferences without regard to how much money they have. In fact, these values have remained consistent even though the material foundations of American middle class life have been eroding in recent decades. We hope and anticipate that this erosion can be reversed, as we will discuss below.

American nuclear families typically have only their homes and their jobs to rely on, with whatever savings they have managed to accumulate. Many rely on the government for assistance at some point or another, and most expect the government to help provide for medical care in their old age. But compared to many countries, we do not have much of a safety net here, and attempts to greatly expand it have rarely met with electoral success.

Most American families are not rich, and most have no one to bail them out if they have a major downturn in life. As a result, part of the American middle class mindset is to recoil from anything that threatens the quiet enjoyment of their homes, or its value as an asset. They are fearful of public disorder or squalor. They dislike and avoid the culture associated with poverty, and have little tolerance for irresponsible or impulsive or violent behavior. Americans are often harsh in imposing this code. They have been willing to imprison a huge percentage of their population, often unfairly and in response to victimless crimes, mainly as a way to insulate themselves from perceived unacceptable conduct. This defensive-mindedness, which can be applied in arbitrary and even brutal fashion, is not our most appealing trait. But it cannot be ignored as a persistent feature of middle-class American life.

Without doubt, some of this conduct over the years has been motivated by simple racism. But much of it has probably been driven by the far stronger force of economic self-defense. The first "white flight" was from Irish immigrants who lived in disorderly and violent slums, and who were despised by their more affluent neighbors. The light complexions of the Irish gained them little, at least at first, in terms of acceptance.

On the other hand, if an individual or family can meet certain fairly minimal standards of middle-class behavior, Americans can be remarkably tolerant. A person who has very strange ideas, or dresses funny, or practices an eccentric religion, but who keeps his yard neat, and does not create disturbances that require the cops to be called, will probably be OK.

**Americans Have an Instrumental View of Government.** The American people do not worship government, and they do not despise it. Rather, government is an instrument, which they have always attempted to use for their own advantage, while also knowing that it cannot solve all of their problems. Ideological anti-statism has never been an American trait, and very few Americans have ever been strict libertarians, let alone anarchists. In fact, from colonial days, local governments in particular have had broad scope to regulate market transactions that were regarded as being against the public interest, usually under the traditional "police power" possessed by states and localities to protect health, safety, morals, and the general welfare. These traditional powers to "interfere" in private economic transactions have been slouching toward Washington, D.C. during the last century or so, but they have always existed.

Despite the existence of these broad powers, the view of the state as a parent, protector, and moral leader in society has not historically been congenial to us. Unfortunately, suspicion and circumspection regarding government power has lost its hold on many of our fellow citizens. Nonetheless, the American conception of the proper sphere of government remains notably different, and smaller, at least in theory, than that of many people, including most Europeans.

Historically, Americans have wanted strong but limited government, which had the capacity to do the things it had to do, but not empowered to interfere in other areas. This sort of optimal or "goldilocks" government was a difficult balance to sustain. Once government power really started growing it took on a life of its own. As a practical matter, the reality of limited government has broken down severely in recent decades, and we now face almost unlimited power, either actually or potentially.

However, the growth of government was not the result of some alien imposition that no one wanted. Flying saucers did not descend on Washington and saddle us with an overbearing government. The American people brought this on themselves, for reasons that are also deeply rooted.

Americans have often demanded that the government do things that helped them acquire a respectable, middle-class existence, and protect them in that status. Historically, they have created programs that benefit the middle class, all the while berating the rich and chastising the poor. University of Chicago economist George Stigler wrote in 1970 that "Public expenditures are made for the primary benefit of the middle classes, and financed with taxes which are borne in considerable part by the poor and the rich." This is not a view that is commonly encountered, but the evidence shows it has, or once had, a large element of truth. This does not mean that government checks were necessarily cut to middle-class families, but rather that the redistributive effects of government policy favored the middle class as compared to the others. Examples include public funding of higher education, farm policy and price supports, social security, tax exemptions for institutions that are favored by the middle class, and home mortgate tax deductions.

Medicare is very much in this mold, as is the drug benefit enacted under the younger President Bush. Uninsured medical expenses for any serious illness are typically far beyond the capacity of most American families to pay, especially older people who need repeated and ongoing care. Middle-class Americans simply have not tolerated the prospect of either being driven to bankruptcy or foregoing medical care they need to survive, through no fault of their own. Instead they have demanded and gotten medical care as well some protection from financial ruin, without regard to arguments about economic efficiency or downstream consequences. They have used the state to protect them from a danger they faced, and they expect that protection to continue.

At one time the American middle class managed to get a decent deal from an expanding government. But this was probably never sustainable and it is clearly less and less so. The inefficiencies and costs of the little-discussed middle-class safety net, among other costs and burdens imposed on us by all levels of government, cannot go on as they have, and what cannot go on, won't.

Americans have also always used the state to build public works. In the century after the Founding, Americans expected the government to undertake large internal improvements that would lead to improved opportunities for everyone. The construction of the Erie Canal is one early and critically important example, and the government's involvement in railroad construction is another. In the early twentieth century, Americans willingly taxed themselves and spent an enormous amount of money building roads and bridges to make their new cars and trucks more useful. The construction of the Interstate Highway System was part of the same pattern, and made it possible to commute to city jobs from the newly arising suburbs.

An additional, enormously important example of the American middle class using the government is the Housing Act of 1949, which provided for the wide-scale construction of public housing. These "projects" ended up mainly housing the poor. They became dangerous vertical slums and symbols of despair. This was not the original intention, certainly. But it must be said that it was an outcome the American middle class was willing to let happen. That part of our story is consistent with the plain fact that the American middle class has been willing to play hardball over the years to get what it has wanted through the power of government. This included protecting itself from perceived dangers, such as from unfavored minorities. Again, this reality is not a pleasant issue to look at, but it is clearly part of our history.

The Housing Act of 1949, beside creating "the projects," had an additional and even bigger impact. The Act financed millions of people moving into private, single-family homes. The Act is nothing less than the founding document of the postwar American suburbs.

**Suburbia Is the Culmination of American Culture.** We claim that Americans are liberty loving, nonegalitarian, enterprising, mobile, and voluntaristic, with middle-class values, and who use the government for practical and self-interested ends. All of these features led to the one of America's greatest achievements: the creation of suburbia. A house that fits one nuclear family, with some comfort and privacy, with electric power and labor-saving devices, and some lawn, and maybe some trees, and possibly a pool or a swingset – this is the heart of the American dream.

Americans, and the English before them, have always wanted a house and a yard of their own, with a husband and a wife and their own children in their own home. Of course, owning your own home has usually been beyond the grasp of most families over the centuries. But it is the life they have chosen whenever they could get it, and they have struggled and sacrificed to keep it. The Roman historian Tacitus observed two thousand years ago this same unusual way of life in the Germanic tribes living across the Roman frontier. Our way of life, choosing to live in single family units whenever possible, and having this life as an ideal even when it was not obtainable, has an observed and documented history over two thousand years long.

These Germanic tribesmen were the ancestors of the Angles and Saxons, who became the English, who were in turn the ancestors of the people who colonized North America. By the time of the American Founding there were many people in the new United States who were not of English descent, but who adopted English-derived American ways. Americans have ancestors from everywhere on Earth. However, they are, with many important exceptions and variations, cultural though not biological descendants of the English and their Germanic forefathers. We will discuss this in detail in the next chapter.

Intellectuals and city planners and politicians have persisted since Tacitus's time in saying it is wrong for us to want to live in dispersed single-family houses rather than some form of dense urban arrangement or even in communal housing. These critics have always berated us for not wanting to live in "proper" towns and cities instead. Virtually the entire class of supposedly knowledgeable people has long despised the way most Americans want to live, calling it "sprawl." There is a lot of bigotry in the word "sprawl." It shows that people with power, or those who influence them, see the homes of millions of Americans and the families who live in them not as fellow citizens living a peaceable life, but rather as a form of pollution. Such critics admire the Europeans, who have far greater restrictions on living in suburbs, and who supposedly know how to live well while crowded together in cities.

The influential French architect Le Corbusier was typical. He visited the USA in 1935, and visited Manhattan and some of its suburbs, and offered this sneering assessment:

> After a stimulating cocktail they [the commuters] pass through the golden portals of Grand Central Terminal into a Pullman which takes them to their car; after a ride along charming country roads they enter the quiet and delightful living rooms of their colonial style houses.

"Corbu" went on to make the wildly erroneous prediction that the future would consist of more of the kind of vertical cities that he liked, with the towers of Manhattan as the exemplar. He condemned the idea and the ideal of single-family homes in green locations away from downtown.

From Tacitus to today, it was supposedly the unsophisticated, the rubes, who wanted to live in their own single-family homes. But there has always been a hypocritical flip-side to this view. The Roman elite had country villas where they could retreat from urban life. The elite in America today also want single-family homes in leafy suburbs for themselves. But they object to anyone else being allowed to have them. The proles should live in apartments and take trains to work, but not them.

This is a remarkable example of cultural continuity in itself. The exact same criticism of our way of life has been voiced nonstop for two thousand years. But we are not going to change.

Americans, and the English before them, and the Germanic tribes who preceded the English, have all demonstrated a related pattern of being "land hungry." Americans and their cultural ancestors have sent out shiploads of settlers, sent their wagons West, loaded up the station wagon and driven away, whenever possible in family units, over fifteen centuries of migration. Whenever the land was available, and we could afford it, we have settled in single-family homes. We are a nation of immigrants, a nation of homesteaders, a nation of land speculators, and a nation of real estate developers and home builders, and we always have been.

The American drive to settle in new places has never just been about getting a nicer house, or a bigger yard, or a more fertile farm. It has also been a search for freedom. Over the centuries, Americans and their predecessors have "voted with their feet" to escape the constraints and taxation and corruption of the older settlements. The postwar construction of suburbia, and the current rise of exurbia, filling in the empty places in our own continent, is only the latest example.

Americans built suburbs and moved there, and stayed there, as soon as they had money and motor transport. The first suburbs were outside New York City and the commute was by steamship on the Hudson. Shortly afterwards, steam railways enabled larger-scale commuting for the upper and middle classes. Philadelphia's prestigious "Main Line" suburbs took their name from the Main Line of the Pennsylvania Railroad than made them possible; imitators abounded. Later, "street car suburbs" grew up around downtown areas, followed by elevated trains and subways. The automobile has been the peak, so far, of this process.

Despite much hostile propaganda, suburban "alienation" is a myth.

Americans have not been especially unhappy in their single-family homes, whether in the farmhouses and small towns of the past, or the suburbs of today. Isolation and alienation are far more common in city apartment buildings, which is where many intellectuals and city planners and politicians want to compel all of the rest of us to live. In suburban communities people are separated enough for privacy but close enough to be sociable. This balance of privacy and neighborliness apparently suits most Americans.

People who dislike America as it actually is, or want to change it out of all recognition, typically have a particular disdain for the suburban life most Americans have voluntarily chosen. But Americans keep building suburbs and living in them because they like the life of the suburbs. Any attempt to change this part of the American way of life is bound to fail. It is a hardy plant, and very, very deeply rooted.

## OUR FUTURE WILL BE BUILT ON OUR EXISTING FAMILY AND CULTURAL FOUNDATIONS

Free and independent human beings don't spring fully formed from the earth. As we have discussed, in American life they have come from families, from parents, from homes that are able to form and raise children, to set them free into the world, and that expect them to stand on their own. In turn, free and independent individuals, and the families that create them, can develop and prosper and be happy only in a society and culture that create a framework of law and security, without crushing out their freedom and independence and individuality. This leaves the way open to economic development and change.

Our American culture grew up on the bedrock of nuclear families and on the institutions that evolved over the centuries in the English-speaking world. That family structure and its associated institutions developed further in America based on our unique historical experience, including the self-selection of enterprising adventurers, who came to America as immigrants. The history of these institutions will be the focus of the next chapter.

Striking a balance between freedom and rules, between independence and security, between individualism and the common good, has been the perpetual challenge of American life. By and large, over the centuries, in the face of many challenges, Americans have gotten the balance reasonably right.

In recent years, however, it has become more and more obvious that the balance has been lost. Indeed, this "unbalanced" political and economic order we live with now, which we call America 2.0 – and is also known as the Blue Model, or the welfare state – is on the verge of falling apart.

The inevitable end of America 2.0 may seem like the end of the world, but it isn't. It is only the end of one, now outmoded, set of institutional arrangements built for a very different world. These inevitable changes to institutional arrangements will not reach down to the level of our cultural roots. Political change, even major political change, can rarely reach to that level. We will rework existing institutions, and build new ones, suited for emerging conditions. This new era, which we call America 3.0, will be more consistent with our cultural foundations than the world that is now fading away.

There is every reason to believe that our culture will continue to grow and evolve for many centuries to come, with both change and continuity, as it has for centuries past. The great historian F. W. Maitland referred to this process of organic development as a "changing same." As we described in our first chapter, we believe the emerging America 3.0 will be an improved continuation of that "changing same."

# Chapter 3
# Our Germanic Inheritance

## GOING BACK TO THE BEGINNING

Our goal is to understand where we are now as a nation, how we got here, and where we are likely to go in the next generation or so. So, we are going to look for the deepest possible foundations of America to get our bearings. As we look back over the centuries, we will not stop with the American Founding, as many people do. Instead we are looking for the deepest roots we can find, and following the thread of continuous cultural and institutional development back as far as we can.

We Americans are rightly proud of our Revolution and our Founding era. We are especially proud of our Founding documents: our Declaration of Independence and Constitution. We should also be proud of another set of documents from the Founding era that had as much impact as the Declaration and Constitution: the Northwest Ordinances. These land ordinances were the blueprint for America 1.0, as we will explain Chapter 5.

Many Americans believe that it is the American Founding, our Revolution and our Founding documents, that makes America exceptional. There is a large element of truth to this. There was indeed a *Novus Ordo Seclorum*, a new order for the ages, established by the Founders of the United States. There had never been anything quite like it before.

But to fully understand the meaning of the American Founding, and of our Declaration and Constitution, we need to go back even farther, to see where they came from. The Founders were not writing on a blank page. Far from it. They made a Revolution because the American people already held strongly to certain principles that they saw coming under increasing threat. And they wrote our Founding documents as a conscious attempt to preserve a valued way of life, at least as much as to make something entirely new.

In the run-up to the Revolution, most of the Founders claimed not to be revolutionaries at all. Many were horrified by the thought of going to war with their king and kinsmen, and did so only as a last resort. Rather than claiming to be rebels, they asserted their right to all the ancient liberties belonging to free-born Englishmen, which the Englishmen of their own day were insidiously trying to take away from them.

Even in the midst of a Revolutionary upheaval, the American Founding was a period of continuity as much as it was of change. The freedom the revolutionaries were defending was ancient, and they knew it was. As we will show, in this as in so many things, the Founders were right – more right than they are given credit for today, and even more right than they realized themselves.

This chapter and the next one provide an overview of the English roots of American culture and American institutions, up to the time of the first settlements in North America by the English. We are well aware that there were other cultural influences on the American colonies, but it is an unassailable fact that the predominant influence on the United States, as the colonies eventually became, was English. The majority of us, wherever our ancestors may have come from, speak English today, and most of us grew up speaking it. Our legal system is derived from the English Common Law, not the Civil Law of continental Europe. The history of England and its influence on America will tell us far more about ourselves than studying any other community, however substantial the impact certainly has been of various other cultures.

The tale of the English settlement of America has been told in many places and in many ways over the years. Its general outline is well known to everyone who has gone to an American public school. Jamestown and Plymouth are familiar names, and we will not tell that story once again in this book. However, we will cast the familiar facts in a new light for many readers. To the authors' knowledge, virtually no one else has applied this sort of anthropological analysis of the Anglo-American family to American history in this way.

In our reinvestigation of this familiar story we applied the study of family structures to our history. We delved into the differences between the more close-knit, authoritarian, and even communitarian family types prevalent for centuries in most of continental Europe and the more loosely knit, libertarian, even entrepreneurial family type that developed in England. Based on the best evidence available today, we concluded that the English type of nuclear family was a critical factor in many of the better-known political, legal, economic, and cultural developments in England, and then in America.

The English are descended from the Germanic conquerors who brought to England the "integrated nuclear family," in which nuclear families formed separate households, but stayed close to their relatives for mutual cooperation and defense. These people were illiterate, so we have no written records from those times, and we cannot know precisely how they organized their family life. But what we do know for sure is that over time the original Germanic family type developed into the "Absolute Nuclear Family," or "ANF," which we have today. It appears that the family type we have now has existed for about a thousand years. Its features include: (1) adult children choose their own spouses, without arranged marriages, (2) adult children leave their parent's home to form a new, independent family in a new home, (3) the parents do not have a duty to leave their property to any child, and they may sell it during their lives or leave it by will to anyone they choose, (4) children have no duty to provide for their parents, and (5) extended families are weak and have no control over personal decisions.

This English family type, which became the American style of nuclear family, changed very little, and only very slowly, over time. This continuity was and is a fundamentally important fact. It was the deepest basis for the development of freedom and prosperity in England, and then in America. Further, the underlying Anglo-American family type was the foundation for all of the institutions, laws, and cultural practices that gave rise to our freedom and prosperity over the centuries.

Another underappreciated fact is the striking element of continuity in the culture that developed in England, and then in America. Certain writers, especially David Hackett Fischer, have demonstrated the continuity of American regional cultures, all derived from different areas of England. Yet for all of the variations in these regional cultures, they are all English-type nuclear families. Fischer has shown that for over four centuries these regional cultures have had a formative influence on subsequent developments in American life. We will discuss this crucial phenomenon in the next chapter. The key lesson from Fischer is that cultures do in fact endure over centuries, with discernible and even measurable patterns. Something that can evolve continuously over four centuries almost certainly goes back further still. Fischer's writing starts with the moment of departure of the four waves of immigration into North America from England. But his analysis points even further backward, deep into the past.

After investigating this insight, initially derived from Fischer, for several years, the authors have found, perhaps more controversially, that there has been a discernible and critically important degree of cultural continuity in England, and over into America, for *fifteen centuries*.

As a result, we have confidence that these cultural patterns will continue to develop and evolve, as they have for so long, adapting to new conditions but changing only slowly and grudgingly. Having looked backward, we can turn around and use these deeply rooted cultural patterns as a guide to likely future developments in America. For example, how Americans will respond to and adapt to – and in many cases generate – radical and transformative technological change will be shaped by our historical roots. The gales of change will blow strongly in the decades ahead, but the foundational culture of America will likely change less than many other features of our common life, and will shape our responses, including our political responses, to a transformed world.

## THE ASSIMILATIVE POWER OF AMERICAN CULTURE

One reason the American type of family, and the individualistic culture it gives rise to, has lasted so long, is its amazing powers of assimilation.

For a very long time now the majority of people in the USA have not been of English origin. Yet the many other groups who have moved to the USA, while retaining many elements of their old ways, over a few generations, have ended up adopting the American type of family, along with the English language. Many factors drove this assimilative process.

People who moved to America often had a desire to fit in, out of practical necessity. In the first generation or two they tried to become as American as possible, as they perceived it. Many people wanted to assimilate, or thought they ought to, and voluntarily tried to do so.

There was also a degree of compulsory assimilation. Public school instruction was in English, and American history was taught in a patriotic way. The Americans of 1880 to 1920, faced with a massive influx met it with cultural confidence. They believed the American way of life was good and better than what the immigrants brought with them, and that it was to their benefit to share, and to impose, the American way of life on the newcomers. The most effective method was the unabashed use of compulsory public schools to push the children of immigrants to become "Americanized." Children born here grew up speaking English and fell away from the cultural orbit of the "old country," wherever that may have been.

A less appreciated factor pushing assimilation was the American legal system, which compelled people to adopt American marriage and inheritance practices. However attached immigrants may have been to their own practices, if they were incompatible with our family culture, they could not maintain them here for more than a generation or two. Other cultural systems could not take root or survive for long in America because the law would not enforce any other system with regard to spouse selection, inheritance, or household formation.

The protection of freedom of choice in marriage partners, especially for women, was critical to the assimilation process. People who moved to America, and more importantly their children, faced no legal obstacles, and few social ones, to choosing their own spouses. In America, parents had no legal authority to interfere with the marriage decisions of adult children, whatever the law and customs may have been back in "the old country." The children of immigrants often wanted to marry someone from outside their ethnic or religious community. They then necessarily formed their own families outside of one or the other cultural milieu they came from, or outside of both.

The story of immigrants coming to America for opportunity and freedom, but feeling they are losing their children to a culture they do not always like or understand, is an old one that has been repeated many times. There is an element of sadness to this. This process of loss of the old way of life may be felt as tragic by the parents, but it has been a triumph for Americans over the centuries. We have peacefully, though not painlessly, assimilated millions of people, one marriage and one family at a time, into a shared culture. It is part of the price, often unrecognized, that many people paid to come to America and be part of it. Assimilation to our culture is not costless, but it has hopefully been worth the price over time, to most people who came here and to their children and grandchildren.

The innate appeal of ordinary life here is a further factor pushing toward assimilation. The American middle class family, living in its own home, with some privacy, is a way of life that appears to have universal appeal, or at least very widespread appeal. Immigrants from all over the world have come to America and many have found the life here to be fulfilling, rewarding, and pleasant. Although they may feel a pang for the warmth and security of their old ways, they find that they want the American way for themselves and their own families.

In particular, the nuclear family seems to be an appeal to many people who come from more tightly bound, extended families. The American style of family life liberates them from the web of obligations imposed by an extended family, which in many cultures is the most powerful force in people's lives. In America's expanding economy, with seemingly limitless opportunity, most immigrants would not have felt the benefits of the safety net provided by an extended family to be necessary, while the burdens were apparent. The tradeoff in warmth and security, which was lost as strong extended families dissolved in America, must be counted as a cost. Nonetheless, the American way of life, with its greatly reduced family expectations, permitted individual achievement and was liberating for many who came here.

American culture has a distinctly demotic character, which makes it attractive to immigrants and to people around the world. In plainer English, America is a country where ordinary people have had money in their pockets, and they could make or buy whatever they wanted. Culture happened bottom up, compared to most places that have ever existed before. For the first time in the history of the world, a large majority of people in a country could truthfully claim to be middle class, not just in their values, but because they actually had disposable income. And the American people spent it on things that they actually liked, usually without too much regard for what the self-selected sophisticates in society considered to be good taste. Tom Wolfe describes this phenomenon:

> They were heading out instead to the suburbs – the *suburbs!* – to places like Islip, Long Island, and the San Fernando Valley of Los

Angeles – and buying houses with clapboard siding and a high-pitched roof and shingles and gaslight-style front-porch lamps and mailboxes set up on top of lengths of stiffened chain that seemed to defy gravity and all sorts of other unbelievably cute or antiquey touches, and they loaded these houses up with "drapes" such as baffled all description and wall-to-wall carpet you could lose a shoe in, and they put barbecue pits and fish ponds with concrete cherubs urinating into them on the lawn out back, and they parked 25-foot-long cars out front and Evinrude cruisers up on tow trailers in the carport just beyond the breezeway.

The *gaucherie* of the American middle-class, especially its "lower middle-class," will forever raise a sneer on elitist lips. But many people who move here prize the ability to do whatever they damn well please in their own homes and their own backyards. The furniture stores in immigrant areas in Chicago feature an abundance of *faux* leopard- and zebra-hide upholstery. This freedom long precedes the postwar suburbs, where it reached a luxuriant phase due to a previously unimaginable level of widespread affluence. This "culture of ordinary people" has helped to draw people here and to keep them here.

To sum up, the American nuclear family, and the English family that preceded it, has been robust over the centuries, both from its own inherent strength and from its ability to absorb and transform many others from every possible background.

### CAN THE PAST PREDICT THE FUTURE?

All of the foregoing provokes an obvious objection, which comes in both a conservative and a progressive variant: "Wait a minute, isn't the American nuclear family falling apart? How can you say the future will be shaped by an institution that is breathing its last?" From the Right there will be regret or anger in the question, or that distinctively conservative type of pessimism that seems almost to enjoy the prospect of an apocalyptic end to all that is good and true in the world. From the Left there is more than a whiff of *schadenfreude*, and a sense that the full liberation of society, and particularly women, from an outmoded way of life is finally on the way, that history is moving in the right direction, though not fast enough. In either case, the question boils down to this: "How can a culture based on a particular type of family, as you claim, continue to exist when its foundations are disappearing before our eyes?"

Admittedly, we are in midst of rapid and even chaotic change in family life in America. By many objective measures, and by simple observation, the world has been turned upside down in recent decades. The birth control pill, a transformative technology on the scale of the steam engine, was a cultural supernova whose blast is still ongoing, and whose effects are still impossible to estimate. Effective antibiotics, which reduced the risk and virulence of venereal disease, had a related and compounding effect. Other changes include:

- the liberation of women from back-breaking domestic work because of the electrification of the home and advances in power machinery,

- the move of many women out of the house and into the cash economy,

- the dissolution of traditional family life,

- the legality and widespread use of abortion,

- the sweeping impact of no-fault divorce,

- the effect of fragmented families on several generations of American children,

- the social acceptance of single motherhood,

- the appearance of a political and cultural movement demanding civil rights and marriage for gay people, and

- the rise of ubiquitous pornography on the Internet.

These and other developments have changed or undermined the family as it was known to Americans two or three generations ago. Each of these phenomena is apparently at odds with our claim that the Anglo-American style of nuclear family will continue to be a major determinant of culture and institutions in America.

Although no one can know the future, we speculate that the momentum built up over many centuries is nonetheless likely to continue for some time to come. In foreign countries political attitudes are still shaped by old family patterns that are no longer as pervasive as they were. People's expectations are shaped by upbringing, language, institutions, and unconscious patterns of behavior that take centuries to form. Remarkably the gay rights movement is currently focused on participating in marriage, and the type of marriage they seem to want is a nuclear-type family.

It is too early to say where the many novel developments we are living through now will ultimately lead. We are in the early decades of changes so massive, not only in family life but in technology and politics, that no one can possibly predict how it will all play out. But although there will continue to be changes to the American family, we do not expect to see a total break with the past. Our attitudes and expectations are still shaped by the momentum of centuries, and that will almost certainly continue to be true for a long time to come. We do not anticipate a basic change in cultural attitudes and expectations among the majority of people, at least not soon.

Furthermore, the prospect of a reassertion or revival of family life along more traditional American lines, either generally or among self-selecting communities, cannot be ruled out in the decades ahead. Patterns of radical change followed by partial retrenchment have happened before and may do so again. Further, more traditional families, and more religiously observant ones, tend to have more children than others. As a result, more traditional families may inherit the Earth over a few generations through a steady demographic shift.

The process of Americans sorting themselves out into communities that are more culturally and politically homogeneous, which is underway now, will also likely continue. In that case, there may be a patchwork pattern of self-selected communities that are more strongly influenced by the traditional family and its culture, whereas others evolve in different directions. Those who want to follow different paths, personally or by voluntary association, will increasingly demand to be allowed to do so and to adopt their own community standards. It's a big continent. There is room for all of us. And the appeal and success, or lack of it, of each community will tell over time.

As a result, for now, we have some confidence in our speculation about

the political and economic arrangements that might arise, and are likely
to work, over the next few decades. These future arrangements will still
necessarily be premised in large measure on our centuries-old family patterns, and the unconscious expectations that arise from them.

Because our purpose in looking back is to explain the present, and to
make educated guesses about the future, we will concentrate in this chapter
on the elements of English history that were later influential in American
life. Whatever fascination the many other facets of English history certainly have, that history already fills entire libraries with worthy books. We
will necessarily remain America-focused. Further, our attention will be
directed to those aspects of our English inheritance that have led to American freedom and prosperity, and which have caused America to be the
cutting-edge civilization for the development of much of the modern world.

## THE ORIGINS OF ENGLISH CULTURE ARE GERMANIC

If we Americans, even the people whose ancestors came from other
places, are the cultural descendants and heirs of the English who settled
here, can we go back even farther? There was a time when there were no
English people on the island of Britain. Do we know where the English
themselves came from? In fact, we do. The English and their culture,
including their family structure, have continuous and unbroken roots
that go back to the conquest of Britain by Germanic peoples – Saxons,
Jutes, Angles, and others – starting in the middle of the fifth century.

Our investigation has demonstrated that the cultural roots of
England, and hence of America, trace back to the Germanic peoples who
overran the Roman Empire, and in particular, the Saxons and other peoples who conquered England.

Thomas Jefferson thought English liberty started with Hengist and
Horsa, who according to the *Anglo-Saxon Chronicle*, our oldest written
record of these events, first brought the Saxons into England. That is where
our analysis will also start. We will trace a non-stop process of expansion
and settlement in a generally westward direction for almost fifteen centuries, with a first migration across the North Sea to England, followed a
thousand years later by a second and larger migration across the Atlantic
to America. Further, we will show that over this immense span of time

there was a high degree of cultural continuity, an unbroken line of development – change within continuity and continuity within change – that lives on to this day.

The ancient Germanic origin of English and American culture is now at best a controversial idea, but that was not always the case. It was once a commonly accepted fact that English life and liberty started with the conquest of England by Germanic tribesmen, usually referred to as Anglo-Saxons, or simply as Saxons. In modern times, the long-established theme of English liberty having Germanic roots has gone out of fashion for many reasons – two world wars and a genocidal holocaust waged by modern Germans not least among them.

However the main reason this idea has faded away is because it was couched in the wrong terms in the past. Writers in the past who asserted the Germanic roots of English liberty often did so using expressions like "blood" or "race." They spoke in terms of an Anglo-Saxon "race" that was especially democratic or liberty-loving. Modern people quite rightly recoil from the openly racist ideas formerly expressed by writers on this subject. Because of the racial expressions used by earlier writers, reference to the Germanic origin of English culture and English liberty is usually seen as suspect or tainted, or as purveying ethnic stereotypes.

Modern people are morally offended by this type of thinking, and rightly so. But even more important, the strictly racial explanation for the Germanic roots of English liberty is simply and demonstrably incorrect. We now know more about human biology and genetics than did the writers of the eighteenth and nineteenth centuries. We know for a fact that there is no genetic basis for the English way of life. There is nothing special in the DNA of any English "race" that especially suits them for liberty. Furthermore, we have now had a long track record of English-speaking societies, including America, that are a mixture of all types of people. We have found that people of all possible races, have, over time, and sometimes painfully, adapted to and adopted the culture they found when they moved to America. Fifteen centuries after the Germanic tribes conquered England, we now see people of every race under the sun speaking English, living in nuclear families, and living under English-derived American laws. Americans of every background do not need any "Anglo-Saxon blood" to live and thrive in America.

Nonetheless, contrary to the current majority view, we believe that the older idea of our cultural origins, once it is stripped of its inaccurate racial elements, is fundamentally correct. Despite the defects of earlier thinking on these matters, in general the Germanic origins of English, and hence American liberty, are historically well founded. Because this historical fact must be stripped of its outdated racialist packaging to be properly understood, older writers, some of whom have valuable insights, must be used with care.

For example, an extraordinary and beautifully written work describing this cultural continuity is Edward Augustus Freeman, "The English People in its Three Homes" from his book *Lectures to American Audiences* (1882). Freeman was a profoundly learned man, and he provides a vivid depiction of the very same continuity across the centuries that we are focused on here. However, Freeman was racist in his outlook, in a way that Victorian writers often are, to the dismay of their later readers.

The historical record as it now stands, based on documents, archeology, and genetic evidence, shows that *the foundations of English liberty were not genetic or racial, but cultural, institutional, legal, and political.* These foundations were set down at the time of the occupation of Britain by its Germanic conquerors, who brought a distinct culture with them when they conquered England. As we will show below, the thread that connected the generations for centuries, from the Saxons to the American colonies, and down to our own day, was the English nuclear family.

## THE AMERICAN FOUNDERS BELIEVED THAT THEIR "ENGLISH LIBERTIES" WENT BACK TO THE SAXONS

The American Founders were well aware of the deep roots of their liberties and appealed to the "ancient constitution" of the English, indeed of the Saxons, as their source. They asserted their right to the liberties of "free born Englishmen," and they took the Germanic roots of those liberties for granted.

The American Founders learned about these ancient roots from various sources. One was Baron de Montesquieu, whose book *The Spirit of the Laws* was a major influence on the thinking of the American Founders. Montesquieu traced the roots of English liberties to their Germanic roots.

Montesquieu thought that the "admirable treatise" of the ancient

Roman writer Tacitus, entitled "On the Manners of the Germans," showed that "the English have borrowed the idea of their political government" from the ancient Germanic tribes.

The accuracy of Tacitus's depiction is disputed by current scholars. Nonetheless, his depiction, made centuries before the Saxon conquest of England, is the only one we have of the life of these Germanic peoples who later overran the Roman Empire. Further, it has been accepted as generally accurate for centuries, including by the American Founders. We also accept it as a generally accurate depiction.

The American Founders also learned about the Saxon roots of their institutions and their liberties from the influential legal historian and scholar William Blackstone. Blackstone wrote a four-volume *Commentaries on the Laws of England* in the decades prior to the American Revolution. The *Commentaries* were universally recognized as a standard guide to the law of England – and the Americans took Blackstone as their guide as well. Blackstone spoke of the "spirit of Saxon liberty" as part of the background of English law.

Thomas Jefferson had a detailed understanding of the Saxon roots of American liberty and American landholding. Jefferson asserted that the Saxon ancestors of the English settlers

> were the free inhabitants of the British dominions in Europe, and possessed a right which nature has given to all men, of departing from the country in which chance, not choice, has placed them, of going in quest of new habitations, and of there establishing new societies, under such laws and regulations as to them shall seem most likely to promote public happiness. That their Saxon ancestors had, under this universal law, in like manner left their native wilds and woods in the north of Europe, had possessed themselves of the island of Britain, then less charged with inhabitants, and had established there that system of laws which has so long been the glory and protection of that country.

Jefferson understood the "laws" of the Saxons to have survived as the basic law of England for thirteen centuries, since the legendary conquest of England by Hengist and Horsa. Jefferson even proposed that the national seal of the United States depict "Hengist and Horsa, the Saxon chiefs from whom we claim the honor of being descended, and whose political principles and form of government we have assumed."

The Founders' assertion of the ancient Saxon roots of their liberties was to some extent political rhetoric. In particular, when the political writers of the Founding era wrote that the Saxons had possessed a pure or perfect constitution, they were indulging in politically motivated myth-making. But, embellishment aside, the Saxon origin of their liberties was indeed a historical reality, and they appear to have actually believed it to be true.

Most modern scholarship dismisses the Founders' claim of the Germanic and specifically Saxon roots of America, and of our tradition of political and economic liberty, as unhistorical, mythical, racist, or politically opportunistic. However, modern scholars are wrong and the American Founders were more correct than they are currently given credit for.

## MODERN SCHOLARSHIP ALLOWS US TO DIG BACK FARTHER THAN DID TOCQUEVILLE

By common acclamation, Alexis de Tocqueville is the most astute student of American culture we have ever had. He undertook to study America, starting in 1837, about two generations after the Founding. As we do, he looked to the English origins of the Americans, seeking the origins of the American way of life in the mother country. He wrote: "If we were able to go back to the elements of states and to examine the oldest monuments of their history, I doubt not that we should discover in them the primal cause of the prejudices, the habits, the ruling passions, and, in short, all that constitutes what is called the national character."

But, at least in *Democracy in America*, Tocqueville expressed skepticism about the possibility of discovering the primal causes of European countries (including England). As he explained, by the time people sought to examine the origin of their countries, "time had already obscured it, or ignorance and pride had surrounded it with fables behind which the truth was hidden." Thus Tocqueville appears to have rejected the possibility of looking back past the few centuries since the English colonial settlement in North America to search for the foundations of the American way of life. Tocqueville was only able to work back in the historical documents to the late fifteenth century. Tocqueville therefore looked mainly at the national character of the English at the time that they first settled in America, as they were about 1600, and in the decades following.

As a result, Tocqueville focused on the Puritanism of the English settlers in America and the geography of the American continent, and did not expend much effort seeking answers from deeper in the past. Tocqueville was familiar with Baron de Montesquieu, who wrote in his book, *The Spirit of the Laws*, that English political institutions could be traced back to the ancient Germans, as depicted in the writing of the Roman historian Tacitus. However, Tocqueville did not rely on these historical arguments in writing *Democracy in America*. Indeed, the word Saxon does not occur in *Democracy in America*, and he referred to those who sought continuities from Saxon times as "antiquarians."

Tocqueville could not have known that the medieval and earlier roots of English culture would become far more accessible in later decades of the nineteenth century. Tocqueville, in his writings after *Democracy in America*, did apparently perceive a deeper and older unity between England and America, extending back before the Puritans. Tocqueville actually visited England only after visiting America. As a result, he noted, for example, that aspects of Saxon legal procedure had survived down to his own day nine centuries after the Norman Conquest of 1066. Nonetheless, at the time he wrote *Democracy in America* the extraordinary continuity of English life from the prior centuries was based more on guesswork, sometimes inspired guesswork, than on hard evidence. As a result, in our view, Tocqueville, in his most influential work, gave too much weight to the strictly Puritan element in the settlement of America.

Tocqueville, by focusing on differences between the settlers in America and the home country, prefigured much modern thinking about the United States and its culture. The unusual features of the English settlers, especially their Puritanism, became his focus, rather than their ordinary Englishness. Furthermore, Tocqueville took the supposedly unique nature of the American wilderness these settlers encountered as the other main factor in America's subsequent development, anticipating the "frontier thesis" of Frederick Jackson Turner, who asserted that the uniqueness of American culture mainly resulted from the frontier conditions encountered by the people who settled and occupied the territory of the United

States. Thus Tocqueville focused on the way the Americans broke with their English past, because, he claimed, they were founded by an unusual minority and because they had to adapt to unique conditions. In contrast, our focus is on the continuity, evident to a degree that Tocqueville was unable to see because many significant facts were not available to him.

In the years since Tocqueville wrote, scholarship has greatly advanced, and we are able to go farther than he could go in tracing the roots of American life. In the 1830s research on the earliest period of English history was only beginning. Since then, generations of historical and archeological research have illuminated the Middle Ages and Dark Ages of England, even back into preliterate times far beyond what was accessible to him. Nonetheless, Tocqueville's advice to look for the "oldest monuments" of our history was exactly correct. We are simply able to look farther into the past than he was able to.

## The Rise, Fall, and Reappearance of a Historiography: Tracing English and American Liberty to Its Saxon Roots

In the generations following the Founding era, there has been a rise, a fall, and the beginning of a new rise in the understanding of a Germanic and Anglo-Saxon foundation to English and American culture and institutions.

Throughout the nineteenth century, in the generations after Tocqueville wrote *Democracy in America*, there was a flowering of document-based, archival scholarship all over Europe. Every surviving written trace of the Middle Ages was examined. In England, the serious study of the medieval centuries advanced rapidly. In fact, English scholars were both blessed and cursed with an enormous volume of written records. On the continent of Europe, after centuries of nearly perpetual war and revolution, the surviving documents were rare and precious, and often fragmentary. But over those same centuries England had been spared from foreign invasion, and its civil wars had been mild affairs by European standards of violence and destruction. As a result, England had preserved a deposit of medieval documents many times larger than those of its European neighbors. Once Victorian era scholars began digging into this historical treasure trove, they were able to create a remarkably accurate picture of English life, especially its legal and political life, far back into the Middle Ages.

One of the overarching themes that arises from this literature is the unbroken development in English law and political institutions over the centuries. The growth and change that occurred were organic, without any radical break between generations.

As an extreme counterexample, the Mongols overran much of the Eurasian landmass and crushed the places they conquered down to rubble. The Mongols conquered both Russia and Mesopotamia, transforming those countries and fundamentally breaking their continuous life and development. Russia was deformed permanently into a land of poverty and tyranny by the "Mongol yoke." Mesopotamia, modern-day Iraq, was devastated, transformed from a lush country, watered by an extensive networks of canals, into the desolate desert that America soldiers came to know and fight in. England, in contrast, never suffered anything to match such devastating "change."

Even the Norman conquest of England in 1066 was more of a hostile takeover of an existing regime than a transformative occupation. It was not a loot-and-pillage invasion. To the contrary, William of Normandy saw England as a valuable asset that he was adding to his portfolio. He wanted to extract a steady and substantial flow of resources from it, not ransack it and ruin it. Therefore, as significant as the Norman invasion was, it did not entirely derail English developments onto any new track.

As the Victorian era historians came to see it, the invasion by the Normans led to a melding of conqueror and conquered rather than a replacement of the conquered by a truly new order of things. Edward Augustus Freeman wrote:

> The Norman Conquest brought with it a most extensive foreign infusion, which affected our blood, our language, our laws, our arts; still it was only an infusion; the older and stronger elements still survived, and in the long run they again made good their supremacy. So far from being the beginning of our national history, the Norman Conquest was the temporary overthrow of our national being. But it was only a temporary overthrow. To a superficial observer the English people might seem for a while to be wiped out of the roll-call of the nations, or to exist only as the bondmen of foreign rulers in their own land. But in a few generations we led

captive our conquerors; England was England once again, and the descendants of the Norman invaders were found to be among the truest of Englishmen.

The Saxon population, in the course of a few centuries, managed in large measure to assimilate even their Norman conquerors and rulers. This absorption was certainly made easier because the Normans themselves (the name means "North men") were only recently descended from Nordic war bands that had mixed with the local Frankish population, much like the Saxons and the Britons had done centuries earlier. Nonetheless this "Englishing" of the Normans is the most remarkable of the many feats of assimilation that the English, and later the Americans, would accomplish over the centuries.

The scholarship on medieval England from the Victorian era is extensive, and much of it is beautifully written. But we will have to take a shortcut to the last and greatest of the Victorian era medievalists, Frederic W. Maitland.

Maitland's life's work was devoted to the history of English law. He discovered early in his career as a historian that an immense depository of medieval court records was stored in the English Public Records Office, which had barely been touched by scholars. He devoted the remainder of his all-too-brief life to investigating these records. He discovered that English law, and the underlying social order, had lived a continuous life as far back as written records existed.

Maitland found that this continuity was particularly marked in the seven centuries preceding his own day.

Hardly a rule remains unaltered, and yet the body of law that now lives among us is the same body that Blackstone described in the eighteenth century, Coke in the seventeenth, Littleton in the fifteenth, Bracton in the thirteenth, Glanvill in the twelfth. This continuity, this identity, is very real to us if we know that for the last seven hundred years all the judgments of the courts at Westminster have been recorded, and that for the most part they can still be read. Were the world large enough to contain such a book, we might publish not merely a biography, but a journal or diary, of English law, telling what it has done, if not day by day, at least term by term, ever since the reign of Richard I (1157–1159); and eventful though its life may have been, it has had but a single life.

The picture Maitland paints is one of continuous and unbroken development in the law. He tells us that "[h]ardly a rule remained unaltered," meaning that that there had been broad and continuous change. Yet over that seven hundred years, the laws of England had possessed a single "identity" and had lived "but a single life." This was one of many strands of unbroken continuity across all aspects of English life.

In one of Maitland's early writings, *The Constitutional History of England*, he examines the law of England before and after various major political and constitutional crises: the Norman conquest, the reign of Henry VIII, the English Civil War, and the Glorious Revolution. In each case, despite severe political upheaval, Maitland found that, once things had calmed down again, the changes to the law had been incremental rather than revolutionary. Maitland confirmed that not even the conquest by the Normans, a foreign people speaking a different language, broke that continuity. William the Conqueror confirmed the existing law at the time he took over England for his own political advantage.

Maitland was cautious about tracing English law and the English way of life far back before the Saxon era. He was a legal scholar who relied on written records. The written records only went back so far, and often in fragmentary fashion, before the reign of the great law-making king Edward I, who reigned from 1272 to 1307.

> Beyond these seven centuries there lie six other centuries that are but partially and fitfully lit, and in one of them a great catastrophe, the Norman Conquest, befell England and the law of England. However, we never quite lose the thread of the story. Along one path or another we can trace back the footprints, which have their starting-place in some settlement of wild Germans who are invading the soil of Roman provinces, and coming in contact with the civilisation of the old world. Here the trail stops, the dim twilight becomes darkness; we pass from an age in which men seldom write their laws to one in which they cannot write at all. Beyond lies the realm of guesswork.

Maitland could not foresee that archeology, anthropology, and other disciplines in the twentieth century would help to deepen the understanding of those dark and illiterate ages. The "realm of guesswork" would be forced to give up some further secrets beyond what he could find in the documents available to him.

Maitland died in 1906. In the ensuing century, there has been a turn away from the idea of the Saxon roots of English institutions, and particularly of English liberty. By the 1970s, it was accepted in scholarly circles that the idea of "the Germanic or Anglo-Saxon origins of Englishmen" was nothing more than "a great national myth."

There were several reasons for the scholarly rejection of the previously universally accepted historical consensus. First, as noted above, the assertions of the "Anglo-Saxon origins of Englishmen" had often been presented and explained in racial terms. Scientific understanding had advanced, and no one any longer accepted the idea that some group or other had a genetic predisposition toward any particular set of political or cultural arrangements. "Race" strictly as a biological and genetic phenomenon had been correctly debunked as an explanation for the events of English history, or its differences from its European neighbors.

Further, the racial explanation had not been presented as a neutral fact, but as a prop for political control. Racial Anglo-Saxonism was used as the basis for nationalism and chauvinism and bigotry. The English, and many Americans, had been taught that as "Anglo-Saxons" they possessed a particular aptitude and right to rule others, that they were superior to other sorts of people. Hence racial Anglo-Saxonism was used as an excuse for imperialism. However, this ideological "Anglo-Saxonism" was not founded on historical fact but on political and ideological convenience, and self-flattery. Anglo-Saxonist ideology probably reached its peak around 1897, the year of Queen Victoria's Diamond Jubilee, when the Royal Navy commanded the oceans, the city of London was the center of all banking and commerce in the world, and the British Empire was at the height of its pride and glory.

But the story of the decades after this glittering apex was one of increasing stress, defeat, and barely averted disaster, none of which suggested any sort of innate superiority. Racial Anglo-Saxonism could not explain the bloodbath of World War I, the relative economic decline of

Britain, or the rise of Japanese and American power in the Atlantic and Pacific. As the British Empire faced new challenges, as colonized people began asserting themselves, any sort of racial self-regard was increasingly repudiated by the evidence. Further, as America became less and less an ethnically English country, racial Anglo-Saxonism in this country fell back to the fringes of culture and politics, and it faded away as a plausible explanation for American success. The Depression and the Second World War provided further blows to any notion of racial superiority on the part of any of the English-speaking countries.

With the experience of the race-driven Nazi holocaust, and the political awakening of the Black and Brown peoples living under European colonialism, any argument for the purported racial superiority became morally abhorrent. Further, during the conflict-ridden period of decolonization, and the civil rights struggle in the 1950s and 1960s, any claim that there was a special English or American aptitude for liberty seemed to be hypocritical and unsupported by certain obvious facts, such as the ongoing scandal of Jim Crow in the American South. In those dramatic times, a response couched as "yes, but . . ." was unlikely to get a hearing.

Ideological and race-based Anglo-Saxonism was also linked to the type of historical writing that came to be known as "Whig Interpretation of History." To greatly oversimplify, this type of writing presented the rise of England and its political institutions, particularly the constitutional monarchy, as the result of an inevitable and even Divinely ordained march of progress. When Britain was at its peak of power, this idea may have appeared to possess some plausibility. But in the years after World War I and Britain's long decline from global preeminence, the idea that Britain's institutions represented the culmination of history was no longer tenable.

The rejection of the "Whig Interpretation of History" blinded people to the fact that political and economic liberty had indeed evolved uniquely in England over the centuries and had an outsized impact on the rest of the world. The Victorian era historians who were accused of holding this view were correct on many points, in particular the continuity of English culture and institutions. Where the "Whig historians" were wrong was in thinking that there was anything inevitable or God-ordained about this fortuitous and fortunate historical record. In fact, the rise of political freedom and representative government was a series of lucky contingencies and several "close calls" where it could have gone much differently, and probably worse. However, by rejecting the Whig historians entirely, later historians lost much that was valuable.

There is yet a further reason that the earlier understanding of the Anglo-Saxon and medieval roots of English institutions and of English liberty came to be rejected. The rise of Marxism as a major factor in the academic world was antithetical to the idea of deeply rooted institutional and cultural continuity. To the Marxist way of thinking, all cultural and institutional phenomena, even human consciousness itself, are simply superstructure resting on an economic base. To a Marxian thinker, as the world advanced from an agrarian to a commercial and then an industrial economic structure, the culture would have necessarily gone through a series of revolutionary transformations. This was an *a priori* understanding among Marxist historians, and they projected it backward onto English history – because England must have been repeatedly transformed according to theory, the facts would be made to fit the model. In this view, English people in the Middle Ages had to have been peasants, not free people who bought and sold land like a commodity, so the historians cherry-picked their evidence to conform to their model. This set of ideological blinders blocked out any conception of cultural continuity from Saxon times. Evidence that England did not fit the Marxist model was downplayed or explained away. Proponents of a contrary view were shouted down or ignored.

As a result of these intellectual changes, the baby was thrown out with the bathwater. The reality of English exceptionalism was lost. The reality of English liberty and its slow evolution over time was forgotten. The continuity of English institutions across the Atlantic and into the American wilderness was downplayed or rejected.

However, there is now at least the beginning of a revival of the parts of this historical legacy that were well-founded all along. The source of this revival is the infusion of knowledge based on archeology and anthropology into the historical analysis. Key figures in this regard include the French anthropologist Emmanuel Todd, the English anthropologist and historian Alan Macfarlane, and the English historian James Campbell. The foremost modern expert on the Saxons, Professor Campbell, has said that the more he studies these ancient people, the more they appear to be simply English, and not alien at all, though they lived in England a century ago.

Professor Alan Macfarlane, in his seminal book, *The Origins of English Individualism*, showed that the Marxist reading of history could not be reconciled with the historical facts. At that point, in 1978, he hinted that Montesquieu's claim that the origins of English culture were Germanic and rooted deeply in the past might indeed be correct. Macfarlane has recently written that "[t]he social and political structure of the . . . Anglo-Saxons, who colonized England had certain features which were to be important over the next thousand years." Macfarlane, as an academic historian, is properly cautious, and does not go as far as we do. Nonetheless, Macfarlane's own findings are consistent with the story we tell here.

Furthermore, as we discussed in Chapter 2, the underlying family structure America inherited from England is the foundation of all the of our culture, our laws, our way of life. We owe this insight about the critical importance and the long continuity of family structures to Emmanuel Todd, who has been actively developing these themes for many years. Notably, Todd correctly predicted the collapse of the Soviet Union years in advance, and his explanation of politics in terms of family structure matches the historical facts almost uncannily well. His analysis of Anglo-American family life and its consequences deserves an attentive hearing.

This academic and intellectual revival of interest in the continuity of English and American culture, and their Germanic roots, is only beginning. Campbell, Macfarlane, and Todd are all still active, and we hope to see much more from them. We cite them specifically because they have had significant impact on our thinking. There may well be others whom we have not discovered yet who are developing these or related themes. We eagerly await further developments in what promises to be a revived field of inquiry.

## HISTORICAL RECORD OF THE SAXON CONQUEST OF ENGLAND

During the Roman Empire, all of Britain was inhabited by Celtic peoples, now referred to as Britons. Most of what is now England had been conquered by Rome, and it was ruled by a small number of Romans and Romanized Britons. Britain was a valuable province to the Romans, and it was stoutly defended. A large army was stationed there, with strong fortresses, and a defensive wall crossing the entire width of the island, Hadrian's Wall, some of which still remains standing two thousand years later.

But as the Roman Empire fell apart, Britain was not to be spared. In 410 the Roman Empire was beset by enemies on all sides. The troops based in Britain were called away to fight on other fronts. After centuries of rule, the Romans abandoned the local people to defend themselves as best they could against whatever enemies might attack them. The Britons who were left behind, without their defending legions, did not have to wait long for the assault.

Britain was soon under attack by Picts (from what is now Scotland) and Scots (who were, confusingly, from what we now call Ireland) as well as from Germanic people from across the North Sea. According to St. Bede, an early English historical chronicler, there was a king in Britain named Vortigern whose people were being attacked by the Picts and Scots. Vortigern held a council that "decided to call the Saxons to their aid from beyond the sea."

Then the nation of the Angles, or Saxons, being invited by the aforesaid king, arrived in Britain with three ships of war and had a place in which to settle assigned to them by the same king, in the eastern part of the island, on the pretext of fighting in defence of their country, whilst their real intentions were to conquer it. Accordingly they engaged with the enemy, who were come from the north to give battle, and the Saxons obtained the victory. When the news of their success and of the fertility of the country, and the cowardice of the Britons, reached their own home, a more considerable fleet was quickly sent over, bringing a greater number of men, and these, being added to the former army, made up an invincible force. The newcomers received of the Britons a place to inhabit among them, upon condition that they should wage war against their enemies for the peace and security of the country, whilst the Britons agreed to furnish them with pay. Those who came over were of the three most powerful nations of Germany – Saxons, Angles, and Jutes.... The first commanders are said to have been the two brothers Hengist and Horsa.

St. Bede's history cannot be confirmed, but much of it appears to hold up well based on other evidence we have.

Exactly when these events happened, to the extent they did occur at all, is beyond recapture. The foremost expert on the Anglo-Saxons, James Campbell, states that we do not really know the correct date of this remote founding moment. "The fifth-century Anglo-Saxons were illiterate and cannot have kept annals. Wherever the material in the [*Anglo-Saxon Chronicle*] came from the absolute dates required by the annalistic form were probably supplied by various processes of deduction and guesswork and are worth little." Nonetheless, we must pick a date for the beginning of this story, and the best we have is Bede's date of 449.

Whether or not Vortigern, Hengist, and Horsa were real men or legends does not matter for our purposes. The indisputable point is that Britain was subjected to waves of invasion and settlement by Germanic intruders.

The Celtic Britons went down fighting, and even counterattacked for a while. The legend of King Arthur comes from that time, and like Arthur, the Celts were ultimately defeated. Within a few generations, and after a few setbacks, the Saxons had taken over all of what is now England. The Saxons and the other Germanic invaders were the last people ever to successfully impose an alien rule and a wholly new culture on all of England. They pushed the Celtic Britons into the edges of the Island, to Wales, Cornwall, and Scotland, or off of it entirely, into the Brittany peninsula ("little Britain") in what is now France. They conquered the previous inhabitants, brought over their relatives, settled down in England, and never left. Over time, these "Saxons, Angles, and Jutes," and their descendants, came to be known as the English. In this book we will generally refer to them all as simply "Saxons."

## WHAT WERE THE SAXONS LIKE?

Because at first the Saxons left no written records, we have only sketchy notions about the early years of their settlement and rule. Nonetheless, we can discern that the Saxons shared certain commonalities with the other Germanic peoples who overran other parts of the Roman Empire.

Some of the Saxons cultural characteristics include the following:

- They were free people. They were independent minded, individually and in their tribal organization. They held slaves, and might fall into slavery due to debt or capture in war, or through gambling their freedom in games of chance, but the majority were not slaves.

- They owned property individually, not communally, and not as families. Adult children and parents had separate and individual rights, not collective rights as a family.

- They traced their lineages through both the male and female line. This prevented clans or extended families from forming and becoming exclusive, as happens when lineage is traced solely through the male line. As a result extended families or clans did not have collective legal rights, or any recognized political role.

- They usually worked together by voluntary association in peacetime, and under coercive authority mainly in wartime.

- In government, they had local rule. They had a confederation of tribes with chiefs, and with limited hierarchy.

- They restricted the authority of their kings. A king's authority extended mainly to war-making, with only limited power in peacetime. Their kings were bound by oath to serve the people and not oppress them.

- They preferred living in the country, or in dispersed homes, rather than living in large towns.

- They engaged in money transactions. They initially used cattle, goods, and other merchandise for trade, but quickly adopted a cash economy as soon as sufficient coinage became available.

These features contained in embryonic form the English culture, and the American culture, of the next fifteen centuries.

To stretch things to nearly the breaking point, this list already shows in very rough form a discernible similarity to the American culture we know today. We can see the outlines of a society of (relatively) free and equal people, who work together on a voluntary basis, who have divided and limited government, who have some degree of representative government, who prefer to live in the country (or at least a suburban mix country and city living) and who are business-minded and money-minded.

We cannot know for certain what type of family arrangements these Germanic peoples had in 449, because of the lack of writing or other direct evidence. But it appears that they had nuclear families, with some loose degree of communal ties and obligations. Linguistic evidence suggests that the Saxons from the earliest times were organized as nuclear families.

Apparently, among the Saxons it was typical for young families to start out living with, or close to, their extended families, and establishing autonomous households over time. This type of family structure, with the nuclear family homesteads generally remaining in proximity to their kin, is technically described as the Undifferentiated Nuclear Family. It is apparently the oldest form of family type known to mankind. The evidence therefore suggests that from the very beginning, an important seed for future developments was the family structure of the Saxons.

We can therefore add as a further characteristic of the Saxon conquerors of England:

- Their family structure was one of nuclear families, generally living in proximity to their relatives.

This type of family was apparently shared by all of the Germanic peoples who overran the Roman Empire, and it evolved over time into the many different types found in the various parts of Europe. Over the centuries the nuclear families in England diverged sharply from the path taken by families on the Continent. In England, they developed into what is technically known as the Absolute Nuclear Family.

England, and its daughter communities, are not strictly unique in this regard. There are three other places outside the Anglosphere where the Absolute Nuclear Family exists: (1) the western districts of Holland near the sea, (2) Denmark, including parts of Sweden and Norway, which were settled by Danes, and (3) parts of Normandy, a province of France but settled from Scandinavia and Brittany also in France. The first two are significant here. Emmanuel Todd includes a map in his book *The Explanation of Ideology*, which has been further confirmed by later scholarship, showing the current locations where the Absolute Nuclear Family predominates.

Remarkably, Edward Augustus Freeman, in 1870, and without bene-fit of modern survey data available to Todd, found that the people of these exact same geographic locations were the most closely related to the English. Freeman reached this conclusion based primarily on linguistic analysis. He wrote that the English language derived from the Germanic root-language called "Low-Dutch." He found that the communities that had a language with the same roots were the people of coastal Holland and "in the second degree . . . the Danish." And, in fact, the Germanic conquerors of England launched at least two of their invasions from these very loca-tions in Europe. For example, the Jutes came from Jutland ("Jute Land"), which is peninsular Denmark. This linguistic overlap between areas where the Absolute Nuclear Family now exists indicates that both the family-type and the language originated from the same root community.

In the English style of family even the weak kinship groupings of the original Germanic family type weakened further. Saxon, and later English, nuclear families became increasingly independent and autonomous, and relied on voluntary associations, contract and market transactions instead of kinship ties for an increasing portion of their affairs. This diminishing reliance on kinship networks contrasts with their European neighbors.

European writers have often been critical of the English nuclear family and the type of society it gives rise to. To select one example, the great nineteenth-century French sociologist and scholar of family life, Frédéric le Play, categorized the English family with the unflattering word "unstable." He condemned it in the following words:

> The unstable family constitutes that regime in which young men submit the least to the influences derived from tradition. The young adults leave their parental firesides so soon as they gain any confidence in themselves. They think themselves in no wise bound to preserve the memories or customs of their ancestors and only hand down such usages as are strictly indispensable to the preser-vation of the race. With such habits fully established the unstable family is seldom met with except among people living in a barba-rous and degraded condition. . . . The children are but little affected by parental influences often less so than those of savages. The adults marry outside of their family circle and they no longer con-nect their future views with the fireside or workshop of their

parents.... Under this system labor exhibits an instability in the extreme. True it is however that this regime frequently leads to rapid improvements in methods and even to the commercial prosperity of manufactories.

This quotation captures the traditional French animus toward the Anglo-American way of life. This animus lives on to this day. Le Play saying that England in 1871 was "barbarous or degraded" was an expression of outrage at the power and wealth of a country that played by a very different set of rules. Nonetheless, stripped of its moral condemnation, le Play provides an accurate depiction of the English family. Le Play was too good a social scientist not to accurately record the salient features of English family life, and to know that France had developed very different practices and even different moral values.

This English divergence, while empirically indisputable, presents a conundrum. Because the whole of Europe was overrun by Germanic tribesman, all with a similar or identical family structure, why did England end up taking an (almost) unique path?

One possibility is that the Germanic invaders who were willing to uproot and sail across the North Sea to England were already more independent minded than those who stayed behind on the mainland. Also, people willing to undertake an overseas colonization may have organized themselves by cooperative agreement rather than based on extended family ties. Hence the initial infusion of Germanic peoples into England may have been composed of exceptionally enterprising and individualistic people from the get-go. To speculate further, perhaps England after 449 was a "nation of immigrants" in much the same way that America is understood to be today, attracting the most footloose, ambitious, and ornery from more settled places. But this thesis is pure speculation.

More likely, the settlers in England were not significantly different from the other Germanic peoples engaged in a continent-spanning *völkerwanderung* – wandering of peoples – that engulfed the Roman Empire in the West. We will probably never know if the Angles, Saxons, and Jutes who settled in England were distinct in their family practices from the Franks, Goths, Lombards, and others who stayed on the European mainland.

Further, when the Saxons conquered England, it was the most "lightly

Romanized" province in the Western Roman Empire. By contrast, the Germanic conquerors on the mainland occupied lands with populations speaking Latin, or a derivative of Latin, and with the prestigious remnants of the Roman state all around them. As a result, the Germanic tribesmen on the mainland became far more "Romanized" from an early date than did the people who settled in England. This fact is proven by the written laws followed by these diverging communities. The Germanic law codes in continental Europe from the earliest date (the Visigothic, circa 480 A.D.) were written in Latin. The sole exception was England, where the first written laws, the Dooms of Aethelbert (circa 560 A.D.) set down the customary law of the Kentishmen of southeastern England in their own native speech.

If the Saxons' family practices did not diverge until after they settled in England, then we need another explanation for the development of the Absolute Nuclear Family. One suggestion has been made by Emmanuel Todd. He indicates that the Absolute Nuclear Family arose in response to the attempts by the Normans to impose primogeniture by law. Primogeniture requires that property always be given intact to the oldest son. This type of inheritance law creates a rigid aristocratic structure and locks up assets, and is a prerequisite for a functioning feudal system. Primogeniture took hold on the continent of Europe, but it never completely overcame the preexisting Saxon way of doing things in England. The most powerful English families adopted this practice. But for most English people this law ran against the grain. They resisted it continually for eight centuries, and finally abolished it in 1850. This is a vivid indication of the strength, tenacity, and endurance of cultural forces against political and legal power where the rules simply do not fit.

A more certain reason for the survival of the nuclear family in England is clear if you simply look at a map. Britain is an island. The Saxons and their Germanic cousins, once planted there, were able to develop their culture and institutions in relative security. They suffered depredations from Vikings, the forcible establishment of a kingdom of Danes on their island for some generations, raids by Scots in the north, and the occasional fight among themselves. And, as noted, there was the Norman Conquest of 1066, which did not uproot the underlying Saxon culture in England. Nonetheless, despite these intermittent bloody travails, compared to their European neighbors, the English have enjoyed a fifteen century-long "peace dividend." Because they lived in relative isolation and relative safety, the English were able to evolve slowly, and to make far fewer changes in their basic cultural composition than their less fortunate, embattled neighbors.

Islandhood and comparative safety allowed the English to enjoy a unique degree of continuity. England has been able to hold onto old-fashioned things to a greater degree than other places. As a result, a distinct characteristic of England is its retention of numerous *retained archaic forms*, which survive and evolve and are repurposed for tasks that are addressed by other means in other societies. The great French historian François Guizot observed that over "the entire course of English history, never has any ancient element completely perished."

The monarchy is a classic and obvious example. There has been a king or queen of England for well over a thousand years. The role actually played by the monarch has constantly changed over that time, yet the form of the institution remains. Another example of retained archaism is medieval constitutionalism, which placed limits on the authority of the king, and provided for local and representative government, where all of these features died out in Europe. Another example is England's ancient universities of Cambridge and Oxford, Cambridge having recently celebrated its 800th anniversary. These universities are altered beyond recognition from what they were in earlier centuries. Nonetheless Oxford and Cambridge have retained their independent life, where the equally ancient universities of Europe long ago lost their freedom and became agencies of the crown, and then of the state. Most important of all, the English type of nuclear family is yet another example of a retained archaism.

It is impossible to overstate the importance of Britain being an island. This was the most important factor for all later developments in England. In explaining the "unusual way" that England developed, Professor Macfarlane has written that there are many causes, in fact "webs of causation." But as he concludes in *The Savage Wars of Peace,* "the single central, necessary cause was islandhood." Because of its natural sea defenses, England "never suffered the total shattering which occurred when, in every other large country in Europe or Asia, with the exception of Japan, a foreign nation conquered its soil and took control." To get ahead of ourselves for a moment, the Americans went one step farther, by conquering almost an entire continent, with oceans on the East and West, and with relatively weak neighbors to the North and South, giving us the ultimate, continent-sized island.

Although we cannot delve into any detail here, England's European neighbors were shaped by the perpetual warfare that raged on the Continent, down even to the bedrock level of the types of families they came to live in. In general, a more authoritarian and communal life was necessary for mutual defense and protection, both against attack from foreigners and against the depredations of their own lawless rulers. The nuclear families of England were free to live without these tight networks because they lived in comparative safety and security.

One significant example demonstrates the greater safety of England compared to Europe: the English use of water mills. In Europe, mills had to be located in places that were secure and even fortified. This limited their use and value. In England, water mills could be located in the best location to generate power, and they were built for efficiency. Security from attack was not a major consideration. As a result, England benefitted from much more mechanical power and developed the most advanced skill in mill technology, machinery, and gearing. This set of skills was of immediate value once steam power became available to drive mills anywhere coal could be mined.

Looking back from our era, medieval England looks very violent and dangerous, and so it often was. But we cannot compare those days to suburban life in modern America that many of us enjoy. The proper comparison is to England's neighbors on the Continent. On that score, England was relatively peaceful, lawful, and secure. As a result, the original tendency toward independent nuclear families survived and developed in England, and evolved into something very different from the family structure of other European countries. Americans have inherited the results of these centuries of (comparatively) peaceful development.

England's location on an island, protected by its "moat" was a necessary condition for most of the important aspects of its later development. Of course, a body of water can be a highway for invasion as well as a moat, as the Saxons, Danes, and Normans proved. Merely being an island did not protect the Irish from the English, for example. To make an island secure, its people need to defend their moat, which means they have to have a powerful navy. As we know, the English, and later the British, did indeed build a navy. Their Royal Navy came for a time to rule the waves on all the world's oceans.

## A FAMILY FOUNDATION FOR FREE INSTITUTIONS

The Germanic invaders brought with them a type of family life that has evolved slowly over the centuries. Shielded by their sea-moat, the English had an extraordinary degree of peaceful and unbroken development. The many distinctive institutions of English life arose and survived because they were fitted for and shaped by this underlying type of family. In the next chapter we will examine some of these English institutions that developed over the centuries and that eventually took root in America.

# Chapter 4
## Our English Inheritance

### DEVELOPMENT OF THE ANGLOSPHERIC "TOOLKIT"

We have now gotten the Saxons ashore, have shown what kind of people they were when they arrived in Britain, and we have asserted that their family life, laws, and culture maintained an unbroken continuity, though of course evolving and developing, over the centuries. We now shift to identifying certain specific elements of English life that most influenced America. This requires identifying a few key facts out of a history of over one thousand years. A chronological narrative would simply reiterate a short version of English history. There are already thousands of books that do this. Instead we are going to break that history into categories and put the main pieces of the Anglo-American and Anglospheric "tool-kit" into those "boxes."

We will place the key features of our English inheritance into four categories used by Alan Macfarlane. He tells us that the distinguishing feature of modern life is the separation of the various spheres of life: politics, economics, religion, and kinship:

> Human life can for convenience be divided into four major spheres, the pursuit of power (politics), the pursuit of wealth (economics), the pursuit of salvation and meaning (religion), the pursuit of social and sexual warmth (kinship). In the normal state of affairs these are fused into one totality, a holistic merging based on the dominance of one sphere to which everything else is secondary. Tribal societies provide this dominance or infrastructure through

kinship, India and Islam through religion, traditional China through kinship and ethics (Confucianism), *ancien régime* Europe increasingly through kin-based politics. What is peculiar about modernity is that there is no institutional infrastructure, or, if it exists, it is provided by the impersonal, contextual, contractual pressures of the 'free' market economy and the ethic of trust upon which it has to be based.

The English were from an early time remarkable in their ability to break up these spheres and keep them separate. In that sense, the English were "modern" before modern times. The state did not control the economy, the church did not control the state, nuclear families and individuals were able to live with a high degree of autonomy, and there was wide scope for free association and civil society.

Most of the key elements of the modern world (especially the Industrial Revolution) began from this original source, appearing in England and then spreading to the rest of the world. Although our focus is on America, the "modernity" that started in England and spread to America has, disruptively and often forcibly, shaped much of the rest of the world for the last two centuries.

We speculate that the separation of spheres, and the institutions that grew up in a "separated" society, are all downstream consequences of the underlying family structure we have detailed above. The autonomous families and individuals produced by the English type of family were already "pre-loaded" for this division. They demanded a role in government and expected fairness in its operations, they were accustomed to deal in market-type economic relations from the earliest days and they have always made their own decisions regarding marriage and family life. The role of religion was bound up with these other elements until relatively late, but even there, it tended to take on an unusually individualistic form in England.

Macfarlane asked: "If kinship was restrained, God was kept out of the market, the State inhibited, how or why should people work effectively together?" The English solved this problem by creating what we now call civil society. A key to the success of the English, and then the Americans, was allowing voluntary association in each realm: political parties, business firms, church congregations, and nuclear families. Civil society associations of all kinds, formed on a voluntary basis, are the essential defining feature of England and later America. It provided the glue that held together the divided spheres.

To achieve the economic and political benefits of modern life, any country, any group of people, must achieve this separation to some degree. That process is a shock to many communities when they are first exposed to it, and some of them cannot manage to adopt it. The other countries of Western Europe were once part of a shared Christendom, and also possess much of England's inheritance from ancient Greece and Rome as well as from the Middle Ages. These neighbors have long had a much higher degree of "separation of spheres" than more remote cultures. Nonetheless, Europe for some centuries experienced a tendency toward the reintegration of these spheres, with the concomitant loss of freedom and faltering economic growth. The despotic regimes of Philip II of Spain and Louis XIV were marked by combined political and religious power, increasing state control of the economy and the near extinction of civil society. But there were still roots, though buried, and in recent centuries Europe has adopted much of the English-speaking toolkit with comparative ease.

The English, and the Americans, achieved and maintained a high degree of such separation many centuries ago. How this separation is linked to the underlying family structure of the English is a question that will require more investigation. But based on our research so far, we are willing to speculate that it was.

## ENGLISH FERTILITY

We have already spoken at length about kinship and will mention only one other factor before we focus on political, economic, and civil life. For many centuries, Western European women married later than did others in the rest of the world. The statistical line dividing early from late marriage age runs roughly from St. Petersburg to Trieste and excludes southern Spain, southern Italy, and Ireland, and is known as the "Hajnal line." Marriage and childbearing soon after puberty were typical outside this zone, whereas within this zone marriage was sometimes put off by as much as ten years.

Where Western Europe was an outlier in the world, England was an outlier in Europe, with typical marriage ages for women in their mid-twenties. In a similar pattern, the number of women who never married was higher in Europe than elsewhere, and highest of all in England. People in England did not marry until they could afford to set up a home of their own, and in many cases this pushed the age of marriage back, or pushed it off entirely. In fact, the English varied their birth rates based on economic conditions from as early as we have records, reducing their fertility when real wages fell.

As a result the English accumulated wealth for investment, permitting a rise in per capita income, and avoided the "Malthusian trap" of consuming all economic gains immediately by feeding a rapidly increasing population. Where population grew faster than per capita wealth, the population growth would inevitably be "corrected" by famine, epidemic disease, or warfare. England avoided this fate.

Also notably, the English apparently adjusted their fertility up or down to adapt to economic conditions to a degree unknown in the rest of the world, mainly by earlier or later marriage. Remarkably, the same English people who had comparatively small families at home, produced very large families once they arrived in North America, where opportunity seemed boundless, the demand for labor always exceeded the supply, and where land to start a new home was easily available. And as the twentieth century progressed and farm life became a thing of the past for most Americans, they adjusted their family size down once again.

## ENGLISH POLITICAL LIFE

English political life and practice derives ultimately from the practices of the Germanic tribes who conquered the country. Lord Acton describes the Germanic roots of free political institutions this way:

> Their kings, when they had kings, did not preside at their councils; they were sometimes elective; they were sometimes deposed; and they were bound by oath to act in obedience to the general wish. They enjoyed real authority only in war. This primitive Republicanism, which admits monarchy as an occasional incident, but

holds fast to the collective supremacy of all free men, of the constituent authority over all constituted authorities, is the remote germ of parliamentary government.

In these Germanic tribes the men capable of bearing arms were the electorate. They would select a king to be a war leader, on an as-needed basis. This was ratified by acclamation, with the warriors pounding their spears on their shields to show their assent. They then carried the newly chosen ruler, standing on their shields, to show him to the people.

Over time, as appealing as this rough-hewn process may sound, political life became too complex for it to continue. Nonetheless, Lord Acton's summary shows the earliest roots of our own concepts of political legitimacy: the right of the people to choose the ruler; the right of the people to remove the ruler; the duty of the ruler to act in obedience to the will of the people; limitation on the power of the ruler, especially in peacetime; the binding of the ruler by oath to a higher authority, first to the people, then to God.

**Limits on War-Making Power.** The role of the king as the war leader is not so central today as was in the past. Personal leadership by a monarch in battle ended, for the English, at the Battle of Dettingen, in 1743, where George II took the field. Yet to this day the British monarch is still formally and officially the head of the armed forces and frequently appears in uniform at public gatherings. The British princes also serve in the military when conditions, and personality, allow. One of the latest generation has seen combat in Afghanistan.

In war time the powers of the king, or of a government acting on behalf of "the Crown," were always broad and loosely defined. The usual practices and freedoms enjoyed in peacetime could be and were curtailed when the survival of the country was at stake. In similar fashion, our Constitution provides that "The President shall be Commander in Chief of the Army and Navy of the United States." The Constitution does not further define the powers of the Commander in Chief, which are meant to be broad and pragmatic in wartime.

However, the large wartime role of the ruler was never accepted as the norm. Instead, political authority was limited in peacetime, greatly enlarged in wartime, but then reverted back to "normal." This practice has been a characteristic of the English and Americans from the beginning and goes back to the Germanic tribes, as Lord Acton depicted them. To the despair of military commanders, whose job is to foresee and prepare for threats, our tendency has been to ramp up sharply to wage war, then to dismantle much of the successful military machine at its moment of glory, once victory was secured. The English, then the Americans, have consistently followed this pattern.

Our "ramp up, ramp down" approach to war mobilization helped prevent the creation of a standing army, which has historically become a tool of despotism in many countries. It also prevented even the prospect of military control of the people by the government, or of a military dictatorship. The downside is that English-speaking peoples have usually had to scramble at the beginning of major wars, which typically get off to bad starts for us.

Our circumstances as of this writing are historically atypical. The USA has gone in a different direction in the last six decades. We have maintained a perpetual, large-scale, expensive, peacetime mobilization in the United States since about 1950. This era is an anomaly, and this unaccustomed policy has had mixed effects. Perpetual military mobilization helped defeat Soviet Communism in the Cold War, an imperative task if there ever was one. But there have been many deleterious consequences, not least of which is the immense, ongoing, and vastly wasteful military-industrial complex. We will offer some proposals to rectify this problem in the chapter on foreign and security policy.

A further distinguishing feature of English and American war powers has been the absence of military conscription, especially in peacetime. The English king could not call men to the colors on his own say-so, but could do so only within specified and limited bounds. This is in contrast to Western Europe, where the military draft became commonplace and where large, conscripted armies were misused by despotic rulers, both for internal repression and for aggressive expansion. Americans inherited an attitude of opposition to conscription, which conflicts with our notions of political and personal freedom.

All-volunteer militaries are part of our tradition. When adequately trained and equipped, our relatively small, professional land forces have usually served us well, particularly in our smaller wars against remote or backward opponents. Otherwise, the English, and the Americans after them, had relied on local militias for local defense. But as early as the American Revolution the militias were seen as inadequate to the demands of serious warfare. The importance of militias declined further as military technology advanced, and as physical invasion receded as a likely possibility. Our modern National Guard and Reserves are adjuncts to the professional military, not true militias. A role for a revived militia-type organization tied to its local community and local government, as we had in the past, is one possible future development.

Britain did not have any military conscription until 1916, in World War I. America had sporadic state-level conscription during the Revolution, and large-scale conscription, on both sides, during the Civil War. In each of these cases, there was strong political and popular opposition, including very large draft riots in New York, led by recent Irish immigrants. The USA introduced conscription for both World Wars, and there was a general recognition that America was in genuine danger and that a draft was necessary. In each case there was nonetheless some public opposition to the draft. We then had a historically unprecedented period of peacetime drafts from 1948 to 1973, during the height of the Cold War. The American public finally withdrew its support for the draft during the Vietnam War.

We have only tolerated conscription where we perceived an existential threat to the nation. Imperial Germany, Nazi Germany, Imperial Japan, and the Soviet Union were threats on this scale. These conflicts required, or could have required, massive land armies. Using draftees for any lesser purpose than national survival was not acceptable, and was finally rejected.

Limiting the king's war-making power was probably the single most important factor in preserving England's political freedoms from medieval times to today. In Europe, the introduction of gunpowder weaponry caused a military revolution, which transformed not only military forces, but governments and societies as well. To survive, rulers needed to arm and train large armies equipped with expensive gunpowder weapons, especially cannon. They also needed to construct large, complex, and very expensive fortifications. These new security demands led to a sharp rise in the royal demand for tax revenue. Any continental European country that did not extract the money to compete militarily was overrun by those that did. In the process, the royal power became unlimited. France, Austria, Spain, and Sweden all went this route. Only England retained its medieval limits on government power through these centuries.

England instead built and maintained a powerful navy, thus securing its "moat," and avoiding the need for large land forces. Although a navy is expensive, its political impact was not comparable to the creating and feeding of huge standing armies, which could also be used for domestic repression.

**Limits on Executive Power.** The critical requirement that the king be "bound by oath" to act in the common interest lived on from ancient times into medieval times. Coronation oaths took on a more compelling force as the barbarians who occupied Western Europe, including the Saxon conquerors of England, became Christian. The coronation oath of medieval European kings limited their powers and established the essential principle that the king is subject to a higher authority, and that loyalty to the king is conditional on his ruling justly and according to law. A revolution against lawless, unjust, and arbitrary rule was allowed, if not required. The coronation oath made the monarch's possession of the crown conditional on respecting the people's rights, and a breach of that duty was not merely an offense against the people but an offense against God.

The coronation oath established very early the principle that the power of the government is subject to and limited by the law, by the consent of the governed, and in the worst case, to replacement by revolution. This "Medieval constitutionalism" died out in Western Europe in the sixteenth and seventeenth centuries, but survived in England.

Medieval customs and laws restricting the king were rejected in Europe, and the idea of Divine Right grew up in its place. To a Divine Right ruler, there was no rule of law; instead the king's own word became law. But the English never accepted that their kings had any Divine Right. Their kings for a time thought otherwise, and one of them was beheaded for his trouble. In England, the subjection of the executive power to a higher law, and all the institutions of free and limited government, lived on from medieval times. It never died out, despite some close calls, and was transmitted to America by English colonists. Regrettably, most Americans are not aware of this inheritance from medieval times, or its unique survival in England, or its importance to freedom in the centuries to come.

Limitations on executive power should not be mistaken for weak or "minimal" government. The Saxon kings claimed the authority to keep the "king's peace," which meant that civil disturbance and banditry were to be put down and order kept, but they could not always achieve it in practice. When William the Conqueror came into England, he and his successors created a strong executive power, which could secure the realm and keep the peace. But the English also insisted on limits of the power of the King beyond these requirements.

The English, like the Americans who came after them, wanted government to be limited in its scope, but strong and effective where it had to be. Where it was needed, the English approved of "energy in the executive," and we inherited this idea. James Madison, the leading drafter of our Constitution, wrote: "It is a melancholy reflection that liberty should be equally exposed to danger whether the Government have too much or too little power. . . ." The English and Americans have had good fortune in finding that balance. Minimalist government, or anarchic nongovernment, while theoretically appealing to some Americans, has no historical precedent.

We also owe to William and his successors a system of regular, orderly taxation and an organized Exchequer with its own courts to enforce tax collection. We are unlikely to want to cheer about the creation of a taxing authority. But it is easy for us to forget that countries cursed with arbitrary and lawless taxation never obtain political freedom or achieve significant growth. A taxing authority bound by law is a blessing few other people have had.

**The Common Law and Civil Disputes.** When the Western Roman Empire went down beneath the spears of its illiterate, barbarian conquerors, the sophisticated, written, Roman legal code fell out of use. No community can live without law, and the ancient Germanic tribes brought with them their own body of customary law. By 1000 A.D., all of Western Europe was governed by customary law, or codifications of the customary law, of the peoples who had settled in the areas once ruled by Rome. This unwritten law was based on the general knowledge, practices, and moral standard of the community.

This customary law became known in England, as the "Common Law." Frederic Maitland wrote that "Common Law is in theory traditional law – that which has always been law and still is law. . . . In older ages, while the local courts were still powerful, law was really preserved by oral tradition by the free men who sat as judges in these courts." Over time, the Common Law, which was founded on Anglo-Saxon customary law, was fused with Christian influences. It became the law that was enforced in the English king's courts as a law "common" to all of England.

After the Normans conquered England, the new rulers established a legal system that required the people to seek justice through the king's courts rather than local courts. As a result, the king's judges "rode the circuit" from place to place, and "held court" there, and imposed a consistent and increasingly uniform set of rules. The Common Law did not start out as a set of written rules, with each case being forced to fit into a preexisting mold. Rather, each case was resolved based upon the customary rules, as they were applied in previous rulings by judges. These earlier rulings established precedents, which had to be applied to all later cases with closely similar facts. This method limited arbitrary power, allowed people to know the law in advance, and to plan and act accordingly. This regularity and certainty is essential to freedom and to economic growth.

Land was the primary productive asset and source of wealth for most of recorded history, and England was no exception. The bulk of Common Law disputes, and the web of rules that grew from them, related to land ownership and disputes about land. But the Common Law also came to govern what we would now call torts (injuries to persons or property) and to the enforcement of contracts.

The Common Law allowed precedent to be applied to new facts and circumstances by analogy. This analogical expansion to accommodate new developments in the economy and in society is a uniquely important feature of the Common Law. This gave the Common Law a "Goldilocks" balance between clearly defined rules and flexibility to fit novel circumstances. The rulings of the King's courts thus became a flexible and adaptable system of law in a "bottom up" and inductive fashion.

We have also inherited from England a belief that there should be equality of all citizens before the law. Everyone appearing in a Common Law court expected to receive impartial justice from the king's judges. Generally, this was true and court procedure was fair in comparison to the rest of Europe. Of course, the Common Law courts were far from perfect. Punishments, including corporal punishments, were harsh. The death penalty applied to an appallingly broad array of crimes. Nonetheless, the Common Law courts developed a reputation for integrity that they held, and deserved, for centuries. George Orwell captured this spirit, which lived on into the twentieth century:

> The hanging judge, that evil old man in scarlet robe and horse-hair wig, whom nothing short of dynamite will ever teach what century he is living in, but who will at any rate interpret the law according to the books and will in no circumstances take a money bribe, is one of the symbolic figures of England.

These judges held onto their independence, and enforced the law consistently, even though the law was often not fair or just according to modern standards.

In contradiction to an ideal of legal equality, during much of English history there was a degree of inequality built into society that we would find repugnant. There was a legal category of aristocrats of varying degrees. The aristocracy was able to obtain various privileges that protected it from the ordinary operation of the law, including the right for its members to be tried by their peers in the House of Lords instead of in the king's ordinary courts. However, importantly, an aristocrat's family members did not share these privileges; they were solely reserved to the titled individual. This made England's aristocracy much different from the noble families of Europe. Frederic Maitland explained it this way:

> The sons and daughters of lords have been from the first been commoners during their father's lifetime, and on his death only his heir becomes entitled to any legal privileges. Whatever social pre-eminence the families of peers may have, has no basis in law: we have never had a *noblesse*.

Under the Common Law, there was never a class of nobles, but individual nobles. This was unlike the rule in France, where all those of "noble blood," the *noblesse*, possessed special rights and privileges. In England, a lord's family members, because of their wealth and power, might indeed have unfair advantages or intimidate jurors or overawe judges. But they were, as a strict matter of law, commoners like everyone else. This limitation on legal privileges protected liberty in England. The apparent rise of legal inequality in America, where the well-connected get special treatment, is a break with this tradition and corrosive to respect for the law and to freedom for the majority of the people.

The Common Law was critical for another reason, beyond its practicality, capacity to evolve, and relative fairness. The Common Law was also a shield for liberty, the emblem and guardian of the rule of law, where the law was more than the will of kings, and the kings themselves would be subject to the law. As the legal scholar Theodore Plucknett wrote, it embodied the "defense against royal prerogative that accounts for that legal principle so crucial to the tradition of Common Law: the King is bound by the law of the realm.... [T]he sovereign is not the author of the law, but the guardian of the law."

**The Common Law and Constitutional Limitations on Government Power.** The Common Law was especially important because England has never had a written constitution along American lines. Americans originated the practice of having a single document setting out the mechanics and the limitations on government power, which is above all other law. England has instead for centuries had a constitution in a looser sense. This "constitution" includes Common Law cases, written documents, especially statutes, as well as customs and practices that have been recognized as mandatory. Some features of the Common Law were recognized as being of "constitutional" significance.

One constitutional Common Law feature was an independent judiciary. The Common Law courts and their rulings became, over centuries, increasingly free from any direct interference by the king. The law, and the courts, came to exist autonomously and finally independently of the executive. An independent judiciary has been and remains a key protection against arbitrary government power and is embodied in the United States Constitution.

Most importantly, from a constitutional standpoint, was the application of the Common Law to the enforcement of the criminal law. The abuse of the criminal law by the ruler presents a grave threat to freedom. It was Common Law precedent that in large measure determined whether a person would be deprived of life, liberty, or property, as a criminal penalty, again based on known precedents. The Common Law required legal process rather than arbitrary rule in enforcing the criminal law. The requirement that the law follow known procedures and known rules became a bulwark of liberty. Trial by jury and the presumption of innocence in criminal cases, as well as the writ of *Habeas Corpus*, were among the Common Law protections that slowly evolved in the king's courts. The decay of each of these safeguards in America bodes badly for freedom in this country.

The freedom from the terror of torture, at the hands of the ruler, under color of law, is now an almost forgotten story. But this crucial liberty is one of our most precious inheritances. Torture certainly did occur in England. There is a rack on display in the Tower of London, and it was used in its day. Torture was employed in particular by the Tudor and Stuart rulers, who aggressively sought to expand the powers of the monarch and issued special warrants permitting torture. But torture was never recognized as a legitimate part of the legal process in England, unlike in Europe, due largely to the English jury system. In Europe it was unlawful to convict a person of a crime unless he confessed to it. Using torture to extract confessions was commonplace as a way to bring prosecutions to a close. Merely being accused, with its prospect of torture, must have led to the arbitrary imprisonment or corporal punishment of countless people over the centuries. But in England, juries were allowed to convict on circumstantial evidence and on the testimony of witnesses, making a confession, and torture, unnecessary. Because the government never had a legitimate legal basis to torture people, the practice was successfully barred in England.

The Common Law was the subject to multiple attacks by the Tudor and Stuart rulers (1491–1649), who were frustrated by limitations on their authority. These were forceful and determined rulers: Henry VIII, Elizabeth I, James I, and they were not easily kept from what they wanted.

One of the great confrontations between the Common Law and royal power occurred on June 30, 1606. Lord Coke, the Chief Justice of the highest civil court in England, was called to appear before King James I to answer some questions. The king had claimed the authority to decide which courts had jurisdiction over certain cases. The king wanted these cases to be heard in courts that did not follow the Common Law, where he could influence or dictate the outcome. King James made the aggressive claim that he could decide individual cases subject only to his own discretion and without regard to the established law. Lord Coke responded that "the King in his own person cannot adjudge any case, either criminall . . . or betwixt party and party . . . but this ought to be determined and adjudged in some Court of Justice, according to the Law and Custom of England. . . ." The outraged king declared that the law was based on reason, and his reason was as good as any judge's. Lord Coke replied to King James in no uncertain terms:

> God had endowed his Majesty with excellent Science, and great endowments of nature; but his Majesty was not learned in the Lawes of his Realm of England, and causes which concern the life, or inheritance, or goods, or fortunes of his Subjects; they are not to be decided by naturall reason but by the artificiall reason and judgment of Law, which Law is an act which requires long study and experience, before that a man can attain to the cognizance of it. . . .

The law, not the king's arbitrary authority, was the only permitted "measure to try the Causes of the Subjects; and which protected his Majesty in safety and peace." Coke, in another setting, and not to the king's face, put the matter even more strongly: "The King by his proclamation, or other ways, cannot change any part of the common law, or statute law, or the customs of the realm."

The supporters of arbitrary royal power also faced a practical problem, even if they were right in theory. The Common Law had grown up organically, and it was not clearly or plainly organized. The Common Law was not a code that could be rewritten or revoked. It could not even all be written down. It was a body of corporate knowledge and expertise, and what was written was scattered across many documents. The Common Law was comprehensible only to the lawyers and judges who practiced it. And of course they clung to their privileged position and resisted any effort to make their expertise obsolete.

As a result, no one could figure out how the Common Law could be gotten rid of, or replaced. To change it, the king would have had to create a whole new legal system from scratch. Piecemeal efforts to bend the Common Law to royal ends were absorbed, worked around, and interpreted out of existence by the bench and bar, and the system carried on. Maitland eloquently wrote:

The English Common Law was tough, one of the toughest things ever made. And well for England was it in the days of Tudors and Stuarts that this was so. A simpler, a more rational, a more elegant system would have been an apt instrument of despotic rule. At times the judges were subservient enough: the king could dismiss them from their offices at a moment's notice; but the clumsy, cumbrous system, though it might bend, would never break. It was ever awkwardly rebounding and confounding the statecraft which had tried to control it. The strongest king, the ablest minister, the rudest Lord-Protector could make little of this "ungodly jumble."

Odd as it may seem, the very fact that the Common Law was at once arcane and indispensable kept it alive. And so the legal foundation for our basic freedoms survived through those perilous times and was transmitted to America.

A significant detail in Coke's confrontation with King James I is that he was an Englishman, and his royal opponent was from Scotland. Through his writing and judicial rulings Coke was considered, even in his own lifetime, to be the very embodiment of the Common Law tradition. But James I of England was also James VI of Scotland. He had ruled the Scots before he also became the king of England. In Scotland, the Common Law had never applied. The law in Scotland was heavily influenced by Roman law, which was increasingly seen as authoritative in Europe. James I got his ideas about the unlimited power of kings from his experience ruling Scotland, and he tried unsuccessfully to import these ideas into England.

How was it that Roman law was relevant in Scotland and in Europe in 1606? The Goths had sacked Rome in 410, twelve centuries earlier. The surviving eastern half of the Empire lived on until 1453, but it was far away and held no sway in the West. The reappearance of Roman law is a strange chapter in European history, which is little mentioned in America. Sir Paul Vinogradoff, the great Victorian scholar of the Roman law, wrote:

Within the whole range of history there is no more momentous and puzzling problem than that connected with the fate of Roman law after the downfall of the Roman state. The story ... is, in a sense, a ghost story. It treats of a second life of Roman law after the demise of the body in which it first saw the light.

What happened was this. In or around 1070, scholars in northern Italy rediscovered a single copy of a compilation of Roman law that had been lost in the West for five centuries. This compiled code had been prepared on the orders of the Eastern Roman Emperor Justinian in 534 A.D. This Justinian Code contained centuries of accumulated Roman law. The lawyers and scholars were awed by it. It was immediately recognized as far more sophisticated and comprehensive than the comparatively primitive legal codes they were using. Universities in Europe, starting in Bologna, Italy, began to study and teach the Justinian Code. Over time, this old Roman law came to be widely adopted as authoritative. The law of continental Europe is still based on it.

This "reception" of Roman law, although it had some advantages in terms of order and clarity, was lethally destructive to liberty. Roman law allowed much greater power to European kings than they had enjoyed before and stripped away the traditional limits on kingly power. After all, Cæsar had been bound by no such limits. The kings of France and Spain and of other, smaller, states wanted what the Cæsars once had, and the Roman law gave them an excuse to seize it. Medieval liberty slowly died out in Europe. European rulers had less and less constraint on their authority, and such unlimited power was inevitably abused.

However, the reception of Roman law, and the displacement of traditional medieval law, never happened in England. Despite the prestige of the Roman law, and the efforts of some of England's kings to use it to justify their despotic actions, it could not take hold. England and its successors retained medieval notions of liberty and the rule of law, despite the near triumph of despotic rule under the Tudors and Stuarts. Foreign conquest by Spain or France might have succeeded in subjecting England to the Roman legal system, but the English, alone in Europe, never imposed it on themselves.

### English Statutes and Constitutional Limitations on Government Power.
Of the numerous statutes enacted in England, a few are considered to be constitutional in significance.

We will mention two that had a crucial impact on political freedom in England and in the United States.

Magna Carta, first enacted in 1215, guaranteed in writing various existing customary rights, which King John had violated. The king was forced by his barons to sign Magna Carta, promising to restore and defend these rights. Most importantly, the king promised his subjects what we would now call due process of law:

> No free man shall be arrested or imprisoned or disseised [have his property taken] or outlawed or exiled or in any way victimized, neither will we attack him or send anyone to attack him, except by the lawful judgment of his peers or by the law of the land.

The king could not take a person's life, liberty, or property on his own. The king had to bring that person before a court, presided over by a judge learned in the law, who would apply the law fairly and accurately, and would grant a judgment against the person only if the facts and the law required it. This language was eventually understood to mean a right to a jury trial, something that did not yet exist in 1215. Magna Carta, in its day, applied only to a part of the population of England. But over time, as more Englishmen became "free men," its guarantees were understood to apply generally.

Some historians have challenged the importance of Magna Carta, and claimed that it was largely forgotten for centuries and brought to light only much later. Maitland, the greatest of English legal historians, thought otherwise:

> The Great Charter stands in the forefront of our statute book ... [a]nd certainly it is worthy of its place. It is worthy of its place just because it is no philosophical or oratorical declaration of the rights of man, nor even of the rights of Englishmen, but an intensely practical document, the fit prologue for those intensely practical statutes which English Parliaments will publish in age after age. What is more, it is a grand compromise, and a fit prologue for all those thousands of compromises in which the practical wisdom of the English race will always be expressing itself. Its very form is a

compromise – in part that of a free grant of liberties made by the king, in part that of a treaty between him and his subjects, which is to be enforced against him if he breaks it.

At the time it was written Magna Carta was understood to be an important guarantee of political and legal rights. It was so regarded in England for more than five hundred years, including by the people who colonized America, as well as by the Founders of the United States and the authors of our Constitution. Magna Carta was the first constitutional document in our history, the first to commit to writing the limitations on government power, the first in a series of "treaties between crown and people."

Over time the symbolic meaning of Magna Carta came to overshadow its actual words. For example it was claimed, without much textual basis, that Magna Carta stood for the principle that "a man's house is his castle." This in turn came to mean that searches and arrests without a court-issued warrant were unlawful, and that "general warrants" allowing search and arrest of unspecified places and persons were also unlawful. To this day we consider it a basic right that a person's home should be his or her castle.

Whatever the king and barons may have put down on parchment in 1215, many in England and America drew on the prestige and general principles of Magna Carta when they argued for limitations on government power. As the legal scholar Leonard W. Levy wrote: "What mattered was not what Magna Carta actually said but what people thought it said or, rather, what it had come to mean. What also mattered was the inspiring imagery that swelled the sense of freedom in the ordinary subject."

Further, all Common Law–type arguments, whether English or American, are similar in structure. Lawyers gather precedents to be used in support of arguments, which are alive and urgent at the time. Lawyers are not interested in history; they are trying to win cases. The meaning of Magna Carta in legal and political conflicts was not an arid matter of historical scrupulosity about an old document. Establishing its meaning was part of a full-blooded, life and death struggle in the here-and-now, on behalf of threatened freedoms. Pushing arguments as hard as possible is what all advocates are required to do.

The Founding generation in America was influenced by both the substance and the symbolism of Magna Carta, especially in drafting our Constitution and Bill of Rights.

The Bill of Rights of 1688 is another key English constitutional document that came to have a major influence on our own Bill of Rights. It consisted of a set of promises by the new king, William III, to the English parliament. William III was Dutch, and he had just successfully conducted a swift, successful, and relatively bloodless invasion of England. This foreign ruler's claim to the kingship was legally dubious at best. Maitland wrote:

> Now certainly it was very difficult for any lawyer to argue that there had not been a revolution. Those who conducted the revolution sought, and we may well say were wise in seeking, to make the revolution look as small as possible, to make it as like a legal proceeding, as by any stretch of ingenuity it could be made. But to make it out to be a perfectly legal act seems impossible.... We cannot bring it into our constitutional law.

William III knew he was on thin ice legally and that attacks on his right to rule by his enemies would be convincing. To appear as legitimate as possible, and to secure the crown for himself and his heirs, William III made a "treaty" between himself and his new subjects. From this rather desperate deal, we Americans inherited much that has been of priceless value.

The Bill of Rights of 1688 stated that "excessive bail ought not to be required, nor excessive fines imposed, nor cruel and unusual punishments inflicted," which is identical to our Eighth Amendment to the US Constitution. It also stated that, "the subjects which are Protestants may have arms for their defence suitable to their conditions and as allowed by law." This is a predecessor to our own Second Amendment. However, our American Second Amendment is phrased quite differently and does not exclude Catholics! The different phrasing between the two provisions is a fascinating study, which we cannot plunge into here. Whatever the language, the concept of a personal right to possess arms is enshrined in the Bill of Rights of 1688, and our Founders adopted it and we have it to this day.

These and other guarantees of personal freedom in the Bill of Rights of 1688 were certainly important. But its most significant effect was establishing the primacy of Parliament over the king. The king could not on his own authority suspend or dispense with laws, nor could he levy money, nor could he raise a standing army in peacetime. Only Parliament could do those things.

The Bill of Rights of 1688 was the final triumph of representative government over royal power in England after centuries of conflict. But the broad grant of power that Parliament extracted from the king itself proved to be defective, precisely because there were no specified limits on that power. Parliament itself became despotic, especially to those who had no say in selecting its members. It was Parliament, far more than the much-reviled George III, which attempted to strip the American colonies of their legal and political rights, to the point that they rose up in revolution, with results we all know.

**Representative Government.** As we noted, at the dawn of their history, the English had a sort of direct, local democracy. As England developed into a single kingdom, direct democracy became impossible. But the kings still needed to consult with the people, or at least the most powerful people, to make laws that would be accepted and especially to levy taxes that would not provoke resistance or revolt in response.

Medieval England was not at all unique in its early development of representative government. In fact, some sort of representative assembly existed in every country of Western Europe that had been conquered by Germanic tribes. However, in the rest of Europe, over time, these assemblies were called less and less frequently, and finally fell out of use as kings became more powerful and arbitrary. What is unique about England is that its ancient Parliament survived from medieval times and developed into a national representative assembly. This survival and victory of Parliament was threatened on many occasions. There was much conflict, including a royal beheading (Charles I) and a foreign-led *coup d'état* (William III). But, as we saw earlier, Parliament eventually displaced the power of the king himself.

What came to be known as the English parliament began as an advisory body to the king, and it did not meet regularly. The word "parliament" comes from the French word *parler*, which means "to speak." Early "parliaments" were one-time events, gatherings of important persons to speak to the king and advise him, especially with regard to taxes the king wanted to impose, or to raising armies for war.

However, as the king's demand for taxes increased, and as new laws had to be enacted to meet new conditions, Parliament became permanent, and it began to meet regularly, and then frequently. It also began to take on the familiar features that existed in England until very recently. Peers and commoners were both represented. Each of these groups had its own "house," which came to be known as the "House of Commons" and the "House of Lords." Each of these houses had its own rules regarding membership. The houses of Parliament had to assent to new laws and to the imposition of taxes, though the king could sometimes muscle them into giving him what he wanted.

Representation was haphazard and limited by today's standards. Local counties and incorporated towns sent representatives to Parliament. But all districts were not equally represented, and only a minority of males, who met certain property qualifications, could vote. Nonetheless, the members of Parliament acted in some measure as representatives of the counties and towns they came from, typically consulting at home before coming to London.

Even though only a minority could directly participate in choosing members of Parliament, Englishmen often belonged to many other types of representative institutions, including their towns, church congregations, or social or professional groups. These groups usually had elected governing bodies. Thus, England had strong networks of self-governing institutions long before universal parliamentary suffrage. The English were accustomed to meeting, voicing their opinion, and voting on matters that affected them, and following orderly procedures to do so. The day-to-day practice of democracy and debate, in government and in civic life, were well established in England long before the colonization of America.

Local government in particular was a crucial school for freedom and democracy. Many English towns were able to obtain charters from the king, giving them a legal existence. These autonomous towns were called "burroughs." Each charter was unique, representing a "deal" between the king and the town. The king granted certain liberties in return for certain taxes to be paid. A common feature of the various charters was that the minority of people who were citizens of each town could participate in electing their civic leaders. As Tocqueville noted with regret, genuine local rule was lost in Europe, where the kings had imposed centralized control by the early 1700s, and towns and counties were reduced to administrative units of the central government, with no life of their own. In England local government largely retained its vitality and freedom from centralized control until at least the late nineteenth century. The degree of local identity and even local patriotism is shown by the fact that as late as Jane Austen's day, the English sometimes referred to their home county as their "country." Further, local officials, including the powerful county sheriff, had to live in the county and be answerable to the local landholders.

The English colonists in America from a very early date established local governments, including traditional features they had known back home. The colonists brought three institutions of more than a millennium's antiquity to America: sheriffs and posses; counties and county courts; and militia-based defense. These institutions ensured that the use of government power in everyday life remained close to the people. Notably the only three traditional personal obligations of England were jury duty, service in a posse, and militia service within the county, and all of these were brought to America. We still require jury duty; and although the sheriff's posse may theoretically exist in some places, it has fallen into disuse; and our militias are no longer locally raised and organized, and in fact are no longer militias. Nonetheless, local governments in the USA are still comparatively autonomous and locally accountable to this day.

Local control of law enforcement is particularly important. Americans have, crucially, retained local control of police departments and county sheriffs' departments. As a result our law enforcement agencies, with all their potential for abuse and corruption, have historically been closely accountable to the people they are charged with protecting. The police are less likely to unlawfully, or even mistakenly, kick your door down in the middle of the night if they are answerable at the next village board meeting. This local control seems to be eroding in recent years in America, which is a dangerous development.

National-level police have been an unaccountable and arbitrary force for tyranny, as the word Gestapo and the initials KGB attest. Americans did not create any police forces above the local level for over a century after independence. The first state police force was in Pennsylvania, in

1905, and the first federal police force, the Federal Bureau of Investigation (FBI), was created in 1908. We will say more about these when we discuss America 2.0 later.

It is impossible to exhaust the subject of the political inheritance we received from England. There are countless books as well on the legal and social aspects. We have limited ourselves to touching on some highlights, which we believe were particularly important, and which we believe will live on through our current troubled times into the future America 3.0, which we are predicting.

## ENGLISH ECONOMIC ORGANIZATION

The distinguishing feature of English economic life has been the dominance of market-type exchanges, made on a cash basis, rather than traditional or customary means of organizing trade and work, or disposing of land and other property. This distinctive feature goes all the way back to Saxon times. Commerce in England has been transacted in cash from the beginning. Archeology shows that even in early days there was a very large amount of coinage in circulation, enough to make cash-based transactions possible across all of England. This is an unusual feature of English life by comparison to other countries. As a result, the English economy has had a "modern" feel to it for a millennium. The English were capitalists in their thinking and practices long before anyone thought of the word "capitalism."

A market economy in land was especially important, and unusual. Ownership of land has, in most cultures, been bound up with particular families. A family would be identified with a particular plot, with strong emotional ties to it, and that family's unique attachment to its bit of land was recognized and protected. This is characteristic of peasant communities, in all parts of the world. But the English have never been this way. They have never been peasants. The English have, for as far back as we have records, treated land as a commodity to be bought and sold, to be subject to rational calculation of its value and its expected return. English land was not bound up in customary, peasant-type ties. Because land changed hands relatively frequently, establishing who owned any particular piece of real estate became a matter of great importance.

When William the Conqueror seized the English crown, he ordered an inventory to be compiled of his new kingdom. William's officers went about the country and took a survey. The result of this painstaking investigation was Domesday Book. It recorded who owned each patch of property, and what taxes were owed on it. It covered almost all of England. Domesday Book is a treasure trove of information about England at the beginning of William's reign. Among the many things it shows is that the bigger landowners owned property in separate lots all over the kingdom, not just in contiguous holdings. Property was purchased for use and for speculation, and ownership was diversified in portfolio-like fashion. And it did not have to be compact for defense, since domestic peace was reasonably assured.

Domesday Book also shows that land, and the fruits of the land, were owned individually and not communally. Maitland asserted that there was no factual basis to any theory that property was owned collectively, for example by a village, and only later came to be possessed by individuals. "No one who has paid any attention to the history of law is likely to maintain with a grave face that the ownership of land was attributed to fictitious persons before it was attributed to men." Rather, the Germanic people who occupied England "brought with them the idea that the cultivable land should be allotted in severalty." "Severalty" means owning property "without anyone else sharing in the ownership," individually. As soon as the invaders had occupied some territory they typically:

> formed villages closely resembling those that they had left behind them in their older home. But to all appearance, even in that older home, so soon as the village was formed and had ploughed lands around it, the strips into which those fields were divided were owned [individually] by the householders of the village.

This pattern went all the way back to the original Germanic settlers "so far back as we can see, the [Germanic] village had a solid core of individualism." Communal forms of ownership developed only later and became common in Europe, but not in England. Patterns of land ownership show that individualism in England goes back to the dawn of its history.

Amazingly, the original Domesday Book still exists. It is the first example of a permanent, written public record. It served as the final word on ownership of property, and chains of title were traced back to it. As such it is the remote ancestor of the record of deeds in each of the 3,033 counties in the USA. It took centuries for the recording of deeds to become systematic and efficient in England. In fact, the USA was ahead of England in this regard, in part because conveyancing attorneys in England wanted to retain their monopoly on expertise in confirming title. Nonetheless, in England, owners of property could always, sometimes after some effort, establish clear legal title to their property, to convey it, or to borrow against it.

The capacity to establish legal title to land, and borrow with land as security, unlocks otherwise "frozen capital." This liberation of capital has been a continuing source of economic progress in England and America. In many other countries, the capital embedded in land remains frozen, because land title is unclear, and is subject to arbitrary government power, and corruption and bribery. England and America have had relatively efficient and honest government, at least with regard to land title, for centuries. Notably, the recent corruption by major American banks of the process of establishing and transferring title, which preceded and partly caused the 2008 economic crash, is thus an unprecedented blow against a long-established pillar of American freedom and prosperity.

Besides surveying his new kingdom, William the Conqueror also established a central government, with himself as the chief feudal ruler. Feudalism is the political and economic system that was common in Europe during much of the medieval period. Generally, it was a system to provide for the military defense of a community, up to the level of an entire kingdom. It bound people as serfs to the land, and established that certain others would be lords, warriors who would subsist off of the work of the serfs. Feudalism was not slavery, and there were rights that ran between lord and serf. Feudalism was a dense web of contracts, with duties imposed on all parties. The lord had a duty to protect and defend; the serf had a duty to work and to serve. In practice, the lords were armed and powerful, and they did not always keep their side of the bargain. But the principle of reciprocal duties was universally accepted.

Under feudalism, land was parceled out so that serfs, working certain land, would provide sufficient support to arm and equip the lords to fight. Unfortunately, lords would sometimes treat their territory almost as separate kingdoms, when they could get away with it. This practice often led to the dissolution of central authority, making the king incapable of maintaining civil peace, and leading to devastating local warfare between the various lords.

Maitland revealingly wrote that England was at once the least feudal and the most feudal in Europe. England was the *least* feudal because the population retained many traditional rights, and they could seek justice in the kings' courts, not just those of their lords. Further, in England, whatever feudal duties a person owed, beyond those obligations, he retained a high degree of personal freedom. This is quite unlike the situation on the Continent where everyone who was not a lord gradually sunk to the level of an oppressed class.

England was, on the other hand, the *most* feudal because every inch of the kingdom was "held of the king." In other words no lord owned his land outright with no obligations to anyone else. Such "allodial" lands existed in France, for example, and the lords there could not legally be compelled to stop fighting each other, or to otherwise obey the king. This was a prescription for chaos, and it was never allowed to happen in England.

When William conquered England, he stripped the Saxon lords who had opposed him of their land, and he gave it to his own followers. The Norman lords took the land and took an oath to serve the king. William also ordered the Saxon lords who fought on his side to give up their land to him, and then he gave it back to them, making them also swear loyalty to him. As a result, every lord in England owed direct loyalty to the king. This prevented internal civil war, and it gave the king the clear responsibility and authority to rule the entire kingdom and to impose his peace to it. Civil peace is a rare and precious thing. Although there certainly was civil war within England, it was never as severe as the internal conflicts in continental Europe. William laid the foundation for England's thousand-year internal peace dividend.

Also, by establishing ultimate land title in the king, William established the system that we have to this day. In England and in America, all land held is held by individuals, but in every case there is the possibility that the land will go back to the state if taxes are not paid on it. In technical terms, such land is held "in fee simple." This gave the king a strong interest in establishing clearly who owned what property, so he could tax them. The spillover effects of having clear title had the powerful positive effects we have noted. Americans relied on this experience when they divided up North America, as we will see below.

William and his successors established strong government. In England and in America, strong government in its legitimate sphere, with limitations on its power, has been the ideal. We have never wanted minimal government, nor have we wanted the state to run everything. In the terminology of Francis Fukuyama, the English, then the Americans have always wanted, and usually had, a state that had great "strength," meaning enforcement power, within limited "scope," meaning limits on the range of "functions and goals" taken on by the government. Civil peace, uniform law, clear title to land, regular and orderly taxation all result from strong government. The rule of law, freedom from arbitrary state coercion, free enterprise, and personal autonomy all result from a government limited in scope. These two factors are the prerequisites to both freedom and prosperity. The English had a "Goldilocks" state that was "just right" from early on. They transmitted the idea and practice of a strong but limited state to America. We came to see this balance as normal and expected, but in most of the world, this rare balance has never been achieved.

As noted above, the Normans introduced primogeniture into England, mainly to force landholdings to be transmitted to heirs intact. This allowed the king to rely on a consistent level of military support and taxation from his feudal lords. As we also noted, the English did not like this system. Further, under feudalism there were duties that prevented the transmission of property by will, including payment of very large death taxes to the crown, or to a feudal lord, at the time of death. This also went against the English grain. The English went to great lengths to work around these obligations, including making innovations in the law. The way they did it had an enormous and unanticipated downstream effect on English and American life. The point is somewhat technical, even in a brief summary, but it is so important that we must tell the tale here.

The workaround the English invented to avoid feudal death taxes was the law of trusts. A person would create a trust while he was alive, name trustees, and transmit the property to the trust, for the use of his heirs. Then, when he died, because he did not own the property, it could not be taxed, nor was it bound to be transmitted to the oldest son according to primogeniture. This allowed him to give his property to whoever he wanted. There was, however, a crippling problem at the beginning: The king's common law courts would not enforce a trust agreement. You literally had to "trust" the person or persons who were appointed as trustees to act on behalf of the beneficiaries. This was obviously unworkable, because if you gave something valuable to someone, and then died, he will most likely want to keep it, whatever he may have promised to do. However, there was an alternative to the common law courts, which could and would enforce trust agreements.

One of the king's senior advisors was the chancellor, who among his many duties could hear cases that could not be heard by the common law courts. The chancellor was a churchman, usually a bishop, and he was supposed to intervene and assure that justice was done where strict law would not provide it. The common law courts could only grant money damages, but the chancellor could make injunctions, ordering someone to do something or not to do something, where justice required. He had his own courts for this purpose, which were not courts of law but were called courts of equity.

In the twelfth century, the chancellors's courts of equity began to enforce trust agreements, which were unenforceable at common law. The reality was as strange as it sounds. The king's own chancellor began to enforce trust agreements, even though they were to the detriment of the king, because they denied tax revenue to the king. Maitland put it this way:

> The Chancellor began to hold himself out as willing to enforce these honourable understandings, these "uses, trusts or confidences" as they were called, to send to prison the trustee who would not keep faith. It is an exceedingly curious episode. The whole nation seems to enter into one large conspiracy to evade its own laws, to evade laws which it has not the courage to reform. The Chancellor, the judges, and the Parliament seem all to be in the conspiracy. And yet there is really no conspiracy: men are but living from hand to mouth, arguing from one case to the next case, and they do not see what is going to happen.

Eventually, Henry VIII, a very powerful and often tyrannical king, tried to put a stop to it. He tried to end the use trusts, and to collect the taxes he believed he was due. But he was too late. The device was too deeply embedded in English life. The lawyers and judges merely paid lip service to Henry's enactment and construed it exceedingly narrowly, to the point that it became irrelevant. This is one case where we can thank the slippery lawyers. Despite a mighty king's best effort, the equity courts kept up their same old business, and trusts continued to be enforced.

If the law of trusts only allowed people to allocate their property at death, it would be a significant matter, though not world-changing. But, it is no exaggeration to say that it did change the world.

The use of trusts over time became increasingly common for an ever-larger and diverse set of tasks. The trust became a way to organize activity, to gather and preserve capital for various enterprises, including business ventures, such as the insurer Lloyds of London, professional associations like the Inns of Court, where England's lawyers were trained, many types of clubs ranging from sports teams to political associations, religious associations with their parish churches and funds set aside for the poor, as well as schools and colleges. Using trusts permitted all the organizations that make up civil society to stand on their own, to organize themselves, to fund and to house themselves.

Most importantly, the trust could be set up by individuals without asking any permission from the king. Any time civil society needs permission from the state for its survival it will not survive long, as we have seen repeatedly in the twentieth century. Civil society had been robust in medieval times in Europe, with guilds and self-governing towns and other groups. But when kings began to rule by Divine right, civil society was virtually eliminated. There was nothing like the law of trusts in European law, and it was unknown to the Roman law. Almost uniquely in England, civil society lived on and flourished. Organized collective action over time could be undertaken purely by free association and agreement. The law of trusts kept the state's hands out of innumerable private arrangements, in a way that simply could not occur in other societies.

Maitland drew a clear distinction between the use of trusts, and the use of corporations to organize group activity. Corporations were granted by the king, by means of charter, and they could be taken away by the king. These charters had very specific limits to what could and could not be done, and what was owed to the king. To this day, a corporation must be created and authorized by the state. This was not true of the trust, which allowed association for a common purpose with no permission from the king or from anyone else.

Other forms of organization, including increasing refinement to the law of partnerships, and the free grant of business incorporation, became the norm in England and in America. Our civil society no longer relies on the law of trusts. Nonetheless, it was the accidental breakthrough created by the law of trusts that allowed the individualistic English, on their own initiative, to freely form large organizations that endured over time and were autonomous from state control. It was an extraordinary thing that the English law permitted individuals to have this much power, a truly king-like power, but we are blessed that it did.

This quirk in English law, which appeared apparently out of pure happenstance, was essential to the later rise of American freedom and prosperity. The revival and strengthening of civil society in the future, including pushing back against the ever-encroaching tentacles of the state, is a critical task for the future of America. The equity lawyers eight-hundred years ago managed to push back successfully, and in our own day and age, we need to find new ways to repeat that success.

The English bequeathed many other things to America that shaped our economic life, notably: (1) openness to science and technology, (2) technical and trade skills in shipbuilding, mining, metal-working, and machinery, (3) sophisticated farming methods, compared to Continental practices, (4) comparatively sophisticated banking and insurance, and (5) legal enforcement of contracts.

As a result of the foregoing factors, and many others we cannot delve into here, England followed a slow but steady path of economic growth and rising per capita income from an early date. By the time America was being colonized, England's European neighbors had sunk into despotism, economic progress had faltered, and the mass of people were not enjoying increasing per capita income. Europe was stagnating.

England was on a different path.

## ENGLISH RELIGIOUS PRACTICES

England was a Christian country, and much of the medieval constitutionalism we discussed above was based on Christian ideals, such as the king being subject to a higher law, and to the separation of religious and civil authority.

In terms of personal faith, England was a country with a devout population for much of its history. During the millennium when England was Catholic, the people were noted for the ardor of their faith and their generosity to the Church and to good works. Nonetheless, the king and people of England were always jealous of their rights *vis-à-vis* the Pope. English Catholicism had a distinctive flavor, marked by many voluntary associations, while also being part of a larger Christendom it shared with Europe. Peter Ackroyd's *The Life of Thomas More*, who lived from 1478–1535, vividly depicts this lost world, where commerce, politics, and religious devotion were already separated, though still more commingled than we would see today. Over the centuries shared Christian beliefs, with English characteristics, provided a generally accepted ethical framework for law, government, and commerce.

When England became Protestant it formed its own Anglican Church with the king at its head. This combining of religious and political authority presented a hazard to freedom, and many were persecuted by the state church. But this admixture did not prove fatal over the long run to English liberty. The more ardent Protestants, including Puritans, Quakers, and Presbyterians, were all initially oppressed by the Anglican Church and the Crown. These "Dissenting" groups formed their own tightly knit communities. The solidarity within these groups, and their collective sharing of hardship, helped them to successfully lead the colonization effort in North America. This solidarity also helped to create networks of high trust among themselves, which led to political cohesion and economic progress, which they also brought to America.

The Reformation was a violent era, and the back-and-forth struggle of the English against the Catholic Church, and against hostile Catholic countries, shaped the English self-identity as the "Protestant Island." Eventually the fires lit by the Reformation cooled. The ideal of freedom of conscience came to be generally accepted in Europe, and in England. Everyone had either suffered at home, or had co-religionists who had suffered in foreign countries. After brutal wars over religion, and harsh persecution on all sides, people and rulers increasingly sought civil peace rather than imposed uniformity.

The English went further than most with this, and England became a haven for (non-Catholic) religious refugees. The Anglican Church itself became a "big tent" that permitted a variety of practices and even beliefs within its flexible parameters. England slowly became a place where people were serious about religion, personally devout, yet increasingly tolerant. Even Catholicism, which was seen as truly evil, oppressive, and tyrannical, eventually became tolerated and accepted in England, though this happened only after the United States had been founded.

One downstream impact of English religious tolerance would have flabbergasted the leaders of the Reformation in England, Anglican and Puritan alike. To paraphrase Tocqueville, Americans can assimilate anything, and he noted that even Catholicism in America was taking on a distinctly American cast. The Catholic Church in America came to promote a tolerant and neighborly spirit among the various churches. As a minority religion, whose members were often poor and excluded, this made practical sense. But interreligious amity also came to be seen as a matter of principle. It was American Catholic scholars, acting on this principle, who promoted the Declaration on Religious Freedom, which was adopted at the Second Vatican Council in 1965. There was stormy debate on this document and the drafting process was protracted and tortuous. The final language included this:

> the human person has a right to religious freedom. This freedom means that all men are to be immune from coercion on the part of individuals or of social groups and of any human power, in such wise that no one is to be forced to act in a manner contrary to his own beliefs, whether privately or publicly, whether alone or in association with others, within due limits.

Over centuries, in a roundabout way, the slow and grudging English religious toleration led to an American constitutional guarantee of "the free exercise of religion," which then "blew back" and substantively impacted the way the Catholic Church itself came to understand religious freedom all around the world.

Protestantism appears to have reinforced the English tendency toward individualism by eliminating or greatly reducing the intermediation of the clergy and eliminating the uniform and universal dogmatic and moral theology instilled by Catholicism. Further, for non-Anglicans, who did not receive government tax revenue, voluntary associations were necessary to provide a church for their congregations. English Protestants brought this spirit of voluntarism and self-reliance to America along with their Bibles. Further, the Protestant settlers of America also brought their medieval constitutionalism with them as well, which they had inherited intact from the Catholic centuries in England. In that sense, and ironically, the colonists carried ancient Catholic notions of political liberty with them into the American wilderness, even though they were the very "Protestants of Protestantism."

England remained a notably religious country until historically recent times, but Christianity no longer dominates public life there today. Nonetheless, the mix of tolerance with personal devotion, an individualistic, personally chosen approach to faith, and communal self-reliance among congregations, all live on to this day in America.

## ENGLISH EXPANSION AND IMPERIALISM

With regard to English kinship, we will elaborate on only one point here. The Saxons, the English, and the Americans, were always land-hungry. The particular way that they have seized, settled on, and hung onto territory arises from their family structure. When they could afford to buy and build, they did. And when they could take land from someone else, they did that. And if they needed to travel long distances to get it, they went. Nuclear families need new free-standing homes, and the prospect of an autonomous life, for each new family in each new generation. There is always pent-up demand for real estate among English-speaking peoples.

The archeological evidence suggests that Saxons waged continuous warfare, and pushed the Celtic people to the edges of Britain, to Cornwall in the south, Wales in the west, and Scotland in the north. Nonetheless, scholars are not sure whether the Saxons actually killed and drove off most of the local people, or over time imposed their culture and language on them. It was almost certainly some mixture of both. In any case, both sets of behavior, conquest, and assimilation are characteristic of the English, and of the Americans who came after them.

The English have always showed a remarkable capacity to incorporate and assimilate foreigners, not only those who move among them, but even those they conquer. They not only take the land from the people they defeat, they also take away their culture and language. This is remembered with some bitterness by the descendants of the people whom they conquered. The English imposed more Englishness on the Welsh, Scots, and Irish than most of them like to admit. A similar pattern has recurred in India today. The grandparents of today's Indians struggled to drive the British out. But once the British were gone they discovered that the English language and much else had been left behind, permanently embedded in the cultural DNA of India.

Conquest and displacement has also been an Anglo-American practice. The English, over the centuries, have taken and settled every piece of territory on the Earth that they could find that was weakly defended by technically backward people. The distinctly English pattern of expansion has been to drive off the natives entirely where that was possible and to move families, and even whole communities, into the conquered areas, as soon as it was safe to do so. Other colonial powers would send bands of adventurers, not whole families, and these conquerors would go native, marry local women, and otherwise fail to transmit their own culture intact and enduringly. But the Saxons took permanent possession of English lands by rooting themselves there. The English later conquered and occupied parts of Scotland and Ireland in a similar way. Once they got oceangoing ships, the English went on a global land-grab. They conquered and occupied vast new territories in North America, Australia, and New Zealand, settling them permanently, pushing the natives to the brink of extinction, and creating entirely new countries in the process. This pattern of seizing and holding land began with the initial conquest of Britain by the Saxons in the fifth century, and it lasted until the destruction of the Sioux and the Apaches by their American cultural descendants fourteen centuries later.

This forcible expansion we no longer see as entirely admirable. A hundred years ago the celebration of the advance of civilization by the expansion of English-speaking communities would have been presented free of much nagging guilt. Conquering the frontier was seen as a glorious tale, and to some degree it was. But today we are inclined to also look at the cost side of the ledger and to try to understand this process through the eyes of the peoples who were defeated in these struggles, as well as the victors. Some today would like to impose a burden of perpetual guilt on the people of the English-speaking world for these earlier annexations and the destruction of communities that could not successfully defend their own land. But what has been done cannot be undone, and there is no one alive today who actually participated in these events. Any contemporary moral judgment of this amazing process cannot change the facts as they exist now. These territories once supported a tiny number of inhabitants in neolithic conditions. Today these English-speaking communities, including the United States, are among the most powerful and wealthy in the world, with millions of inhabitants. They are not going to go away, and perpetual hand-wringing over the past is a waste of time, and apologies for events that happened before anyone now living was alive, are mere moralistic posturing.

In the process of conquest and occupation, the English brought with them a "toolkit," which made them particularly effective colonizers. When groups of families arrived in the new countries, they would organize themselves into a political body, based on the towns and counties they knew in England. They would adopt rules and a process for electing officers, including sheriffs, the most ancient English office. They would establish a legislative body, which in a small settlement or town would often be a town meeting composed of the free men therein. They would organize a militia, bearing their personal weapons, and select leaders for it and rules for regulating and training it. They would build a church and make provision for its governance and upkeep. They would use the Common Law, to the extent they could, as an agreed set of rules and principles to resolve disputes, even before they had courts, and even before they had any law books to rely on. They often came from England with a written charter for a new colony, which was often organized as a for-profit business, with shareholders back home. They would keep written records of their own enactments and ordinances, and of who had title to property. This successful toolkit was adopted in turn by Americans as they expanded over North America.

One of the problems that English colonists faced was the ambiguity of their legal status in relation to the home country and its government. Colonists tended to adopt a broad view of their rights as "free born Englishmen," but there was a problem with this. The legal rights of Englishmen applied only to English subjects while they were living in England, not elsewhere. No less an authority than Lord Coke held this to be correct, and as galling as it is for an American to say it, he and those who followed him had the better case as a strict matter of law. This issue arose starting in the 1200s, as English colonists established communities beyond the borders of England proper. In Wales, in Scotland, and especially in Ireland, the problem of what rights were retained by Englishmen outside of England was a nagging problem in English constitutionalism. This legal ambiguity was a critical factor in bringing on the American Revolution. When the time came, the Americans resolved the ambiguity, in their favor, with swords, muskets, and cannon.

# Chapter 5
# America 1.0

When Charles-Louis de Secondat, Baron de Montesquieu visited England in 1729 he found "a country which hardly resembles the rest of Europe" in terms of its great wealth and freedom. At the same time the English were settling North America, they were getting the big things right at home. Transplanting this success across the Atlantic was the challenge of the Colonial era.

The English colonists succeeded in bringing their cultural and institutional inheritance, which were the foundations of their wealth and freedom, with them across the Atlantic. That culture took root here and adapted itself to the frontier conditions of North America. We have seen that the story of England was one of a slow change within many centuries of continuity. England's history was shaped mainly by its being an island, or the dominant part of the island of Britain. Relatively secure from attack, England preserved "archaisms," old things that lasted for centuries, from medieval times and earlier, including premodern notions of limits on government power. English institutions tended to be complex, with many accretions from earlier times. For example, English Common Law relating to real property was a complex maze that only skilled lawyers could navigate. The colonists, with the sea behind them and the trackless woods and mountains before them, could not afford the luxury of unnecessary complexity. For them, it was do it yourself, or do without.

The colonists and Americans of the early years of the Republic took their inherited English institutions and stripped them to their essentials so they would function in the hard conditions of frontier life. Tocqueville noted this comparative simplicity in America: "One could compare

America to a great forest cut through by a large number of roads which all end in the same place.... But in England the roads cross, and you have to follow along each one of them to get a clear idea of the whole." Alan Macfarlane addressed this point when he wrote: "England is an old country, where there are contradictions and inconsistencies, and the winding tracks of a thousand years of history." William the Conqueror had "set up a consistent system of government" but "over time it had evolved and twisted into new shapes. In America, with its sparse population and short history this had not happened." Politics, law, business relations, land ownership, even religious life developed into simpler, more practical, and more robust forms in America.

Americans took the basic patterns from the home country and simplified, generalized, and universalized them until they became a versatile template that could quickly convert expanses of raw land into new, functioning, self-governing communities. America had a "second-mover advantage," which allowed us to start out with a thousand years of cultural and institutional evolution already at hand. Soon after their arrival, and constructing their homes, Americans were able to act as citizens, jurors, legislators, militiamen and volunteers, vestrymen and congregation-members, entrepreneurs, and self-actualized persons. By keeping things simple, they were able to bring people from other backgrounds "up to speed" rapidly.

## FOUR WAVES OF SETTLEMENT

The English-speaking settlers of North America came in four major waves. Each wave of immigrants brought its own distinct cultural characteristics to America. David Hackett Fischer, in his classic book *Albion's Seed*, identified these four groups

> During the very long period from 1629 to 1775, the present area of the United States was settled by at least four large waves of English-speaking Immigrants. The first was an exodus of Puritans from the east of England to Massachusetts during a period of eleven years from 1629 to 1640. The second was the migration of a small Royalist elite and large numbers of indentured servants

from the south of England to Virginia (ca. 1642–75). The third was a movement from the North Midlands of England and Wales to the Delaware Valley (ca. 1675–1725). The fourth was a flow of English-speaking people from the borders of North Britain and northern Ireland to the Appalachian backcountry mostly during the half-century from 1718 to 1775.

There were numerous other settlements, including the Dutch settlement in New York, which we will discuss below, but these were the four "hearth cultures," which went on to shape the regional and national culture of the United States to this day.

Each of these groups brought a love of liberty, as they understood it, to the wilderness. Each group came as a result of defeat and persecution at home, and was determined to stick to its principles in the new country. We have inherited a mix of good and bad traits, as we now see things, from each of these groups.

Fischer notes the common features of these groups: "These four groups shared many qualities in common. All of them spoke the English language. Nearly all were British Protestants. Most lived under British laws and took pride in possessing British liberties." However, Fischer's book does not look at these groups in comparison to foreign cultures, and hence he focuses on the diversity between them and the differences between American regional cultures. Nonetheless, each of these settling communities had family practices, for all of their variations, which were of the Absolute Nuclear Family type, with the features we have discussed above.

The Puritans settled in Massachusetts and founded towns all over what is now known as New England. Over time, the Puritans lost some of their religious fervor, and people from this region began to be called Yankees. These Yankees went on to settle the Upper Midwest, creating a distinct cultural zone from Maine to Minnesota, with pockets farther west. This Yankee diaspora out of New England may be the single most important event in American history, with a truly global impact, as we will discuss below, but it is little appreciated today. In the American South, a Yankee is a Northerner, but in the rest of the world, a Yank or a Yankee came to simply mean an American.

The Puritans who founded New England fled to America because they were persecuted by the Anglican Church in England. They believed in equality before the law, for people in their community, and in democratic participation in town meetings to govern themselves. We inherited a commitment to the rule of law and to democratic accountability from them. The first written constitution enacted in America was the Massachusetts Constitution of 1780, which was written by John Adams. It is still in force, and is the oldest continuously operating constitution in the world.

However, the Puritans and their Yankee descendants who followed them did not believe in a small or minimal state. They believed in and built a comparatively intrusive and paternalistic government. Americans owe their tradition of activist government, ultimately, to them. The Progressive tradition of securing "freedom from want" by government action did not arise only with Franklin D. Roosevelt's New Deal. FDR got this idea from his Progressive and Liberal contemporaries, but he also got it from his Yankee ancestors.

The Puritans and Yankees were paternalistic, but they were not tolerant, as we understand that term. They believed in freedom of religion only if it was the "true" religion, the same one they had been persecuted for, the one they went into the wilderness to practice. The Yankees brought the Puritans' moralistic, all-or-nothing spirit into their politics. The American Revolution started in Massachusetts because of this unyielding, principled (or dogmatic) attitude. The Abolitionist movement that led to the Civil War started in New England as well. Once they had made up their minds, the Yankees were sure of God's will and flatly refused to compromise with the evil of slavery. As one Southerner accurately put it, "When you see those damned psalm-singing Yankees turn out of their churches, shoulder their guns and march away of a Sunday, you may know that hell is going to crack shortly."

The downside of this principled and uncompromising Yankee spirit is seeing political opponents as not merely mistaken, but evil. The Yankees and their cultural descendants often give their political views a religious intensity. This is increasingly so as religious belief has faded out among them. This Puritan-Yankee attitude is the distant but clear ancestor of the modern notion of "political correctness," which cannot tolerate dissent, is assured of its own perfect righteousness, and seeks to shame, to punish, and to silence opposing views.

The Yankees had several wealthy and powerful individuals and families. The names of some of the earliest successful settlers can be found on the rolls of Massachusetts political and business leaders four centuries later. Nonetheless, the Yankees tended to have a large plurality of self-sufficient individuals living on family farms or working in trades – not rich, but not poor either. There was, to use Tocqueville's term, typically an "equality of conditions" among the New Englanders. The idea that there ought to be a nearly universal "middling" class of people was spread westward by the Yankees, and has shaped America ever since.

New England has poor soil. The ground is not composed mainly of dirt, but of dirt liberally admixed with rocks, lots of small rocks, and plenty of big ones as well. The picturesque "field stone fences" of New England are composed of thousands of large rocks, dug out with shovels and hauled away by wheel barrow, before any seeds could be planted. The amount of labor this took is almost unfathomable. As if the dirt weren't bad enough, the climate is not favorable, either. Because farming was difficult, and was never adequate to sustain a Yankee family, they had to get into other lines of work as well.

> The Yankee farmer had to find subsidiary occupations, such as lumbering in winter, gathering and refining maple syrup in earliest spring, running a forge, distillery, or woodworking or farm shop, perhaps a small foundry or grist mill. The New England farmer had to use his wits to stay on his land.

New Englanders went into fishing and whaling. They also built ships, for use and for sale, and barrels for shipping goods. They made cloth and shoes, and made cast iron tools and ship fittings.

The curse of poor soil and bad weather became a blessing over time. First, the use of wage labor and cottage industry prepared the Yankees for industrial development in the future. Secondly, these conditions formed the Yankees into plain, practical, businesslike, technology-minded, and go-getting people. Once the interior of the continent opened, much of New England was simply abandoned as the Yankees made their way to places with better soil.

The settlers of Virginia, and the Chesapeake Bay area generally, were very different from the New Englanders. They were from the defeated Royalist party in the English Civil War. They had supported the king, who lost his head. Many of his followers went to America rather than suffer under the new Puritan rulers in England. This community went on to settle most of the lowland South.

These Southerners brought with them a notion of "freedom" that has died out in America. They believed that freedom was a privilege for the few, and that most people were meant to live as subjects. They did not believe in equality. A famous Virginian politician, John Randolph of Roanoke put it simply: "I am an aristocrat. I love liberty, I hate equality."

They brought to America many indentured servants, people who were bound to work for a term of years. Personal work and effort were not particularly admired in this region, because hard work was done by an inferior class of people. This community was ideologically "pre-loaded" to employ slave labor, once African slaves were available.

A small number of families formed a wealthy elite, among servants, slaves, and relatively poor neighbors. This was the only group of settlers who practiced primogeniture. The eldest sons inherited large estates, plantations, that tended to stay intact from generation to generation. These plantations produced cash crops for export: tobacco, rice, indigo, and, most importantly, cotton. Large plantations allowed economies of scale in farm work, which made the use of gangs of relatively unskilled slaves profitable for their owners.

Samuel Johnson asked, at the time of the American Revolution: "How is it that we hear the loudest yelps for liberty among the drivers of negroes?" Perversely, these Southerners loved their own freedom because it was rare, and because they had before their eyes what a life of slavery meant. They had a touchy pride and were acutely sensitive to their status, especially their status as "freemen." Southerners also held as an ideal that to command others, they must have self-command as well, and be courteous, unhurried, and hospitable. No doubt most slave owners fell short of this ideal in practice.

The settlers of the Delaware Valley, in what came to be known as Pennsylvania, were predominantly Quakers. They left England to escape religious persecution. Unlike the Puritans, they adopted the idea of "liberty of conscience." The founder of Pennsylvania was William Penn. He had personally suffered persecution, including imprisonment, for his beliefs, as had thousands of Quakers in England. Penn and his fellow

Quakers believed that no religion should be persecuted. Fischer tells us that Penn's "own sufferings convinced him that the coercion of conscience was not merely evil but futile, and deeply dangerous to true faith." "They subvert all true religion," Penn wrote, ". . . where men believe not because 'tis false, but so commanded by their superiors." This commitment to religious tolerance came slowly to be universally accepted in America. The Quakers were committed to the traditional "rights of Englishmen," but they gave a broader interpretation to this idea than any other group of English settlers. They believed that liberty should be universal for all people, and that any liberty a person demanded should be willingly granted equally to others. This was a radical idea in its day. As a result, the Quakers were among the earliest and firmest opponents of slavery. Quakers were also strong supporters of the Civil Rights struggle a century later.

Pennsylvania, unlike New England, was blessed with good soil and decent weather. It became a productive source of grain, hogs, cattle, and sheep for export. Pennsylvanians engaged in numerous trades, such as shoemaking, glassmaking, woodworking, and pottery. They had good mines and early on developed a substantial business in metalworking. Pennsylvania was well positioned to become, as it did, an economic powerhouse. The world-renowned American steel companies of later years were based in Pennsylvania and had their remote origins during colonial days.

German Pietists, fleeing religious persecution, also settled in Pennsylvania. Quaker openness to other religions attracted them, as did the natural wealth of the Delaware Valley. These German settlers built the well-known "Pennsylvania Dutch" farms and barns. However, as the Pennsylvanians pushed into the interior, into the valleys of the Appalachians, they would often find, just one valley over, something quite different. Instead of broad, cleared fields and substantial houses and large barns with stone foundations, there would be log cabins, patchy fields with stumps, and hogs running semiwild. These "backcountry" areas had a distinct flavor of their own.

The settlers in the backcountry, which includes much of the highland area east of the Mississippi, came mainly from the border counties of England and Scotland, by way of Northern Ireland. These areas were plagued by endemic warfare, much different from the relatively peaceful parts of England. In the violent world these Borderers came from, mutual defense was necessary for survival. As a result they had a more authoritarian family type, with stronger extended families, known as clans, unlike the family types in the other areas of settlement. These people were slow to extend trust much beyond their family networks. This has been true for centuries, and continues to this day. They have also had notably low marriage ages for women, relatively low rates of literacy, high rates of violent crime, and a generally intolerant attitude toward strangers or strange ideas of any type. As a result of these features, this group has always been among the most economically backward in the United States for all of our history.

The people of the backcountry have been called many things over the years, mostly derogatory: Crackers, Hoosiers, Rednecks, Hillbillies, and more clinically, Scots-Irish. They have made a critical contribution to American life. The love of liberty among these people was and is the most radical to be found in any part of America. Their idea of freedom sprang from the anarchic conditions of the Scots Borders. Men there had to be willing and able to fight to survive. Personal arms bearing was essential, and was a mandatory element of freedom. The Borderers in the old country had suffered under oppressive royal power, and "rack-renting" landlords. The people of the backcountry carried these memories with them, and saw all taxation and most government as suspect at best, and reflexively opposed both. The prickly attitude toward encroachments on freedom, which many Americans have today, can be traced back to this source. Patrick Henry, who said "give me liberty, or give me death," was a son of the backcountry, and although Captain Gadsden was apparently not from the region, his flag with its rattler and "Don't Tread On Me" motto is emblematic of these people.

The Scots-Irish were the pathbreakers into the wilderness. The explorers and Mountain Men who first probed far into the interior were often from this group. The other communities clung to the seacoast for a century after arriving in North America. The Scots-Irish set out into the hills and over the Appalachians almost as soon as they arrived. They were willing to go knife-to-knife with the Indians. They took land and cattle when they could get it back in Britain and Ireland, by fair means or foul. They did the same thing here. This is not a pleasant part of America's story. The Scots-Irish did much of the dirty work of pushing out the indigenous people, allowing more orderly, organized, and respectable communities to settle peacefully in their wake.

The Scots-Irish, with their fighting spirit, have contributed a disproportionate share of America's soldiers over the years. Many famous American warriors came from this stock, including Alvin C. York, Chuck Yeager, and Lewis "Chesty" Puller. The hardships of military life were often less severe than day-to-day living in the mountains. Powder was expensive, the hill people were poor, and each shot counted when hunting game. This same precision sharp-shooting that brought meat to the table brought down many of America's enemies all over the world, as well as many men in Union blue during the days when Americans were shooting at each other.

As an aside, it is beyond dispute that African Americans were essential to creating the music that dominated not only America but the entire world in the twentieth century. This musical current, like a river originating in West Africa, and swelling through the years of slavery, poured over its banks beginning in the early twentieth century, was one of the main components of America vernacular and popular music. This inundation led to a harvest of jazz, blues, rock'n'roll, and hip hop and their spinoffs and variants in all their limitless variety. The other critical contributor to that mainstream was the music of the American mountain folk, bluegrass, country, and Western. America's poor people of all colors have made the most glorious contribution to our popular culture and brought unalloyed happiness to countless millions of people in the process. But few would have heard it, if it weren't for the entertainment industry that was born and based in New York.

New York City is not counted as one of Fischer's hearth cultures. In terms of immigration into the interior of the continent, this is correct. People who moved into the Midwest from upstate New York were usually transplanted Yankees from New England. However, New York was the hub of the American economy for many years, and its banks came to dominate the country and the world. New York was the leader in America's cultural life, both high and popular, and has dominated book publishing for most of our history. New York's unique identity had an impact far out of proportion to its size and numbers, and its elite were the de facto managers of the country and its economy for many years.

New York is unusual because its main cultural heritage is not English at all.

New York's tradition of pluralism began with its Dutch founders early in the seventeenth century. It combined a policy of official toleration with intense ethnic rivalry and bitter religious conflict. Bonds within ethnic groups tended to be close and warm, but relations between them were distant and hostile. These patterns appeared as early as 1624 and still persist in New York City, which for sixteen generations has been a place of extreme ethnic diversity, conflicted class relations, turbulent politics, intense economic competition, enormous energy, abrasive manners, and abusive speech. In all these ways, Manhattan in the twenty-first century is remarkably similar to descriptions of old New York in the eighteenth century, New Amsterdam in the seventeenth century, and even old Amsterdam in the Sixteenth century. The urban folkways of New York City, for all its highly cultivated habits of historical amnesia, have strong linkages to the distant past.

New York City has remained a world unto itself all these years, and many have commented that it is somehow not really "America." There is some bigotry to this, but also some truth. New York is an odd fit with the rest of America because of its Dutch origins. That initial Dutch influence, its wide-open and hustling style and focus on money, its tolerance or indifference to varying cultures so long as they don't get in the way of business, and the competing ethnic enclaves that began during the Dutch era, have shaped the New York City ever since.

Each of the groups that migrated to America made a contribution to what we are: The New England town meeting, the Quaker Liberty Bell, Southern hospitality and gentility, the hard-nosed and hustling city of New York, and the frontiersman with his Bowie knife and Kentucky long rifle. These are all threads that make up America before we broke with England, and have lived on ever since. We will speak below about the long-suffering and resilient African Americans, and later immigrants.

As the Saxons had crossed to England, the English had crossed to America. The Absolute Nuclear Family was successfully transported across the Atlantic and rooted in North America. The key institutions of political and economic freedom had made it across, as well, and were adapting themselves to the new country.

In each of the settlement areas, despite their many differences, the basic English "toolkit" was employed. There was participatory local government, at least for free people or people of means. Towns were organized, usually adopting practices carried over from England. There was representative government, with people being sent to the colonial capital from the various localities. Land was surveyed and property rights were defined to facilitate the buying and selling of real estate. Courts were established, judges were appointed, and the Common Law began to be applied, though in a rough and ready fashion. Counties were formed, and sheriffs selected. Public order began to be enforced, and miscreants punished. There were jury trials, though with local variations. Business enterprise was permitted and encouraged. Limitations of sales to "market days" or limited market locations were eliminated, and America was open for business most of the time, almost everywhere. Congregations built churches, selected ministers, and spread the Word.

But in the midst of all these accomplishments, there is the tragic note of slavery.

## SLAVERY

Unlike the English and later immigrants, African people did not come to America voluntarily, but by force and in chains. They and their descendants spent 250 years as slaves, and a further century under "Jim Crow" and lynch law. Their very survival in the face of centuries of brutality is an extraordinary saga. The majority of African Americans have begun to be formally included in American political life only since the passage of the Civil Rights Act (1964) and the Voting Rights Act (1965). Historically, that's just yesterday. It is only about 12 percent of the time elapsed since the first African slave was auctioned for sale in America in 1619.

The African American story serves as a counterpoint to our main theme of English-speaking freedom and cultural continuity. African Americans were cut off from their own past, yet forcibly excluded from participating as equals in America, even as a matter of law, for 350 years. Nonetheless, it was ancient principles of freedom embedded in American life, usually strengthened by religious conviction, which at long last ended slavery, and ended Jim Crow a century later.

As we discussed earlier, England managed to avoid the reception of

Roman law, thus avoiding a mortal threat to freedom. But there is one massive exception, which had evil and long-lasting results. In the 1700s, English settlers on the island of Barbados, in the Caribbean, owned large populations of slaves. This presented difficulties, because there was no existing English law that could be used to govern this slave-owning society or regulate the ownership and sale of their human property. In England there had been slavery in Anglo-Saxon times. But from a very early date slavery faded away in England. It came to be considered part of the English constitution that there could be no slavery in England. In 1772, on the eve of our Revolution, an English court held in the *Somerset* case that there was no lawful slavery in England, and that a slave setting foot there was a free man.

Slave owners in the colonies could not rely on English law to protect their property rights in slaves, so they wrote their own slave codes. In the Caribbean, English local governments adopted legal codes based in large part on the slave code of Mexico, which was a Spanish colony. The Spanish law used in Mexico was derived from Roman laws. Slavery was a universal practice in Roman times. Spain and Portugal, unlike more northern European societies, never saw all slavery turn into serfdom. Slave markets operated continuously from Roman times, through Muslim rule, and through to modern time. Spanish law regulated the use and disposition of slaves. Most importantly it included a rule that a person born of a mother who was a slave was automatically a slave. This rule created a permanent system of slavery. Slaves became a class, and a race, condemned to treatment as property and deprived of all legal rights.

South Carolina was the only American colony that was not settled directly from England. It was settled from Barbados. The Barbadian slave owners brought their slave code with them. South Carolina came to have the largest slave population relative to its free population of any state. It became the "market leader" with regard to the practice of slavery. From South Carolina the law of slavery spread to other Southern states. At first, in the American colonies, slaves were in a legally ambiguous position, often being held for only a term of years. With the imposition of the Barbadian/South Carolinian slave codes, the legal chains were forged and unbreakable.

Presumably, the slave owners would have found some way to make slavery work profitably for themselves. Greed usually finds a way, and money can change the law to its own advantage. Nonetheless, the preexisting English law provided no framework for slavery, and they had to invent a new system. It was only by installing provisions from a foreign system, derived from Roman law, that slavery was made to work for the slave owners.

The nature of the tobacco and later the cotton crop made slavery practical. Both required constant tending of the crops in the fields and processing after harvesting. Agricultural labor on the South's cash crops was constant, not seasonal. As a result the Southern slave owners could keep their slaves profitably employed. Farming in the North did not require the same sort of full-time labor force. Although there were some slaves in the North in the colonial era, the system did not predominate simply because it was a poor use of capital to invest in slaves there.

If the continent of North America had been ten degrees of latitude south of where it actually is, slavery would have been profitable in all of the colonies. There would have been economic pressure to keep it going, and moral objections would not have been sufficient to eliminate it. America would have been entirely based on slave labor, and the world would have taken a very different course. Instead, by pure geographical happenstance, the line dividing climates where slave-based agriculture was profitable from those where it was not passed roughly through the center of the colonies, and through the later United States.

By the time of the Revolution, slavery was deeply entrenched, profitable for its owners, with a legal and political structure built upon it. Many people, including many slave owners, would agree that slavery was wrong. Many understood that slavery was incompatible with their own notions of liberty, or of Christianity. But they were not willing to suffer the costs or provoke the conflict necessary to change it. Because slave agriculture tended to exhaust the soil where it was employed, many reconciled themselves to slavery by believing it would eventually die out on its own. This prediction proved false, due both to technological change and to the opening up of the interior of the continent after the War of Independence was won.

The Declaration of Independence put down in writing what the war with England was about, and why it had broken out. But it was apparent from the beginning that the claims in the Declaration of Independence that "all men are created equal" and that "liberty" was God-given to everyone, could not be reconciled with slavery. Thomas Jefferson, who drafted the Declaration, was a slave owner, but throughout his life he condemned slavery as evil. He attempted to put strong anti-slavery language into the Declaration, condemning the king for violating the "sacred rights of life & liberty in the persons of a distant people who never offended him, captivating & carrying them into slavery in another hemisphere, or to incur miserable death in their transportation thither." But Jefferson's proposed language was voted down. Jefferson and others of like mind made the pragmatic decision to win the war, gain independence from England, and start a new country. They put off any fight about slavery for another day. That fight was long in coming, but it came.

Many of the Founders did believe that they had, in effect, written gradual emancipation of slavery into the Constitution by banning the importation of slaves after 1808. Slavery was for the most part so destructive that most slave populations did not reproduce at the replacement rate; new supplies of cheap slaves had to be continually imported from Africa to replenish the workforce. Only Virginia and Maryland produced a surplus, possibly because of the legacy of the improvised slave codes they had created in the 1600s, which were arguably less harsh than the Barbardian codes.

Even without a specific condemnation of slavery, the words of the actual Declaration equipped later Americans to undermine and uproot the slave system. The words of the Declaration were subversive. They set a flag in the ground beyond where America was at the time. But the flag of freedom for "all men" was visible on the horizon, and it served as an inspiration in America and around the world. Jefferson's assertions were like a bit of rogue code left in our national software by its first programmer. It went viral and ultimately transformed the entire system.

Frederick Douglass, the freed slave and champion of the anti-slavery struggle, was asked to speak to a group of abolitionists on the Fourth of July in 1852. He had hard words for them:

> What to the American slave is your Fourth of July? I answer, a day that reveals to him more than all other days of the year, the gross injustice and cruelty to which he is the constant victim. To him your celebration is a sham; your boasted liberty an unholy license ... your shouts of liberty and equality, hollow mock...."

But Douglass later came to see the Declaration and the Constitution as, on their face, being documents of freedom. He chose not to reject them, but to hold them up to the white men of America and demand that they live up to their own standards. This ultimately proved to be the workable way forward. Saul Alinsky's cynical but effective "Rules for Radicals" includes Rule 5: "Make the enemy live up to its own book of rules." But this need not be merely a tactic; it can be a genuine moral correction. Martin Luther King, Jr. took this approach, and achieved significant though incomplete success with it.

In 1935 the African-American poet Langston Hughes wrote:

> Let America be America again.
> Let it be the dream it used to be.
> Let it be the pioneer on the plain
> Seeking a home where he himself is free.
> (America never was America to me.)

America had indeed never been America, for him and for his fellow African Americans. But that dream was not a lie: It was true but incomplete. The solution was not, and is not, to conclude that the dream of "seeking a home where he himself is free" is false because not everyone was able to share in it. The answer is to make "America be America" for everyone. This project still has a long way to go. But our hope is that the changes that are coming to America will move us farther toward a future where "opportunity is real, and life is free, equality is in the air we breathe."

## REVOLUTION AND FOUNDING

The details of the American Revolution and the Founding era are well known and ably discussed in many other books. As to the war itself, we will have to avert our eyes from the stirring events of Lexington, Concord, and Battle Road; from Washington's midnight crossing of the icy Delaware; from the sharpshooters at Saratoga; from the midnight raids of the Swamp Fox; and from Cornwallis's doomed garrison at Yorktown stacking its arms while the fifes played "The World Turned Upside Down."

From our vantage point, the most important fact about the American

Revolution and the Founding era is that the political break with Britain was not a break with our cultural and institutional inheritance from the mother country. In fact, by the time of the Revolution, Britain had become a Parliamentary oligarchy, which ruled with few limits on its power other than custom and the self-interest of the powerful. Britain, for the benefit of its leading families, was imposing itself on Ireland and India, and making subjects of their inhabitants. This was the same fate they intended for the Americans. By breaking with Britain the Founders preserved our inheritance of freedom, which was faltering in its original homeland and in Britain's growing empire.

The Founders did more than preserve the "rights of free born Englishmen." They invented a more general and more elevated idea of "Liberty." The American vision of liberty was expansive and forward-looking and universal, as against an English one that looked back to its ancient constitution, and was limited to England and the jurisdiction of its own courts. The new idea of Liberty was cited as a God-given right in our Declaration of Independence, which was, on its face, applicable to everyone, everywhere. This was indeed a "re-imagining" of the old ideas, but it was a continuation and expansion, not a break with the past.

Building a government that could preserve this expansive liberty was a difficult challenge. At the time of the Treaty of Paris, which ended the war with Britain, the United States' national government was carried on under the Articles of Confederation. The Articles are typically discussed as merely an unsuccessful prologue to the Constitution we still have. But the government under the Articles accomplished something of decisive importance for the future of America, which was of equal importance to the Constitution: the passage of the Northwest Ordinances.

The Constitution is rightly revered as the foundation of our political life. But the Northwest Ordinances were of equal importance as the foundation of American economic life.

## DIVIDING UP THE CONTINENT

One of the chief causes of the Revolution was the British attempt to prevent the settlement of the interior of the continent, beyond the Appalachians. The British Proclamation of 1763 attempted to prevent settlement

in the Trans-Appalachian lands. The goal of the proclamation was to preserve the Indian tribes, Britain's allies, in the possession of their
lands. The colonists were outraged by this attempted limitation of their
settlement into the interior of the continent. Nuclear families need land,
and there was a lot of it for the taking, just over the mountains.

During the war, the United States sent successful military expeditions
into what were then called the "Northwest Territories." This area com-
prises the Midwestern states of Ohio, Indiana, Michigan, Illinois, and
Wisconsin and a large chunk of Minnesota. As a result of these American
victories the British conceded that the United States would take possession of all the land between the Atlantic and the Mississippi, with the
exceptions of Florida and Louisiana, which were at that time owned
by Spain.

The United States government had to determine how this land was
going to be settled and incorporated into the new country. Thomas Jefferson took the lead on resolving these questions, and was the lead
drafter of the Northwest Ordinances of 1784 and 1787. Jefferson wanted
to dispose of the land by sale, and not keep it in the hands of the national
government. He knew that the government lacked the power to police
and control the territory. If the government tried to retain ownership,
settlers would simply move in without permission and they would end
up in conflict with each other and with the national government. Jefferson also saw that the government should not be permitted to own such a
huge and valuable territory and operate it as a landlord. A government
with that much power would be unaccountable and would inevitably
engulf the freedom of its people. In any case, the land was a valuable asset
and the new government needed money, so it had to be sold.

The Ordinances provided that the land would be scientifically divided
by celestial survey, using latitude and longitude. The process of surveying
this immense wilderness was extremely difficult, but it was eventually
accomplished. The land was divided into uniform, six-by-six mile squares,
designated as townships. Each such township was divided into 36 square-
mile sections.

Most of the territory west of the Appalachians, continuously to the
Rockies, and in parts to the Pacific where topography permitted and prior
Spanish title did not conflict, was surveyed and sold by township and
section. As a result, most of the United States is composed of counties

that are either square or have right angles, except where their borders follow rivers. This process led to entire states being square or rectangular in the western half of the country. "The Northwest Ordinances were the colonial Americans' institutional thumbprint on the American continent all the way from the Ohio River to the Pacific."

The survey methods used to carve up the interior were meant to support nuclear families, with each family having enough to sustain itself. A 160-acre quarter-section was considered to be the amount of land necessary to support a single-family farm. The Ordinance was written with an embedded assumption that the country would be turned into millions of single-family farms.

The United States government sold these territories through its General Land Office. The sales did not go as well as the surveys. The phrase "land office business" captures the insatiable demand for land, and the difficulty the government had trying to keep up. There was notorious fraud and corruption in the process of selling off this land. Inevitably, there was speculation, with booms and busts in land values, and large fortunes were made and lost in the process.

However messy, the mechanism set up in the Ordinances led to the disposal of public land into millions of private hands, with clearly established title established by survey. It is impossible to overestimate the importance of this process, which, in the words of Jonathan R. T. Hughes, was "a great gift to the future. The world today is still strewn east to west, from the *taiga* of Russia to the deserts of South Africa, with nations whose political malignancy reflects failure to solve the problems of land ownership with secure titles for individuals."

The Ordinances also specified the rights that the new owners would have in the land, in technical legal terms, the "tenure" of the land. They carried on the type of tenure used in the original colonies but, as was typical, in a simplified way. The land tenure adopted came to be known as "fee simple" and it is the main type of land tenure in use in America to this day. It provided that the land was held without any condition other than payment of taxes on it, that the owner has unconditional use of the property as well as unconditional power to dispose of it by sale, or to anyone by will. Ownership, buying, and selling of land were made simple.

An expert on the Northwest Ordinances, economic historian Jonathan

R. T. Hughes, speculated that they were the foundation of all later American capitalism:

> American agriculture from the beginning meant popular ownership and control of productive resources – the nursery of ubiquitous American capitalism. . . . For future generations, ideas about rights in property of every kind including services evolved from the one form of property ownership so widely experienced, the ownership of agricultural land.

Hughes was certainly right that the creation of millions of individually owned farms, each one a small business, helped turn America into a business-minded, enterprising country based on private property. However, the "nursery of ubiquitous American capitalism" is the nuclear family, with its aspiration to personal autonomy and a home for each family. The creation of millions of family-scale farms built on, and fulfilled, the deepest material aspirations of the Americans of the day.

## THE CONSTITUTION AND LEGAL SYSTEM

The Constitution and the Bill of Rights permeate American life and thinking, as symbols and as law. The Constitution has been studied, written about, and used as legal authority, and has generated an incalculably large literature.

From our perspective, the Constitution and Bill of Rights restated, simplified, and clarified the limitations on government power the Founders already believed they had inherited from England. There was little that was truly novel. In particular, virtually all of the provisions in the Bill of Rights were based on long-standing English law. Hence, the Americans of the day insisted that these provisions be included in the Constitution. Because they were time-tested rules, American lawyers and judges had a clear idea of how to put them into concrete operation.

The Americans did make one very important innovation. The very concept of "constitutional law," as we now understand it, with our highest law embodied in a document, was made in America. It was an attempt to lock-in the rule of law by placing the highest law outside the reach of ordinary politics and by providing clear limits on government power. In effect, it attempted to replace the king's oath to be subject to a higher law with a written higher law that would not need human intervention. This has worked imperfectly over the years. It is never possible to entirely remove the human element from government power, and it is always a question not of "if" there will be a final decision maker on what is lawful, but "who" that will be.

The remarkable degree of religious toleration set forth in the First Amendment was a step beyond English practice. It protected the free exercise of religion from interference by the new national government, and barred the establishment of a national church. At the time of the Founding, the colonies typically had a taxpayer-supported church, as the English and the Scots did. However, early in our national life, taxpayer-supported churches died out. America filled up with a variegated, though still overwhelmingly Protestant, religious believers who did not want to pay for someone else's church. The Founding generation wisely saw that with many disparate groups mixed together tolerance was a necessity. Civil peace is like oxygen: You only notice it when it is gone. Interreligious conflict can be the bloodiest kind. Compared to many foreign countries, religious differences have provoked very little bloodshed in America, in part because of this constitutional protection.

The Constitution also protected America from foreign predation and attack, which was perhaps the greatest fear of the Founders, though usually forgotten today. It created a unitary foreign policy, so that foreign enemies could not divide and conquer by negotiating with the several states. This turned the Atlantic into a moat, and prevented any foreign power from gaining a foothold within the existing union. The Constitution created a single military and naval power, and provided a secure tax base for their funding. This naval and military power was to be directed by a single commander in chief, who could draw on the militaries of the states in wartime. The USA soon went from being a weak and divided group of colonies to a significant power, with great latent military potential. America's Constitution made America into a defensible "artificial island" allowing us to enjoy a large peace dividend, as the English had before us.

The traditional English right to keep and bear arms was also embedded in the Bill of Rights. This right has had many challenges over the years. Southerners, after the Civil War, wanted to keep freed slaves from having guns, and they were the first to argue that the right is not a personal one. In modern times people have tried to impose gun prohibition, misnamed "gun control," on a people who believe in self-defense as a right and who know that "when seconds count, the police are minutes away." In recent years, the Supreme Court has reasserted this right forcefully. In Britain, where the right did not have constitutional protection, the people have been deprived of their right to keep and bear arms. This critical liberty has faded away in its original homeland, but was preserved here by the American Founders.

The Constitution also turned the entire country into a huge free-trade zone, and a single national market, with all the economies of scale and comparative advantage that entailed. This was an absolutely essential prerequisite for future economic development, which we enjoy to this day and take for granted. Even with a national Constitution, we might have ended up with a fragmented internal market because of variations in the law among the states. But the creation of a single market was a conscious decision that did not have to happen.

We ended up with a common American legal culture for reasons beyond the Constitution. In the early years of the country there was popular animosity toward anything English and some resistance to relying on the Common Law and English precedent. American lawyers and judges rejected this notion and created an American style of law that was continuous with England's, though not the same. They managed to keep this system roughly consistent across the entire country by relying on legal treatises that were considered authoritative. The most important example was James Kent's *Commentaries on American Law*, which went through many editions.

The variations from state to federal court, or between state courts, were largely matters of detail. Of course to a practicing lawyer those details would mean the difference between defeat and victory. But as a matter of legal culture, any lawyer going from one state courthouse to another, reading the statutes and reported cases of another state (partially excepting Louisiana), or drawing up contracts, deeds, or wills, would have been able to understand the laws of the other states. It is very much the same today. As a result, through no planned process, the United

States acquired a largely uniform legal system, which allowed people to trade or to relocate within the United States with confidence that they would not face a radically different set of rules.

## NEW STATES

When Americans think of the Constitution these days they are unlikely to focus on the critical provision allowing for the admission of new states. The first line of Art. 4, § 3 of the Constitution reads: "New states may be admitted by the Congress into this union." The United States was founded as a machine for the systematic settlement, annexation, and incorporation of the entire continent into the original union.

Native Americans were pushed aside in the process. Tocqueville describes how the mere presence of fixed agriculture drove off the game the Indians needed to survive. More direct methods to force the Indians from their land were also employed. Courageous resistance could win tactical victories, and Tecumseh and Crazy Horse are remembered as fierce and wily opponents. But in an endless war of attrition against a juggernaut, the Indians were slowly but inevitably crushed. It is interesting to speculate on what would have happened if the Indians had a foreign sponsor to arm and equip them, but there was no such help, and they fought and died alone. The United States was able to conquer most of a continent for virtually no cost at all. The US Army spent more time and effort surveying and mapping territory than it did fighting the original inhabitants.

Once the procedure for selling the land was established, there remained a significant political question. As settlers began spontaneously forming new, self-governing communities in the territories, what would prevent them from building new governments on a larger-scale, and even creating new countries, possibly adverse to the United States? It was to preempt this hazard that the Northwest Ordinances and the Constitution established an orderly mechanism for new states to be formed and added to the Union.

Together, the Ordinances and the Constitution created incentives for settlers in the new territories to remain bound to the United States. The people settling in the new territories would be entitled to military protection, which would prove significant in conflicts with the Indians. The

Ordinances also guaranteed the settlers their liberties, including free-dom of religion, trial by jury, and application of the Common Law. The Constitution provided a guarantee that any new state would have to have a "republican form of government," providing a further incentive for set-tlers to incorporate new territories into the United States.

The American Founders knew that expansion into the interior of the continent could not possibly be controlled directly by the government. So, in the words of legal scholar Daniel Hulsebosch, they "attempt[ed] to control a space by law that could not possibly be controlled by men." The Colonists' assertion of freedom, to simply march into the wilderness beyond the jurisdiction of the Crown, could not be incorporated into British legal thinking, and this in part provoked the war. After the Revo-lution, the new government wisely did not oppose the process, but tried to channel it in ways that would strengthen the country and make it pros-perous. Without overland mobility and spontaneous settlement

> the Union's greatest resource – land – remained worthless. And without ties of cultural identity, foremost among which was con-stitutional identity, much of that land might not have become part of the United States. People moved west, acting out what they believed were their liberties; their governors called them Ameri-can; lawmakers incorporated them into the Union; because that incorporation offered the settlers the prospect of equal citizen-ship, they accepted it. In retrospect it is manifest destiny.

In effect, the Americans resolved the conundrum the British had failed to resolve, regarding the status of colonies.

> Thus a new colonial policy was inaugurated, based upon the prin-ciple of equality. The time-honored doctrine that colonies existed for the benefit of the mother country and were politically subordi-nate and socially inferior was repudiated. In its stead was estab-lished the principle that colonies were but the extension of the nation, entitled, not as a privilege, but as a right to equality.

Americans had demanded political equality with the mother country, and they granted that equality to new settlements they made themselves.

Looking back, it is easy to assume that steady creation and incorporation of new states was inevitable. But this process of peaceful expansion did not have to happen. The fracturing of the continent into multiple new centers of political authority, with inevitable conflict between them, was also possible. That did not happen because of the foresight of the Founders.

A continent-scale country happened because its government mostly got out of the way. Government facilitated settlement, with its surveys and public works, but did not direct most economic activity. The land-hunger of people, their enterprising spirit, their own deal-making and work, built the United States.

## EXPANSION AND CONFLICT

The first Northwest Ordinance of 1784 was drafted by Thomas Jefferson. His original draft would have excluded slavery from all lands west of the Appalachians. Slavery would have been restricted to a strip of land along the Atlantic. This provision was defeated by *one vote.* Jefferson wrote:

> The voice of a single individual ... would have prevented this abominable crime from spreading itself over the new country. Thus we see the fate of millions unborn hanging on the tongue of one man – and Heaven was silent in that awful moment.

The Northwest Ordinance was passed in 1787, barring slavery north and west of the Ohio River. The Constitution recognized and permitted slavery, thereby opening the remaining public lands to settlement by slave owners.

Two main waves of migration worked their way into the new western territories in the early years of the American Republic. In the north, the settlers were mainly New England Yankees. They settled along the southern shore of Lake Erie, in what is now Ohio, and pushed on further into northern Illinois and Indiana, southern Michigan and Wisconsin. Many New Englanders abandoned their rocky hillsides for the deep topsoil of the Midwest, sometimes abandoning entire towns in the process. This

"Yankee Diaspora" was composed mainly of well-organized groups who set up local governments, schools, and churches upon arrival. This Yankee movement necessarily passed through upstate New York. There the Yankees become mixed with people from many locations, who had come up the Hudson on their own way into the interior. There was also a movement of "Midlanders" from Pennsylvania, generally settling south of the Yankees as they moved westward. As a result, the new midwestern states were not pure Yankee, but a mix of peoples, probably the first whose identity was simply "American."

This northern tier of settlement, after some trial and error, focused on the production of wheat. Wheat production required a seasonal labor surge at harvest time, a smaller one at planting. The wheat crop required little or no labor the rest of the year. As a result, family farms could do all the work needed most of the year, supplemented by seasonal wage labor hired from the growing towns in the region. The high cost of this seasonal labor created demand for labor-saving farm machinery, which pushed industrial development and manufacturing in the region.

Getting the products of the Midwest to the outside world, past the Appalachian Mountain barrier, was a severe bottleneck in the development of the region. Bringing farm products out by wagons was expensive, and transport by barge via the Ohio and Mississippi rivers was risky, expensive, and time consuming. Tapping the immense latent wealth of the Midwest required superior means of transportation.

The opening of the Erie Canal in 1825 transformed the regional economy. It connected the Great Lakes with the the Hudson Valley, allowing Midwestern products to be carried cheaply by barge and steamboat to New York City, for further shipment to the hungry cities of the East Coast, or across the Atlantic to Liverpool, to make the bread for Britain's growing industrial workforce. With the cost of transport greatly reduced, wheat prices rapidly dropped for Midwestern wheat and other products. The strong demand for Midwestern wheat allowed millions of family farmers to make a profitable living. In the decades after the Erie Canal opened, many other canals were built. Soon thereafter the railroads began to operate between the Midwest and the East Coast, allowing goods to be transported even when the canals and lakes were iced over.

The Erie Canal was financed by the state of New York, and is a classic example of the pragmatic American attitude toward government involvement in the economy, to create public works with clear and widespread benefits, which could not be realized by private initiative.

On its thriving agricultural base, this "Greater New England" of the Midwest began to transition into being a modern economy. We will leave the details of that story to the next chapter. The basic shape of the American North for a century was falling into place in the years before the American Civil War. In the Midwest, abundant and low cost grain, meat, and other farm products moved by canal and rail, to feed the new factory-cities mainly around the Great Lakes, as well as the rest of the country. Much of this development was financed by New York banks, raising capital from around the country and from London, then the financial capital of the world. East Coast cities, especially New York and Philadelphia, engaged in specialty manufacturing and processing of raw goods. The American North, including the Midwest, was rapidly growing into an agricultural and industrial colossus.

The settlement and growth of the South followed a much different pattern. Slave-owning Southerners moved westward, down the Ohio or over the Appalachians. Slave owners had most of their capital tied up in their slaves. They undervalued land, which they used up by overplanting. The slave labor force would then be moved on into new land. As a result, the slave system required constant expansion to survive. Southerners had little incentive to invest in public works, or even to build towns, under this system. Southerners grew most of their food crops locally, in addition to their cash crops, and did not need to participate in the national economy for their subsistence. The South remained distinctly rural by comparison to the North.

Southerners focused their production on cotton, which produced multiple crops per year and required full time hoeing and weeding, as well as much hand-processing. A slave labor force was kept employed all year, either with cotton or with provision crops. The US Constitution had outlawed importation of slaves after 1808, limiting supply in a time of increasing demand. As a result, slave owners found that raising human beings for sale was a significant source of profit in itself. Demand for cotton suffered boom and bust cycles, and with all chips bet on a single commodity, the entire regional economy was highly speculative. Cotton production was a gamble, and huge fortunes were won and lost. The Yankee spirit of steady application, maximizing land value, and constantly seeking improvements in technique and better machinery was not replicated in the South.

Cotton production was profitable for slave owners, despite the high risks and occasional catastrophic losses, because of two innovations. First, Eli Whitney's famous cotton gin massively reduced the cost of cleaning seeds from the cotton fiber. A second less-appreciated factor in the spread of slave-produced cotton was the introduction of new hybrid plants that could grow in higher elevations and colder parts of the region. Productivity per slave did not increase incrementally, but was multiplied by a factor of 4.6 between 1820 and the start of the Civil War in 1860. This explosive productivity growth using slave labor made the South the world's dominant, low-cost supplier of cotton. The South's immense cotton production found a ready market. Britain's industrial revolution was creating virtually unlimited demand for Southern cotton, which was spun and woven into cloth in the mills of Lancashire and then resold around the world.

There is a persistent myth that slavery was dying out on the eve of the war. This is too simple a characterization. Slave prices were rising steeply in the two decades before the war began, as the cumulative effects of the importation ban of 1808 made them scarcer. Slave owners were becoming wealthy because of the growing demand for cotton, and they expected this growth to continue. But, as William Freehling points out, the demographic crisis of slave reproduction and the southward creep of emancipation gave the Deep South only a few grim choices. Half of Maryland blacks were free by 1860; one fifth of Virginia's were. When free soil is near, many owners found it more effective to emancipate their more skilled slaves and hire them rather than risk losing all their value by having them run away. They could either have the slave trade reopened, which seemed unlikely, or they could secede. South Carolina wanted to secede, but they needed to spur their neighbor states into seceding with them. Many in the South were vocally calling for expansion into Mexico, Central America, and Cuba to create new slave states, either within the United States or by leaving the Union. Slavery was at a crisis point. The slave states could secede, or they would have to face eventual emancipation.

The build-up to the Civil War and the war itself are well-known stories. The growing sectional antagonism eventually broke out in open warfare. The Southerners' aggressive pursuit of fugitive slaves in the

North was one source of antagonism. The Northern insistence on a tariff to protect their industries imposed a much-resented cost on the South, especially because the revenue was spent on public works in the North. Repeated attempts to compromise between the Southern and Northern sections, as new states were added, did not bring any final resolution but merely delayed a fight that few wanted but that seemed increasingly inevitable. Open fighting broke out between slavers and free-staters in the new Western states, increasing the mutual anger between North and South. Still, none of this would have been a sufficient cause for a cataclysmic war. On cost-benefit terms, the war made no sense. But the war was not a matter of cold material or political calculation. The expansion of slavery became a moral question that made any final political deal impossible.

The Yankees of greater New England, once embarked on a moral crusade, do not count the cost. They destroyed a national political party, the Whig Party, and created a new one, the Republican Party, over the issue of slavery. They provoked and sympathized with John Brown's guerrilla-style attacks in Kansas and his abortive effort to start a slave rebellion in the South. The abolitionists, based in the old Puritan hearth-city of Boston, raised an increasingly fervent cry against slavery. Although most people in the North did not agree with the stridency of the abolitionists, they did not like slavery, either. The Abolitionists moved the political goal posts. Their radical stance made Lincoln's position, a political call for containing slavery within its then-existing bounds, appear moderate. The Southern response was to speak more and more openly of secession from the Union in response. This threat in turn mobilized the more moderate voters in the North, who would tolerate slavery, but would not stand by and see the country broken up. This cycle led to the election of Lincoln on a "containment" platform. His election provoked an escalating and protracted war that ended up destroying slavery, despite the original intentions of all parties.

Ending slavery did not end the suffering of the "Negro" as they freed slaves were called. The US government was not interested in limitless costs of a long-term occupation of the well-armed South. Without federal protection, the effective re-enslavement and oppression of blacks in the South went on for another century. However, the ability of the South to expand its slave system, and to determine the fate of all of America, was destroyed forever. It became a region that kept to itself and missed most of the industrial development that was to sweep the North in the decades after the Civil War. The South would be economically backward until after the Second World War.

The main result of the American Civil War, from our long-term perspective, is that the unbroken traditions and ideals of family autonomy and self-reliance, personal liberty, civil rights, representative government, and the rest of the English-derived "toolkit" survived and continued to develop in the North, in the newly developing West, and ultimately in all of the United States.

## A LONG, SLOW FADE

America 1.0 reached its peak and began to fade away at the end of the Civil War. Lincoln had been a man of the old world, a self-made man who grew up among pioneers, and who appealed to Americans as a rural rail-splitter. But Lincoln had spent his adult life practicing law, not farming, and his most lucrative clients were railroads. Lincoln personally bestrode the two ages, with America 1.0 already taking on a mythical air.

During the war, in 1862, Congress passed the Homestead Act, which literally gave away 160 acres of land for free if the homesteader was either the "head of a family," or was "twenty-one years or more of age" or was a veteran of the Union Army or Navy. The Act was also meant to suppress land speculation. The homesteader had to swear that the land would be "for his or her exclusive use and benefit . . . for the purpose of actual settlement and cultivation, and not either directly or indirectly for the use or benefit of any other person or persons." The traditional single-family farm lot was invoked, and the intent of the law was to spread the Midwestern pattern across the rest of the continent. But this was not possible.

By the end of the Civil War the best farmland in the USA had already been sold off. The increasingly marginal lands west of the Mississippi would never be as productive as the Midwestern heartland. The 100th meridian cuts through North and South Dakota, Nebraska, Kansas, Oklahoma, and Texas. West of this line, crop-growing is difficult without substantial irrigation. It was not known at the time, but the initial settlements west of the 100th meridian were made at the top of a multi-decade wet and dry cycle. The newly settled lands proved to be a trap. The Dust Bowl in the early twentieth century showed that these areas were better suited for ranching and mining. Only large infusions of federal money could keep these areas operating as farmland.

The days of westward expansion, which began with the initial colonial settlements, was at an end. The Census Bureau announced in 1890 that there was no longer a frontier region in the United States. However, the expansion of the American people into new territory never stopped. As we will see, there were subsequent waves of internal settlement. Each new development in technology, agriculture, and transportation has changed the value of land and allowed it to be repurposed The Americans would move in response. Nonetheless, the heroic age of the pioneer was over.

More important than the closing of the frontier was the rise of the new America that had been long in developing: the America of railroads, factories, and big cities. The railroads and factories had at first been blessings to the farmer, getting his crops to market and making his work more productive with labor-saving equipment. But over time, the ever-improving machinery made farming so efficient, and drove prices so low, that family farms could not survive. The railroads were monopoly suppliers of transportation, and the farmers saw that their profits were being eaten up by railroad rates that they could not control and could not avoid paying. Agriculture faded out as the main employer of American labor. The rise of industrial America, America 2.0, largely destroyed the middle class of America 1.0, which had existed since colonial times, and it was not clear that a new middle class could be built in its place.

There was a long and unsuccessful rearguard action by Populist politicians on behalf of the fading world of independent family farms. There were tactical successes, including federal regulation of railway rates, and failures, like the attempt to coin silver to inflate away farm debt to Eastern banks. But the demand for inexpensive food doomed the traditional family farm, and the small-town life that was part of it. Young people could not make a living and moved away. As the number of farmers declined, the land under cultivation actually increased and productivity increased sharply, but it required a shrinking workforce. The federal government became increasingly involved in the farming sector, providing price support and determining what could be grown and how. In effect, the declining America 1.0 was bought out in the early twentieth century.

Industrializing American agriculture generated more and cheaper food, but eliminated a way of life that many felt to be the "real America." Rural America, which was disappearing, was seen to possess virtues beyond mere economic efficiency. It was the repository of individualism and freedom and personal responsibility, and it has remained so in memory and legend.

Let us close this chapter by imagining two teenage girls, around 1860. One is Caroline Quiner, who became Caroline Ingalls, the mother in Laura Ingalls Wilder's *Little House* books. Caroline was born in the rural Midwest, in Wisconsin, on a family farm. She spent much of her life with her husband and children, building homes from scratch in the wilderness. The life depicted in Wilder's books is the final generation of America 1.0, a hard life of individualism and self-reliance. And an adult reader will notice that Charles Ingalls worked very hard, suffered many setbacks, and never achieved much material success. But his life and his family's life seem to epitomize America, or at least an important part of America.

We don't know the other girl's name. She is from a Yankee town in the hills of New Hampshire or western Massachusetts. Her small town has little to offer. Many people of her father's and grandfather's generation had gone out West. She moves down to one of the mill towns, perhaps Fall River, Massachusetts. She is hired to work in a factory where cotton thread is spun. The work is paid by the hour, and she must adjust herself to the rhythm of the machinery, and work by the clock, not by the sun. The pay is good, at first. Life in the town is not as hard, day by day, as life on a farm, and there is more to do there, and more things to buy. And if her factory closes in one of the periodic economic busts, they will all close, there won't be any work, and she has little to return to. Her world was the world of the future, the world of America 2.0.

# Chapter 6
# America 2.0

## The America 2.0 Revolution

Industrial America, America 2.0, first began to be visible in the Northeast, in the period between the 1830s and the Civil War. The Americans in the Northeast – in Yankee New England and upstate New York, Quaker Pennsylvania, and the Anglo-Dutch New York City – had developed many businesses in addition to farming, including metalworking and machine-making. Connecticut was famous for its clocks, and the Yankee tinkerer was a well-known stereotype. The capacity to make, repair, and operate mechanical equipment was widespread.

To operate an industrial economy you also need a literate and numerate workforce. The Puritan and Quaker traditions had stressed the need for every Christian, male and female, high and low, to be literate in order to read the Bible. From the beginning they had spent tax money on education and required schooling to make that possible. Fischer, in *Albion's Seed*, relates how Massachusetts has consistently spent four times the amount per capita on education than Virginia from 1630 to today. People in the Northeast were on average more literate than they were in the South.

For these reasons the Northeast had the prerequisites for industrialization well in place as the nineteenth century got rolling. Perhaps the least visible of these preconditions, however, was the Absolute Nuclear Family (ANF) system, which allowed and expected children to support themselves and form their own families and to be free to move to another city or state if they desired. At the same time there was no guaranteed inheritance at home to keep children tied to the family land, and no stigma in selling any inherited land on the market if they did inherit. The mobility of the ANF population made it comparatively easy to move off the land, away from family, and into the factory towns.

By 1830 this change had become visible, at first appearing slowly, and soon with disorienting rapidity. Steam engines arrived from England, and soon steamboats were afloat in American waters. They began serving the inland waterways, providing faster, safer, more comfortable, and cheaper transportation along the Hudson and the Ohio rivers, and around the "little Mediterranean" trade regions formed around Long Island Sound, in the Chesapeake Bay, and throughout the Great Lakes. For the first time, it became possible to travel reliably and comfortably over distances of one or two hundred miles on an overnight basis, do a day's business at your destination the next day, and return on the boat that same night. The telegraph allowed trips to be set up on short notice. Thus the business trip was born. These regions were rapidly knit into a recognizably modern economic pattern.

After the 1830s, railroads began to provide fast and cheap transportation even where navigable waters did not run, first to extend the range of steamboat lines, and then supplanting them. Managing these far-flung enterprises, which required centralized control, was a challenge that no private business had ever faced before. There was only one engineering school in the United States: West Point. The routes of early railroads were surveyed and mapped by the US Army Corps of Engineers, who brought their managerial practices from the Army to the new railroad businesses. In this way, the Army also provided the railroads and other large businesses with its own management "software," the *General Regulations for the Army*. This was a 400-page volume that provided sample documents and procedures for the regular flow of information within an organization. It contained forms for monthly, quarterly and annual reports. The Army at that time was "a modern, reasonably effective corporate bureaucracy, more advanced and better organized than any contemporary social, political or business organization in the United States." American big business started out with military bureaucracy and regimentation.

Production was revolutionized when powered looms began turning out large amounts of cheap cloth in water-powered mills along the fall line from New Hampshire to New Jersey, suddenly making clothes cheaper and far more available than ever before. Iron forges and foundries expanded from the small blacksmith shops of Revolutionary times to large industrial operations.

By the time of the Civil War, America had developed not just scattered industries, but an entire system to mine and produce the coal and ore, forge the metal, invent the machines, and manufacture them into a wide variety of tools and goods that together began to transform everyday life. Wire and electric batteries created the telegraph to convey information instantaneously from one end of the country to the other. Steam-powered rotary presses made possible the cheap mass-produced newspaper, to print the news and opinions disseminated by the new telegraph networks. The Declaration of Independence, the signing of the treaty of Paris that ended the Revolutionary War, the ratification of the Constitution – all of these events were conveyed by horse and rider, and took weeks or months to reach the corners of the nation. The election of Lincoln and the shelling of Fort Sumter were known from Maine to Florida within hours of those events, and created the headlines in papers across the continent the next morning.

## THE FIRST INDUSTRIAL WAR

Up to the Civil War, the political system of the United States was still recognizably that of the America 1.0 for which the Founders had written the Constitution. Industrial workers, although a growing part of the population, were still a distinct minority, and the concerns of the government still revolved around the need of individual farm families on their own land. It was the Civil War, and particularly the mobilization of men, war materiel, and money required that created the initial outline of America 2.0.

For the first time in US history, a military draft required young men to serve directly in the Army. For the first time in US history, an income tax was levied directly on individuals. And the United States incurred an unprecedented, enormous debt to finance the war. (The Confederate government, supposedly dedicated to states' rights, also found it necessary to match all of these centralizing acts before the end of the war.) With the vast funds raised, the armed services placed enormous orders for ships, guns, uniforms, equipment, and food, which required a correspondingly vast expansion of industry to provide it.

And, to the amazement of foreign observers, it worked. The US Army and Navy, which had been minuscule and not particularly well-equipped before the war, were expanded to a size that dwarfed most European armies and navies.

The Navy was equipped with cutting-edge, armored warships with rotating turrets and large-caliber guns firing explosive shells. Naval experts had believed that it would be impossible for Lincoln to enforce his blockade proclamation against the Confederacy's long coastline. They were wrong. The Navy proceeded to commandeer ferryboats and coastal steamers, stuff them with the latest cannon, and create a near-airtight blockade that only a handful of specialized, ultrafast steamers could slip through.

At the beginning of the war, the US Navy had only three ships available and suitable for blockade duty out of its 42 in active service, and the Confederacy had 3,500 miles of coastline and 180 ports that needed blocking. The Navy immediately seized and armed 140 civilian ships and put an additional 52 under construction by the end of 1861. As they captured Confederate blockade runners, they armed suitable ones and pressed them into service as well.

On land the army was transported and sustained by rail, coordinated with telegraph lines, and equipped with rifles and cannon from Northern factories. The Northerners innovated in weapon design and manufacture, equipping their troops with lever-action rifles, to pick one example. Ironically, the Union Army rifles were made using the "American System" of interchangeable parts originally devised by Eli Whitney, the inventor of the cotton gin. Whitney's invention of the cotton gin may have made the war inevitable, while his factory methods made Northern victory all but inevitable.

Regiment after regiment was raised, and raised again after they were decimated in the meat-grinder battles of attrition of the Washington-Richmond corridor. With its smaller population, the Southern government found that a Confederate soldier, once lost, could not be replaced. A Union soldier lost could be replaced, if by nobody else, then by any of the steady stream of young emigrants who continued to flock to the Northern ports throughout the war, sometimes walking down the gangplank of their ship from Cork or Bremen straight into the arms of the draft officers.

Not least among the new institutions thrown together at a moment's notice during the war were the federal bureaucracies needed to oversee the equipping, arming, feeding, training, and transporting of these forces in numbers larger than had ever been attempted in North America. The only available solution for such a problem was a centralized bureaucracy, so the United States created one. It worked. It furthermore gave a young generation the experience of seeing a large government accomplish large things quickly. At the same time, it also taught a generation of business-men another lesson – that the large amount of money raised quickly and seemingly effortlessly by the war bond and the printing press would be dispensed quickly, in large amounts, and with minimal accountability. The Civil War was the true start of many of the great fortunes of the sub-sequent Gilded Era.

## THE INDUSTRIAL ARMY AND ITS CAPTAINS

The Civil War trained an entire young generation in the school of mili-tary discipline and obedience. Sanctified by a cause held sacred, whether in the North or the South, they saw that a team working together under unquestioned leadership, sacrificing individual interests to a common cause even to death, and throwing the whole weight of the nation behind their efforts, could accomplish great things, things that could be accom-plished by no other means. That generation became the true founders of America 2.0, and their entire subsequent life was marked by the quest to apply the lessons learned from the war to other areas of life.

For example, the military-bureaucratic model was at that time the only available model for managing large, geographically dispersed enterprises that required precise synchronization. The old trading corporations like the East India Company operated on the model of the premodern navies: each remote unit was by necessity self-administering, within a frame-work of rules and policies. Like a navy captain at sea, a factor administer-ing an outpost in, say, Calcutta could not wait for an answer from London, which might take a year to arrive. He had to decide on his own initiative.

The new railroad companies emerging after the Civil War, on the other hand, could not use this approach. Trains operated over distances of five hundred or a thousand miles, and their departures and arrivals needed to be timed to the minute. A problem in one remote location was not merely a local problem; anything that might impede the passage of a single train could affect traffic across the system, and so must be reported and dealt with at the system level, calling if need be on special resources from across the system. The telegraph permitted, for the first time, information to be exchanged nearly instantaneously across those distances. Most of the men organizing and administering these companies were Civil War veterans, and they found it very natural to apply quasi-military forms of organization and discipline to their operations.

Passenger-train crews and station personnel wore military-style uniforms as a matter of course, both to impress upon the public that the personnel were disciplined and therefore likely to operate trains safely, and for the sake of inspiring *esprit de corps*. France's colonial wars in Algeria in the 1840s had caught the popular imagination of the time, and American militia uniforms started to imitate French styles; thus American troops went to war in 1861 wearing French-style képis. Postwar railroads modeled their uniforms on Civil War models, and never really changed. Thus, until the coming of Amtrak, American railway conductors wore the headgear of French officers. It is perhaps fortunate that the founding influence had not taken place during the Franco-Prussian War, in which event they might have worn spiked helmets.

A military ethos also helped to encourage the substantial personal transformation that the railroads needed from their workforce. It is harder to appreciate it from the perspective of our times, but the coming of the Industrial Revolution substantially raised the demands on the ordinary workforce from that typical of America 1.0. In particular, railroad work required that at a minimum, all operating personnel have substantially more literacy, numeracy, punctuality, and on-the-job sobriety than the average workforce, or for that matter, the average population. Any operating job (train crew, signalman, yard crew, etc.) had to be able to read instructions and signs, fill out simple account forms, tell time, and be on time. Showing up for work drunk or drinking on the job was grounds for immediate dismissal. By comparison, in the maritime industry, sailors had historically received part of their pay in hard liquor and consumed it on the worksite.

These demands helped make railroad workers the lead sector of the industrial workforce. The increase in productivity and safety from following these rules became obvious to other employers, so the management system of the railroads became the model for all of industry. The discipline and regimentation of the industrial system became a key part of the shaping of America 2.0.

However, this transformation, although introduced by industrialists, had other repercussions less to their liking. When workers found themselves at the bottom of an industrial hierarchy, taking orders from all above, rather than farming for themselves or in a small, informal workplace, they naturally turned to the military principles of organization and solidarity as an antidote. Labor unions had begun in the 1830s and 1840 as small local organizations of skilled workers, such as carpenters and plumbers. These trades demanded a substantial investment in skills and training.

Their practitioners discovered that if they formed an agreement among all the skilled workers in their town, and refused to work for less than a stated amount, it was not easy for people needing their services to find adequate replacements on short notice. The agreement was needed to avoid the prisoners' dilemma situation of an employer offering a bonus to one tradesman in return for agreeing to work. Because the skills were genuinely scarce, this tactic was usually successful, and such skilled craft unions became part of the fabric of the emerging America 2.0. They also suited the individualistic personality types of Americans; these organizations were based on voluntary agreements among individuals and merely seeking to act as agents for their members in arriving at contracts with employers.

As the railroads and other new industrial employers increased their scale of operations, workers with scarce and specialized skills were able to make the same tactics succeed at their workplaces – but only for themselves. The great majority of less-skilled workers were easily replaced, and couldn't manage to achieve a union contract, and mostly never tried.

Railroads were the first major exception to that rule. As railroads required a higher set of qualifications than the average worker of the time, employees had greater bargaining power as a group. Locomotive engineers had a highly specialized skill and were in charge of valuable capital assets that could quickly be destroyed if operated by somebody who didn't know what they were doing. With this leverage they were able to force recognition of their union first. The engineers worked as a team with their firemen, who kept the engines fed with coal. This was also a job that required specialized knowledge, and firemen were also part of their union.

Because train crews worked over a wide geographical area they tended to organize not just locally, as tradesmen had, but would organize the entire railroad at once, requiring a regional scale of organization. Because engineers tended to sympathize with the other crewmen they worked with, their unwillingness to cross a picket line of other railway workers allowed the other positions, even with less exclusive skills, to organize in turn. Thus, railroads became a unionized industry decades before any other, just as they became regulated before others.

The emphasis on sobriety and responsibility in hiring also played a role in the early organization of railroad workers. Members of temperance churches, typically congregation-governed, and temperance leagues tended to be favored for hiring by the railroads. Such organizations, the lifeblood of civil society, gave their members the organizational skills and institutional templates to use in forming the early labor unions.

It would be a mistake to assume that with these advantages, railroads were organized easily, quickly, or without opposition from their management. Some of the most bitter strikes of the late nineteenth century were railway labor-management strikes. They were also the first strikes in which the Federal government found itself required to take a stand, as US mail moved by rail and the government had a constitutional mandate to keep it in operation. And in these strikes, the military virtues learned in Civil War service shaped the responses of both sides.

Over the decades of the 1880s, 1890s, and early 1900s, the characteristic bargain of America 2.0 took shape. The industrialists organized themselves into large hierarchical corporations that poured lavish sums into Congress and state legislatures to buy favors – tariff bills to protect themselves from foreign competition; railroad charters giving them the right to force sale of land to themselves; and the use of militia to suppress strikes. Later, they discovered that by imposing licensing and regulatory standards on industries the big corporations could prevent smaller and newer companies from entering the marketplace and competing with them. It seemed natural to industrial workers to organize themselves into unions to counteract this power, particularly when they saw organized workers receive better pay, security, and working conditions than unorganized ones.

And just as industrialists used their economic power to seek favors from the government, the emergent labor unions found that their ability to summon large numbers of loyal voters gave them clout as well, and they began to use it to seek favors for themselves. Early victories included laws excluding Chinese and Japanese immigrants as they were considered competition to the unions' members. Unions also joined with employers to support high tariffs to protect their jobs from foreign competition. Later, unions also supported legislation intended to improve workplace safety and conditions, and to support pension programs, ultimately resulting in Social Security.

## NEW CITIES, NEW NEEDS

As these changes unfolded, the big organizations that had begun to dominate America started to transform the material culture and ways of life of most Americans. Industrialism began to transform the rural-urban balance in two different ways. The growth of factories pulled people off of their farms by the lure of better pay and the better amenities of urban life. At the same time, the cyclic nature of weather and agricultural prices also served to push people off farms, pushed by drought, market crashes, or price fluctuations. Meanwhile, the onrushing industrial revolution produced more and more farm machinery that reduced the once-great demand for farm labor. In 1860, 20 percent of Americans lived in urban areas, and the other 80 percent lived in rural areas. By 1900 the proportion of people living in rural America had halved to 40 percent.

America 1.0's cities were small port and mercantile towns. Philadelphia (ca. 40,000 at Independence) was the largest town, and most were substantially smaller. The completion of the Erie Canal in the 1830s, linking New York City with the newly populated interior of the country, led to a growing urban population, particularly in the northern and midwestern states. By the 1840s, these cities were populous and prosperous, and filled with manufacturing, trading, and financial enterprises.

Although these cities were great places for making (or losing) money, they were horrible in most other ways. Foreign visitors were generally appalled. With few exceptions, they were filthy, with no effective sewage systems, clean water supplies, or organized garbage collection. Tobacco chewing was widespread and the sidewalk was their spittoon. Most families kept a cow or goat in their backyard to provide fresh milk, as commercial supplies were generally unsafe. One family's outhouse would sit uphill from its neighbor's well. There were few public spaces – mostly militia drill-grounds – and almost no parks. The Boston Common was still used for its original purpose of grazing cows. There were no restaurants in the modern sense, only crude taverns where basic meals might or might not be available for travelers. Theaters and other cultural amenities were scarce.

Nor was a stroll along the streets necessarily pleasant or even safe. The streets were crowded with recent migrants from the countryside who had no urban habits or civility or even basic cleanliness. Even more problematic were the hordes of foreign immigrants, many with no English or understanding of how American institutions worked. Many of these joined criminal gangs that killed, robbed, and controlled vice activities almost without challenge, except from each other. Law and order were provided by a handful of town constables, usually wandering around in ordinary civilian clothes, armed if at all with personal weapons. Criminal gangs also collaborated with local political organizations to steal elections at will, subsequently plundering the city treasury.

During the Civil War these problems began to come to a head. The military draft was robustly resisted by the Irish population of New York and other cities, culminating in a weeklong riot in 1863 that required rushing Union troops back from the front to suppress, at the cost of hundreds of rioters and innocent civilians killed in the crossfire.

The generation returning from the Civil War began to ask whether these situations could be tolerated any longer. Some problems began to be addressed by private actions. But in general, there arose the feeling that America's 1.0 institutions had proven themselves inadequate to the task. Their wartime experience also suggested to them that whatever solutions might be found would probably require the same kind of organization, centralization, planning, and control that had yielded such surprising results in the Civil War.

The growing wealth of the USA after the war, and the growing sense of national mission began to transform American life, but particularly in the cities. Aqueducts brought clean water from distant, unpolluted sources; sewers began to solve the waste and disease problems, as they began to be hooked up to new flush toilets; cable cars and elevated railways introduced the first generation of urban mechanical transport, and new public buildings and parks started to give the citizenry, working and middle classes alike, some place to spend the spare time that new shorter working hours had brought. Proper uniformed police and fire departments began to make streets and houses safer, and public health services began to bring the periodic plagues that had always been the accompaniment of urban life under some kind of control. Enormous public works were built for these cities, like the Croton Aqueduct (1890) that supplied water to New York City and the Brooklyn Bridge (1883). Chicago reversed the course of its river, treated its sewage in its immense water reclamation plant, and then dumped it into the Chicago Drainage Canal (finished 1900), which was far bigger than the Panama Canal.

Meanwhile, these cities began to develop suburbs, serviced initially by streetcars, later by elevated trains and buses. The old American middle class of farmers and craftsmen gave way to a new kind of middle class, based in towns and cities. This middle class was composed in part of business owners and skilled laborers. Even in the era of mass production, there were innumerable small or medium businesses serving many needs and wants, from wedding cakes to mother of pearl buttons, furniture making to machine tools. Business ownership or skilled work made a middle class existence possible for many such people.

But the rising middle class of the era was also composed of the employees of large corporations. They focused their effort on their careers, and tried to rise within the businesses that employed them. Their middle-class status and respectability were based on their salaries, the value of their homes, where they lived, and their access to credit, and "intangibles – reputation, appearance, personal habits, local prejudices – mattered a great deal." The attempts to keep the disreputable at bay led to increasing physical separation between middle-class people and the poor, foreigners, blacks, Catholics. The seemingly natural equality in a country where even the well-off often worked with their hands faded away.

## MEN OF STEEL: THE TRUSTS AND THE TRUST-BREAKERS

By 1880 it had also become apparent that the various industrial enterprises that had been transforming everyday life were coming together to form what was in effect an integrated industrial system on an entirely unprecedented scale. At the heart of this was the introduction of large-scale, low-cost steel production made possible by the new Bessemer and open-hearth (Martin-Siemens) processes. Once the new large-scale facilities of Andrew Carnegie and other entrepreneurs came on line during the 1870s, cheap, plentiful steel permitted a massive upgrade of railroads, bridges, ships, and almost all other manufactured products. To feed these steel mills, huge iron ore mines were opened in Minnesota, ore freighters (requiring the construction of complex canal and lock systems) hauled the ore to Great Lakes ports on Lakes Erie and Ontario, and hundreds of miles of high-throughput railroads of unprecedented capacity hauled Minnesota ore and Pennsylvania and West Virginia coal to the new steel-making centers that stretched from Indiana to New York and Ontario.

The steel-making centers themselves were enormous facilities developed on a scale matched nowhere else for decades. As the scale rapidly increased toward the end of the nineteenth century, the capitalization needed to build this complex rose above the capabilities of small companies to finance, so there was a rapid consolidation into a handful of very large corporations, which often owned mills, mines, ships, and railroads alike, the better to finance and coordinate their activities.

To organize these businesses, lawyers used an ancient device, unique to Common Law systems – the trust. From medieval times onward, the trust provided a means for third-party management of funds that did not, unlike the Roman-law device of the corporation, require prior government permission and approval to establish. Suddenly, judges and legislators found that the ancient legal devices that had been put to a variety of uses over the centuries, could now be used to manage the vast new enterprises of America 2.0. As Frederic W. Maitland observed at the time, "out in America the mightiest trading corporations that the world has ever seen are known by the name of 'Trusts'."

Furthermore, the steel that this system produced quickly became an essential – quite probably *the* essential – supply of modern life. National strength began to be measured not only in men under arms or ships in service, but now in tons of steel produced. For at the same time that large amounts of affordable steel became possible, its rapid adoption in military technology made it essential. Sir Henry Bessemer, whose "converters" were a breakthrough in manufacturing large quantities of steel, was primarily a munitions maker. His firm developed the first practical process for large-scale steelmaking, making it possible to build large cannon to fire the explosive shells he had invented.

Between 1890 and 1910, a new revolution in military affairs developed, using the new high-power turbines made possible by steel, the heavy plate armor also made possible by steel, and the large-caliber steel cannon firing high-explosive shells The new battleships enabled by these technologies could sweep anything else from the seas. Furthermore, it was quickly realized that a fleet of such ships could show up by surprise at any coastal town in the world and, if undefended, such towns would quickly be reduced to ruins. This threat of sudden strategic devastation was a new thing, and very frightening to a world unaccustomed to it.

In 1893, a dispute on the border between Venezuela and British Guiana flared up, thanks to an excitable American press looking for something to sell papers, and some talk of war between Britain and America, which considered Venezuela to be within its sphere of influence. Suddenly the inhabitants of American coastal cities realized that Britain's modern fleet was based only a few days' steaming away in Halifax, Nova Scotia, and could, in the event of war, be bombarding New York almost immediately. The Atlantic was no longer the several months' buffer from European problems Americans had always taken for granted. America's fleet was just beginning its modernization and would have no chance of stopping it. US Navy Captain Alfred Mahan's influential book on naval power, advocating the creation of a strong navy, had been published only a few years before and was mandatory reading for naval officers around the world. The circumstances called for a powerful American navy, and Mahan provided the theoretical basis for its construction and use.

Naval construction was greatly expanded. As a result, steel was not just an economic item; the ability to produce large amounts of steel thus became an essential national-defense capability. This cut two ways for the steel industry. On the one hand, it ensured that the government gave it everything it needed to flourish, in particular, a high tariff to protect it from foreign competition. On the other hand, being a national asset meant that the government began to take an interest in how the steel industry was managed. This mix of public and private responsibility persists to this day in the American defense industry, and the military-industrial complex is one of the most deeply rooted institutions of America 2.0

## THE STRESS AND STRAIN OF TRANSITION

To many thoughtful observers, the original successful structure of the Constitution seemed inadequate as America began facing unanticipated problems and situations under the pressure of industrialization, mass immigration from novel sources, and unprecedented urban growth and densities. By the time New Mexico and Arizona had completed the conversion of the contiguous continental land to statehood, the Industrial Revolution led many concerned Americans to believe that the old formula for America was no longer working.

The Civil War and emancipation resolved the contradiction between an individualistic American ideology and the alien system of chattel slavery and large plantations, which had spread to North America from the original Spanish system of the Caribbean. In the process, however, many more Northerners went into the factories to build the munitions of war, many experienced conscription for the first time in American history and the regimentation of military life, and all experienced the income tax, federal paper money, soaring public debt and inflation, and other centralizing and bureaucratizing measures. These were tolerated as a war necessity, and were quickly abandoned in peacetime. Yet a generation of intellectuals was permanently marked by the idealism and shared purpose of wartime, and awed by the ease with which collective action could accomplish great tasks.

At the same time, new problems caused Americans to worry that the old political mechanisms of the Republic were inadequate to handle the needs of the new era. As we saw, massive cities arose, with sprawling quarters of slum housing breeding crime, disease, vice, and corruption of a type and on a scale never known before in the small, familiar seaports of the old republic. The elected sheriffs and handful of deputies and constables who had kept the peace in the past were entirely overwhelmed by the challenge of large immigrant gangs speaking impenetrable languages and bound by exotic cultural practices such as the oath of silence. Immigrants from clan-based societies with no concept of public loyalty or civil society looted public treasuries and ran the already-inadequate public services into the ground. The crony-based legislatures were highly amenable to bribery, so a generation of railroad-builders and other capitalists learned to turn bribery into protection from competition, and thus gain and keep massive fortunes. Soon, both domestic and immigrant workers began organizing militant unions and engaging in pitched battles with state militias. These militias were often composed of farm boys with no sympathy for the immigrant hordes they faced, and no training in crowd control or urban warfare. From the great national railroad strike of 1877, which saw dozens killed and sections of cities burned to the ground, through the passage of the Wagner Act in 1936, labor violence, often with an ethnic component, created what was effectively a low-grade, endemic civil war in America's industrial cities and mineral districts.

Against this background, intellectuals and public reformers believed the old structures and the old constraints of the Constitution had become obstacles to the successful rebuilding of America along lines that could address its obvious problems. They looked to Europe where a newly united and rising Germany had dealt with such problems with a combination of strict regulation and control of society through a quasi-militarized police force, and delivery of welfare benefits such as pensions and medical care. Thus the Progressive movement stood for a new, centralized, and theoretically more efficient form of nationwide regulation and reform. Teddy Roosevelt tackled crime, gangs, and filth as police commissioner of New York, and he became emblematic of a movement that, nationwide, replaced the old deputy or constable with a uniformed, quasi-militarized police in sufficient force so as to intimidate gangs or strikers on sight. Gone was a simple badge, civilian clothes, and civilian style of policing. The new model was military in appearance and intent.

Investigative commissions determined that bloody steel and coal strikes in Pennsylvania had been aggravated by the amateurism of deputies and militiamen, and that immigrants from the Austro-Hungarian and Russian Empires had often failed to obey them because they didn't realize they were police officers, rather than the company's private guards. Thus the Pennsylvania Coal and Iron Police was formed (the antecedents of today's Pennsylvania State Police) and care was taken to train them well and outfit them with impressive uniforms, broad-brimmed "Smokey" hats, and high black boots, a look that state police forces cultivate to this day. Other states soon created their own state police forces.

The first wave of problems began to be addressed by engineers and planners newly empowered by novel technologies and new forms of social organization. Massive engineering works delivered fresh water to

Manhattan and other cities and sewers carried away waste, greatly curbing epidemic disease. Cities began to create sanitation departments; cable cars and elevated railways offered more efficient transportation free from the pollution of horse manure; bridges and paved streets, urban parks, and eventually electric lighting transformed the urban landscape into something citizens could show off with pride. Soon they began to create World's Fairs to do so. These public functions, it seemed, could be performed only by enlightened government.

All these physical and social changes began to transform the character of American daily life. By the early twentieth century, the typical American was no longer a member of a farm family cultivating land they owned, but rather a member of an urban family renting a home and dependent upon employment for a living. Employers took the form of increasingly large corporations. These, starting with railway companies, and then followed by others, had modeled their internal management styles after (and often hired as managers and workers veterans of) the military organizations they had known from the Civil War. At that time, military organizations were the only available example of organizations capable of managing large groups of people who must be closely coordinated while dispersed over long distances. Management was often bureaucratic and authoritarian, and many employees concluded that only a counter-organization, the labor union, could protect their individuality from arbitrary treatment. Despite the usual assumption that unions were primarily attractive for economic reasons, much early union literature stressed protection from arbitrary and unfair management treatment. Also, many industrial workers were recent immigrants from cultures that prized security and/or equality of outcome as values over individual autonomy. Unions and progressive regulations both sought to promote security and egalitarianism and were willing to sacrifice individual autonomy to gain it. The closed union shop, which made union membership a condition of employment, was an example of such a strategy.

Some corporate executives and investors fought this trend. But others astutely saw that their corporations could also successfully trade freedom for security. They were also able to overcome the varying laws imposed by the states, and face only one set of applicable rules. By acceding to overall federal regulation, the larger corporations were able to protect themselves against smaller, more nimble companies threatening to overtake them, because the bigger, more established corporations could better afford to bear the cost of regulatory compliance. They also had more lobbying power to ensure that regulations favored them over their competitors. Big business made peace with big government, then embraced it. As big business gained experience with the regulatory game, it was frequently able to "capture" the regulators completely.

## WOODROW WILSON'S LAWYERS, GUNS, AND POWER

The political movement that arose to address the problems of urban squalor and monopolistic business was known as Progressivism. Progressives remembered the Civil War days very well, because many of the first generation of Progressives had fought in it. The Progressive era did not, for the most part, have the globalist, pacifist, and antimilitarist flavor of the late-twentieth-century political left. Rather, they were nationalists, militarists, and imperialists who saw building a big fleet as an industrial-policy tool, to both promote and also control (through awarding large contracts) the steel and other cutting-edge industries like electrical equipment, and as a tool of spreading their ideology abroad. "We will teach them to elect good men," as Woodrow Wilson said when he dispatched America's new fleet to bombard and occupy Veracruz, Mexico.

By the early twentieth century Progressives had implemented many parts of their agenda piecemeal. The Interstate Commerce Act had created a commission to regulate the railroad companies closely. The movement to build a strong navy had succeeded in integrating the steel and shipbuilding industries into the initial seeds of the permanent military-industrial complex, with the unionized employees of those industries eventually added as junior partners. The assassination of William McKinley had placed Theodore Roosevelt, one of their own, in the White House, and he had important allies in Congress and the state legislatures.

However, many Americans were still strongly attached to America 1.0 values and institutions. The Progressive ideal of a strong central government guided by apolitical technical experts, regulating and deploying social resources, including the citizens themselves, as science dictated, still faced many roadblocks, particularly as the Supreme Court still strongly supported an individualistic concept of rights. The Interstate Commerce

Commission (ICC) as first established was solely investigative, and could refer a case to the courts only if it detected a violation. The first peacetime income tax was struck down by the Supreme Court. Judges trained in the Common Law were indifferent to sociological arguments if prior precedents pointed the other way.

To address these perceived obstacles to remaking America in the 2.0 model, Progressives pushed on all fronts for what amounted to a new constitutional order, implemented over the next four decades. The first major change was the trust-busting legislation and enforcement actions pursued by Theodore Roosevelt, capped by the spectacular breakup of the Standard Oil Company, led by John D. Rockefeller, and one of the biggest companies in the world. Further significant changes came in several distinct waves. The first of these waves came in 1913, with the passage of the Sixteenth and Seventeenth Amendments, authorizing, respectively, the federal income tax, and mandating the direct election of senators. In that year, also, the Federal Reserve Bank system was created, providing for the nation's first peacetime governmental paper money system, and insulating it from the direct influence of Congress.

Collectively, these changes amounted to a substantial revision of the constitutional order. Had we been France, we would have called it a new Republic and given it a number. Although America 2.0 began, socially and economically, before the Civil War, 1913 marked the first real turn toward a state run fundamentally from Washington rather than from the state capitals. The income tax gave it a large revenue stream that could be further increased with no further actions by the states. The Federal Reserve System allowed theoretically unlimited leverage on paper money without even the acquiescence of Congress, and the direct election of senators removed the ability of the states as political bodies to limit Federal power.

The changes of 1913 gave the federal government an impressive new toolkit. But it took World War I and Woodrow Wilson's distinct style of Progressivism to convince a general public still in many cases clinging to the assumptions of America 1.0 to allow politicians and bureaucrats to use these tools. The Civil War saw the first huge expansion of federal power, with the accompanying industrial mobilization and sudden wealth for favored cronies. World War I saw another such expansion, with the difference that the mechanisms of state control were not dismantled as quickly or thoroughly as after 1865. Upon American entry into the war in

1917 there was a much more concerted effort at intellectual control by the government, with censorship not only of militarily sensitive information but of any dissent from war aims, methods, or of course the decision to go to war itself.

In terms of industrial control, the government seized unprecedented power. The railroad system was placed under government control; rationing controlled food distribution, and the Inter-Allied Shipping Board, a transnational organization beyond the power of any one Allied government (and having on its staff the future architect of the European Union), distributed raw materials and finished goods as it saw fit among American, British, French, and Italian users. Just as Progressives had advocated, panels of government experts seized control of many areas of life.

The immediate postwar era was a disappointment to Progressives. Wilson's legacy was repudiated at the polls in 1920 with the victory of Warren G. Harding and his running mate Calvin Coolidge over James Cox and a young Franklin D. Roosevelt. Harding has been reviled by Progressive historians for the ultimate Progressive crime: giving the voters what they wanted instead of what Progressives thought was good for them. Harding promised and delivered a "Return to Normalcy" – basically undoing Wilson's wartime Progressive state, abolishing controls and bureaus, and freeing many of the opponents Wilson had jailed, like labor leader and conscription opponent Eugene V. Debs. Harding's rhetoric was largely based on individualistic themes drawn from an earlier era. But what Harding actually returned to was the Progressive state as Teddy Roosevelt had built and advocated. Harding kept the income tax, the Federal Reserve, and anti-trust law. He did not turn back the clock, but simply slowed the breakneck advance of Progressivism that Wilson's wartime administration had pursued.

## THE GERMAN PATERNALIST STATE, THE FAILURE OF THE WILSONIAN LEFT, AND THE EVENTUAL VICTORY OF ROOSEVELT'S SOCIAL LOCKEANISM

Wilson, as was true of many Progressives, was an ardent admirer of Germany, where the government had early taken a large role in providing for the economic security of its citizens. Wilson wanted to build an American version of this German "social state," based upon German-style social democracy. However, America is based on an Absolute Nuclear Family system, where the Germans were not. In Germany, most people are in an Authoritarian Family (AF, also known as "stem family"). Just as the English and Americans had been shaped by their type of Absolute Nuclear Family, German society and culture was founded on the authoritarian family. In pre-industrial AF societies, the larger social system is treated as an extended family in which the father maintains lifetime control over his adult sons, their wives, and unmarried daughters. At the father's death, the eldest son inherits all the family land and becomes the new head of the family, whereas the younger sons work for him and are obliged to obey him. At the time of the Industrial Revolution and the emigration from the land to the town, the eldest son in a rural family was unable to carry out his duty of care to the sons who left, and the role of the father was transferred to the employer or the state. The welfare state, in which the state provided security in return for obedience, thus took the place of the father or eldest brother. German politics was organized around the question of whether the corporation had a role as the father for some purposes (the position of German conservatives) or whether the State was to be the father in everything (the position of the Social Democrats). These German ways of thinking did not exist in the English-speaking world.

German unions were devices for the loyal younger brother (i.e., the working class) to demand proper recognition for his loyalty in the form of benefits and security. Many of them would have preferred that the State be the father in all things, but so long as the corporation was the father for work purposes, they would render loyal service in return for proper support. They could be militant when they felt their loyalty had not been fairly rewarded, but they were also diligent about ensuring that their service was loyal and of good quality. This pattern has continued into the present day. When in the 1990s and 2000s German corporations made the case to the unions that benefits must be cut back and productivity increased, many were surprised that the unions, once they were satisfied that the need was real, complied willingly and effectively.

Wilson and many early Progressives had been very influenced by German social democracy, and many had studied in pre-World War One Germany. They mistakenly believed that America was not fundamentally different from Germany, at least not in ways that the Progressives couldn't mold through education and influence. Ironically, it was the war against Germany, one marked by insane Germanophobia, that provided them with the chance to impose a German social model on America. Harding's victory in 1920 was a repudiation of wartime Wilsonianism. The enthusiasm with which Americans grasped the Return to Normalcy – actually the Rejection of the German Model – made an impression on Franklin D. Roosevelt, the losing Democratic vice-presidential candidate in 1920. FDR was less intellectual than Wilson had been, but he was probably the most politically astute politician America has ever produced. He had the intuition that the Progressive agenda could never be sold to the American public on its own terms. The key phrase of American Declaration of Independence. "life, liberty and the pursuit of happiness," had been inspired by the writings of English philosopher John Locke. Roosevelt saw correctly that the Americans would only accept a Progressive political program if it was packaged as an updated form of Lockean liberalism.

## THE GREAT DEPRESSION AND THE PEAK OF AMERICA 2.0

In the Great Depression, the US economy suffered a cyclical recession, a monetary contraction, and a one-time major shift in the nature of the underlying economic base,

> throughout the Depression, behind the dramatic backdrop of continued high unemployment, technological and organizational innovations were occurring across the American economy, especially but not exclusively in chemical engineering (including petrochemicals and synthetic rubber), aeronautics, electrical machinery and equipment, electric power generation and distribution, transportation, communication, and civil/structural engineering. . . .

As a result, old jobs did not come back, and the process of recovery was exceptionally slow and painful, even though, paradoxically, the foundations for future growth were being laid. This economic transition would have been painful under the best of circumstances, but it happened under the worst of circumstances.

When Roosevelt was elected President in 1932, in the depths of the

Depression, he got his chance to advance his version of Progressivism, cast in patriotic American terms. He made sure it was presented in a format that could be justified in terms consistent with values based on American family life and our expectations. None of Roosevelt's programs were sold as automatic entitlements, that is, something that was coming to you by right because it was your share of the national patrimony, because Americans did not believe in a national patrimony. Social Security and unemployment insurance were presented as *insurance*, a contract like any insurance contract, where you paid a premium to the insurers and received a benefit under stated circumstances. The government claimed that, like any insurer, they were maintaining a trust fund to insure that when the assets were needed for the payout they would be there. It was a very Lockean program, and entirely acceptable under ANF cultural assumptions. The corollary, of course, was that everybody believes they have, in fact, earned and paid for their benefits, and will be not merely be disappointed, but enraged, if they are not paid out as promised. Economists like to refer to the payouts under Social Security and other pay-as-you-go programs as "entitlements," which they are in economic theory. But it is a poor idea for politicians to use that term. They have been construed as contractually obligated property and most Americans think of them that way.

By presenting many of the programs of the American social-democratic welfare state in the guise of a (classically) liberal contract (in what we might call "Social Lockeanism"), the progressive forces were able to construct the fully realized 2.0 state. This new American polity raised security and egalitarian redistribution higher in its scale of values. It redefined individual autonomy not as actual possession of the physical means of independence, but rather as participation in a series of organizations and structures, mostly governmental or government-protected, that guaranteed access to a specified package of rights, privileges, and benefits.

This hybrid mixture of centralized corporatist and social democratic institutions, borrowed eclectically from Mussolini, the German Social Democrats, and the British Labour Party's theorists, the Fabians. By constructing it within voluntary and contractual framework comprehensible to American culture, the New Dealers and their successors wisely left room for individual initiative and entrepreneurship. And the entire package worked well for quite a while.

FDR's Social Lockean state had seen its principal institutions created and installed by 1938, particularly the cartelized corporate structure capped by the Securities and Exchange Commission, the junior partner of the labor movement protected by the Wagner Act, and the social welfare relationship established by the Social Security Act. However, the costs of these institutions pushed the country back into a second recession, and Republican gains in the off-year elections of 1938 appeared to signal a coming Republican presidential victory in 1940. This threatened to uproot FDR's new establishment before it had time to dig itself in so deeply that it could not be uprooted by a hostile administration. What rescued the administration was the far deeper crisis that had developed in Europe.

The German state, based on authoritarian family relationships, was deeply destabilized by the consequences of the Versailles Treaty at the end of the First World War. A mildly social-democratic movement had created a liberal republic, but under the pressure of postwar inflation and the Great Depression it could not hold the trust of the nation. An authoritarian father must provide, and when he cannot provide he is subject to rebellion and replacement with a new father figure that can provide. Emmanuel Todd has characterized the German Nazi movement as "social democracy in the hysterical mode," and the events of military defeat, hyperinflation, and depression had driven the Germans into this hysterical reaction. By August 1939, the Germans had plunged Europe into war, and Americans grew nervous and afraid. The nation that had been ready to elect new leadership in 1938 turned instead to the familiar and comforting voice of FDR in 1940, and elected him to an unprecedented third term.

From August 1939 to December 1941, FDR gradually moved the US from neutrality to all-but-open intervention on the Allied side against Germany, against the wishes of a substantial portion of the electorate. However, it was Japan's unilateral attack on Pearl Harbor that brought America into the war with full-fledged popular support. Hitler's foolhardy decision to declare on the United States four days after Pearl Harbor allowed the United States to focus first on destroying the Third Reich.

Roosevelt found it easy to take the new centralized bureaucracy of the New Deal era and turn it to war making. The labor movement ensured that the workforce would be disciplined, pledging no strikes until victory (though the coal miners, led by John L. Lewis did strike during the war). The industrial cartels, first brought together under the National Recovery Administration, divided up work smoothly as peacetime industrial capacity was converted to war use. Wages and prices were controlled nationwide and rationing was imposed on food, fuel, industrial goods, and clothing. Auto plants stopped making civilian cars. The nation was placed on year-round daylight savings time ("War time") and a thirty-five mile per hour speed limit was imposed on all roads. Military conscription had begun well in advance of the declaration of war, and it was extremely thorough. Americans in large part accepted these controls for the sake of victory, with less dissent that in any war before or since.

A less-well-understood factor was the rise of a more disciplined version of the Left in the form of the Communist Party USA. From the 1880s through the early 1900s, the American Left was primarily old-fashioned socialists with an extreme fringe of anarchists, and was characterized by rebelliousness and a certain antinomianism. A great many of the activists of the Left opposed the First World War and the conscription and regimentation (including a strike ban enforced by troops and prison sentences) that came with it. After 1919, many of the more hard-core leftists joined the Communist Party USA, attracted by its call for immediate revolution and the prestige of the Soviet government. The CPUSA was much more strictly disciplined than earlier radical movements and was under the control of, and financially dependent upon, the Communist International (Comintern) in Moscow. The CPUSA had gained substantial influence and membership among labor officials, intellectuals, and high-level government bureaucrats by 1941. After the signing of the Nazi-Soviet pact in August 1939, the CPUSA switched instantly from opposing Nazi Germany to opposing any involvement in the Second World War. For example, Communist sympathizer (and later member) Dalton Trumbo wrote the moving anti-war novel *Johnny Got His Gun* in 1939, but as soon as Hitler invaded the Soviet Union in June 1941, Trumbo withdrew the book from print. Similarly, the CPUSA then supported the war effort wholeheartedly, which meant that their union leaders, intellectuals, and government employees suppressed any anti-war sentiment that threatened to emerge, and supported the prosecution and imprisonment of the leftist groups that did attempt to oppose the war.

The prestige of its victory in World War II made the new American state, and a people organized according to Progressive principles, look like the wave of the future. But just as the 2.0 vision of America seemed to be on the road to its final triumph, a surprising thing happened.

America began to execute a U-turn.

# Chapter 7
# The Great U-Turn

## THE GREAT U-TURN AND THE TRANSITION TO AMERICA 3.0

The end of World War Two was the moment of maximal centralism and minimal individual autonomy in America. Mid-twentieth-century Americans had undergone a series of experiences and influences, particularly the Depression, the unionization of industry, the increasing bureaucratization of business, the decline of independent farming and small business, and the experience of military service and/or war-related work during World War I, World War II, and Korea, all of which raised the values of patience, obedience, sharing, and co-operation, and stigmatized standouts and rebels. Those reluctant to join a union or honor a picket line were denounced as "scabs" and "finks."

On top of the regulatory structures of the Progressive era and New Deal, the war had entrenched a massive structure of controls over everyday life. Industry was run in reality by a tripartite structure of management, union bosses, and government administrators, setting prices, wages, and production amounts and types. Everyday commodities were rationed, conscription was near-universal for young people, and a large percentage of industrial jobs required union membership. The Communist Party was influential, and launched a campaign to solve the wartime housing shortage through massive construction of government-owned workers' apartments.

However, the older sentiments of individualism were far from dead. Americans had accepted a great deal of regimentation for the sake of victory in wartime, but they made it clear that with the coming of peace, they wanted something different. The Democratic Party had controlled both houses of Congress from 1932 through 1946, voting reliably for the centralizing policies of Franklin D. Roosevelt. The first postwar election of 1946 returned the Republicans to power in both houses. The new House, under Speaker Joe Martin and Senate leader Robert Taft proceeded to undo most of the wartime controls and return the country to a more market-oriented economy, while keeping popular New Deal measures such as Social Security. Most importantly, the 80th Congress passed the Taft-Hartley Act in 1947 over Truman's veto. This outlawed a number of abusive union practices, and most importantly, the Act permitted states to pass laws forbidding the practice of requiring employees to join unions. Instead of launching massive government housing programs, the new Congress expanded the veterans' home loan program, which enabled millions to own their own homes, and the veterans' college voucher system, which enabled a new class of young veterans from blue-collar backgrounds, many second-generation immigrants, to obtain a college education and professional credentials.

Dwight Eisenhower was elected president in 1952. Ike has been misunderstood by commentators and historians for decades, partly because so many of his significant actions were done under the cloak of security classification. Eisenhower saw his primary job as consolidating the social gains of the 80th Congress; meeting the military, infrastructure, and economic challenges of the Cold War; and restabilizing the country after decades of wrenching and traumatic experiences. Eisenhower also launched a series of initiatives that turned America from, in effect, a metropolitan core in the Northeast that dominated politics, finance, and manufacturing, with the Western and Southern states as semi-colonial farming and mining regions, to a genuinely continent-wide national economy. Most significant was the Interstate Defense Highway System, to give it its original name. However, other advances, particularly the completion of transcontinental coaxial-cable networks to permit simultaneous distribution of television programs, direct-dial telephone networks, and expanded air transportation, soon to transition to higher-speed jet aircraft, permitted activities to take place on a genuinely national scale.

The final critical development in the Eisenhower era was cheap air conditioning for home and commercial buildings. Taken with the Taft-Hartley Act and the creation of rapid, cheap national-scale transportation and communications, air conditioning effectively opened up great reaches of the South, Southwest, and West as practical places to live and work with full access to the national economy. As this became possible, many Western and Southern states, where unions had always been weaker, began to pass right-to-work laws as permitted by section 14b of Taft-Hartley. This created a virtuous circle whereby smaller and newer companies located or relocated in right-to-work states, which then reinforced the pressure for deregulatory and low-tax politics in those states, thus making them more attractive to yet more companies and employees.

The effect of this pattern was to set up a national movement from the Northeast to the Sunbelt (which included the entire West and the Pacific Northwest) that had profound long-term electoral implications. Every ten years, the census redistributes House seats and Electoral College votes. Each census affects the presidential elections beginning two years later. The migration from the northeastern states to the Sunbelt began to affect this distribution as early as the 1960 census, and, arguably, even the 1950 census given the substantial movement of population to California during and after World War II. Voters who chose to move to right-to-work states were generally more conservative than those who remained; thus, the shift in electoral votes and House seats to Sunbelt states began to give Republican candidates an extra edge over Democrats, and within the Republican Party, to give conservative candidates an edge over centrist and liberal ones. Barry Goldwater's election as a Republican senator in historically Democratic-leaning Arizona was a result of this shift, as was his subsequent nomination for President in 1964. Neither would have been likely to happen with the population distributions of 1940. Similarly, northern transplants to the Deep South were one factor in the transition of the South as a predominantly Democratic region to a predominantly Republican one. White southerners had remained Democrats so long as the implicit bargain continued, by which Democratic presidents would not take significant federal action against the southern system of racial segregation. Once segregation was a dead horse, the southern white population gradually switched to the Republicans as more congenial to their cultural traditions of religiosity, military service, and social conservatism.

The population shift to the Sunbelt also accelerated the trend toward sorting of populations, in which like social, political, and religious groups tended to predominate more in particular regions. This had always been a feature of American life, of course, but the centralizing trends of the early twentieth century had started to mitigate it, as mass media began to create a national consensus of opinion and leading elements of all population elements tended to move toward a small number of dominant urban areas, most particularly New York and Los Angeles. "Middlebrow" magazines and authors had a broad appeal across the nation, while as late as the 1950s New York City could treat the revival meetings of Billy Graham as a valid event, without the crushing condescension that would now meet any prominent revivalist.

The social transitions of the 1960s marked the breakdown of the long trend toward centralization and the relative privileging of security over individual autonomy. This was very much the result of the coming of age of the Baby Boom generation, who, unlike their parents, were not scarred by depression and total war. Raised on a sense of nervous optimism – nervous because of the awareness of the potential for a general nuclear war, but optimistic because of the general prosperity of the 1950s and the excitement of the new technologies of space exploration, computing, and medical breakthroughs – the Boomers came of age with high expectations, yet were also inexplicably disenchanted with the life that their parents generation had prepared for them.

The GI generation had been delighted to go to college at all, and the fact that they were usually going to a Southwest State University that had just been jumped up from a Southwest State Teacher's College didn't bother them. The makeshift dorms and classrooms hurriedly constructed to accommodate them were after all better than the makeshift barracks and wartime housing they had just spent five years in. It was the Boomers who noticed that many of these expanded schools had to make do with mediocre professors who had jumped at the chance to gain tenure. The GI generation had been happy to land technical and administrative positions with the big corporations. The corporate discipline was less harsh than military discipline, and the frequent moves on company orders were still less frequent and more comfortably conducted than wartime military changes of post. It was much less attractive to Boomers, who had their own ideas of what and how to do things and chafed at the reality that the still-young GIs would occupy almost every responsible position in industry, government, and academia for decades to come. So, a wide variety of alternative courses of action were attractive to Boomers, a small fraction of which were exotic and attracted media hype, but many more of which were less colorfully a way of striking out beyond the trodden path of institutions.

A series of gross policy errors by the GI Generation once they had taken the real levers of power – Vietnam, urban policy, race relations, the economy – also led to a general erosion of the once-strong faith the previous several generations had had in the emerging technocratic elite – the so-called "best and the brightest." Much of the praise of the "Greatest Generation" has to do with their achievements in the Second World War, as soldiers and junior officers. Yet the direction and conduct of the war (and the early Cold War as well) was entirely in the hands of men who had matured in the late Victorian era or the very early twentieth century. Winston Churchill had served Victoria as a cavalryman fighting fanatical jihadists in the Sudan and the Pashtun country of what is now Pakistan. Eisenhower had grown up in a Kansas where the adults had all lived through Indian wars. Though they have been lauded as the "Greatest Generation" once in power the GI Generation presidents, Kennedy, Johnson, Nixon, and Bush Senior, screwed up almost every major initiative they undertook, with the partial exception of some of Nixon's foreign policy. Most particularly, the Vietnam War soured the Boomer generation's belief in the trustworthiness of American political leadership, whether they had avoided service or participated in it. The veterans were probably more cynical than the protesters.

Today the Boomers are known primarily by media stereotypes created by people, mostly in Hollywood and television, who were generally of prior generations and who actually had little contact with representative Boomers. Their mistakes in drug use and the breakdown of strong families have been multiplied by subsequent generations. Most of the theorists of the drug and sexual revolutions – Timothy Leary, Hugh Hefner – were of older, prior generations and drew on bohemian and progressive themes that went back to the late 1890s.) Yet the positive aspects of Boomer individualism and nonconformism have contributed strongly to the final leg of the great U-turn – the turn away from large units, dependence on the state, and maximizing of security, and a turn to entrepreneurism, small local units, and maximizing of individual autonomy. The organizational and motivational skills learned from organizing an SDS chapter or TM meditation group, or even a garage rock band, were frequently applied in the subsequent decades to organizing entrepreneurial companies or electoral political campaigns.

It is also the case that Boomers divided along the way into two streams. The majority merged with the mainstream of American life, with some idiosyncratic additions in some case. The hippie backpacking was for many educational and not all that different from their grandfather's generational wanderings on boxcars. They begat a wide variety of entrepreneurial businesses and organizations that are now part of the American mosaic, and in many cases their experiences have anchored them firmly on the political right, and at a minimum made them suspicious of governmental power.

A small minority, mostly having roots in the "Red Diaper Baby" wing of the New Left, grew more dedicated to socialist ideology, and developed a contempt for the bulk of the New Left precisely because of their individualism and libertarianism. Abandoning mass-movement politics, they adopted a long-term strategy of burrowing into government, media, and above all academic institutions. There they formed the core of the rising new governing class.

Lyndon Johnson's Great Society program constituted the last successful major expansion of the American state. Medicare, the War on Poverty, the creation of a vast civil rights bureaucracy, and other expansions of state power were reasonably popular at the time they were passed, and Medicare at least has become an expected entitlement of the middle class. However, Medicare, although popular, has turned out to be far less sustainable than originally expected, both because of medical costs rising far faster than projected, and demographic patterns producing far fewer young workers to support retirees than originally expected. Almost all other initiatives turned out to be costly disasters that were at best useless and at worst, such as urban renewal, actively harmful. At the same time liberal social and policing policies resulted in a major upswing of violent street crime and disorder, such as aggressive begging in public places, that rendered major urban centers all but unlivable and unvisitable for middle-class people, and the schools unacceptable for their children, rapidly accelerating the existing trend toward suburbanization and exurbanization.

In the 1960s and 1970s, the long-term effects of stagnant union work rules and complacent oligarchic corporate bureaucracies led to the collapse of major sectors of American manufacturing, first in coal and railroads, then in steel, and finally in automobiles. The urban blue-collar working class, once comfortably housed and fed, secure in well-paid unionized jobs in established, protected industries, and located in gritty but lively industrial towns where several generations of family had put down roots, found themselves in a surprisingly short time out of work with few prospects, out of pensions because of bankruptcy of employers, and forced to sell their houses at a substantial loss because of rising crime rates and misconceived social policies, like forced busing for racial quota purposes, that made neighborhoods and schools unusable.

Neither Lyndon Johnson, nor Richard Nixon, nor Gerald Ford, nor Jimmy Carter had done anything of any use for such people, and they did many things to harm them. Nixon got the votes of some, and some of his symbolic actions were appreciated, but nothing he did made the economy more competitive or saved their jobs, and he made no substantial changes to the social policies they objected to. By the time Jimmy Carter gained election over a wounded Republican party, he mistook his narrow victory for a mandate to continue moving along the track toward a European-style social democracy, basically following the trajectory of Britain and Canada, even to the extent of adopting the metric system. Carter envisioned moving toward fully government-provided medicine, a government-dominated energy sector enforcing strict energy rationing, and a federally dominated school system promoting governing-class values.

It was the defeat and frustration of the Carter administration's plans that made the U-turn, long in process, visible to perceptive observers. Carter and his political supporters still viewed their program as one that, properly promoted by a sympathetic media, would be genuinely supported by the majority of the population, and set in place a new generation of Democratic dominance. Resistance was attributed to white working-class racism, and the substantive objections of the American middle class were dismissed as trivial, uninformed, or selfish. Thus, Ronald Reagan's solid electoral victory in 1980, based on an unequivocal rejection of Carter's program and its fundamental assumption, came as a profound shock. By contemporary standards, Reagan's domestic program was quite moderate and constrained, not really disassembling any major parts of the federal machine, and merely slowing the rate of increase of federal non-defense spending (which was characterized as a "savage cut"). Indeed, Reagan devoted the bulk of his attention to foreign affairs and implementing his principal insight – that the Soviet Union was hollowed out from within and supported primarily by Western financing. Reagan understood that one period of sustained pressure would be sufficient to cause the Soviet empire to collapse without a shot being fired, and proceeded to provide that pressure, with, indeed, that very result.

Further, the 1970s saw the beginning of a set of explicitly decentralizing developments. The Nixon administration began taking some small, low-key steps to deregulate parts of the economy, setting in train, for example the demonopolization of COMSAT, the quasi-utility communication satellite corporation. During the Carter administration, substantial initiatives such as the deregulation of the air transport and freight rail industries were set in motion by Congress. During the Reagan administration, this process was taken further, although not as far or aggressively as Margaret Thatcher privatized Britain; for example, she privatized the air traffic control system quite successfully, while Reagan balked at such proposals during the US air traffic controllers' strike. Another major blow occurred when the AT&T telephone monopoly was struck down by the courts; at one time, even a privately supplied cover to the AT&T-owned phone book in subscribers' houses was described as a "foreign (i.e., non-AT&T-supplied) attachment." The resulting drastic reductions in the price of rail freight, air, and phone service made it substantially easier to do business nationwide and indeed worldwide independent of location; an often-overlooked factor in the entrepreneurial takeoff and continuing decentralization of the Reagan years.

The Reagan administration, and particularly his massive re-election victory in 1984, convinced many in the new governing class that their program was genuinely unpopular among the American middle class, and that merely improving campaigning finesse would be insufficient to restore the dominant Roosevelt coalition. One branch began to pursue the tactic of accepting to some degree the middle class's desire for less expensive, less intrusive government, and concentrate instead on promoting a smaller, more carefully targeted set of government interventions, while pursuing a more efficient use of the resources the electorate was willing to finance. These elements formed the Democratic Leadership Council (DLC) and began promoting the smarter, more effective governors already pursing this strategy: Michael Dukakis in Massachusetts, Bill Clinton in Arkansas, and allies in the Senate such as Al Gore. The other faction remained obdurately devoted to a massively interventionist, leveling government, combined with an active partisanship for anti-American populists and nationalists throughout the world, but especially in Latin America and the Middle East. These could not hope for electoral victory, but rather followed a strategy of burrowing into government, media, and academia, and pursuing their agendas by stealth.

The first try of the DLC in 1988 pitted Dukakis against the bland and conflicted George Bush, Sr., who nevertheless won through a combination of Reagan's aura and Dukakis's unsuitability for campaigning outside of Massachusetts. Bush failed to follow up effectively on Reagan's agenda or themes, and fell victim to a politically more astute DLC type in 1992, the supremely competent politician, Bill Clinton.

Unfortunately for Clinton, he did not at first fully stick to the DLC strategy. He fell victim to the strange assumption that persists among many Democrat politicians that Americans genuinely want government-run health care. Clinton permitted his wife to craft a complex plan to that effect, which met defeat in a more cautious Congress. This and other examples of over-reaching convinced the American middle class that the new Democrat agenda of the DLC was not all that new, and was still inimical to what many believed to be the "American way of life." The new, aggressive leader of the Republican opposition in the House, Newt Gingrich, astutely crafted a platform document, the Contract With America, that successfully called upon classic themes such as individualism, patriotism, and optimism, and in the 1994 elections captured control of House and Senate for the first time since the days of Joe Martin and Robert Taft.

Bill Clinton, cleverly adapting to the latest electoral turn, defeated Gingrich tactically, which ensured that no major rollback of the federal government would ensue. He then worked with Congress to come up with a set of results that could demonstrate that New Democrats like himself could reform government, while giving the GOP congressional majorities enough of what they were seeking to gain their votes. Welfare was formally declared to not be an entitlement, and states were given a finite time period to move most permanent welfare clients off the welfare rolls. This was successfully accomplished without the predicted humanitarian disasters. However, in general, the Clinton years passed with little change to the massive entrenched oligopolistic interests that were entangled with both parties.

At the end of the Clinton years, a combination of his personal failings, a declining market due to a collapse of a stock bubble, and the general political incompetence of the pompous and wooden Democrat candidate, Al Gore, led to the victory of George Bush, Jr. Bush was a well-intentioned political figure who had operated successfully in Texas state politics, serving two terms as governor. But his search for a "compassionate conservatism" that could be somehow distinguished from Reagan's conservatism was confused from the start and failed to generate an effective or coherent plan of action. Bush 43's presidency was marked from almost the beginning by the Islamist jihadist attack on the World Trade Center and the search for an effective response to it. Americans believe strongly in a proactive response to enemies and were generally supportive of his initial actions to seek out Al-Qaeda in Afghanistan, and, with more reservations, to support the removal of Saddam Hussein, a genuinely evil tyrant. However, the subsequent attempts at nation-building in Iraq and Afghanistan, and a strategy that appeared to consist of nothing but absorbing casualties with no end in sight, violated Americans' requirement that wars involving a mobilization of militia and volunteers on a large scale be purposeful and that failing war leaders be promptly removed. Bush's dismissal of Rumsfeld and a new surge strategy was too little, too late to preserve his support. Meanwhile, the Republican Congresses, after a decade, lost any connection to the reforming Congress of 1994 and had slumped into oligarchic favor-trading.

With the collapse of the credit and housing bubble in 2008, the massive bailouts performed in the final days of the Bush administration appeared to remove any difference between Republicans and Democrats. The electorate pursued the traditional American strategy of punishing the failing party and giving the other side a chance. Unfortunately, the electorate didn't get just another New Democrat in the Bill Clinton mold, but a member of the other wing – a president committed to strengthening the centralizing, directive state and to creating a new permanent governing coalition.

Whatever travails may beset us in the years ahead, we believe that an attempt to "double down" on the Progressive vision will ultimately fail, if only because it cannot possibly be paid for. This failure may provoke the crisis that will complete the Great U-Turn. However contemporary events play out, we anticipate a new, third era in the history of the Republic, re-synthesized on the original vision and principles of the Founders.

It is important to realize that, at every turn, Americans were motivated primarily by the desire to do what was best for themselves, their families, their communities, and their nation, as they saw it in the circumstances of the time. For the most part, they were not pushed off their farms; they were pulled by the lure of a higher standard of living and more certain pay. They did not join unions out of class appeals or a desire for socialism; they joined to alleviate the arbitrary management practices of the early Industrial Revolution and to improve their pay and conditions. They saw centralized bureaucratic organizations improve their lives significantly. The Post Office implemented Rural Free Delivery and created the revolution of mail order catalogs, the Internet business of its day. This greatly improved their choices of goods and lowered their costs. Eventually Henry Ford's mass-produced Model T, FDR's Rural Electrification Administration, and Theodore Vail's AT&T phone monopoly with its goal of uniform and universal service made rural life almost as convenient as city life – ironically laying the groundwork for the exurban revolution of the late twentieth and early twenty-first centuries. Finally Eisenhower's Interstate Highway System, and his NASA and DARPA agencies, led to the highway networks, communication and broadcasting satellites, and Internet that made it almost as easy to do cutting-edge, innovative work in dispersed exurban locations.

America 1.0 laid the groundwork for the country's rapid industrialization through universal education and the establishment of a firm rule of law that permitted capital markets to arise. Eventually, unintended consequences of that industrialization created problems that led Americans to create the centralized and bureaucratic institutions of America 2.0. They solved existing problems, or appeared to, but they too had unintended consequences that have given rise to the problems we face at the time this book is being published. Now it is time to discard or transform the broken institutions of America 2.0 and turn to for inspiration to the decentralized and individualistic America of the Founders, but in a new and updated implementation – an America 3.0.

What follows is a discussion of the ways and means of achieving this end.

# Chapter 8
# Domestic Policy

## THE DOMESTIC POLICY OF AN INDIVIDUALISTIC SOCIETY

We have described the fundamentally individualistic, nuclear-family culture of America, throughout its history, and before. We have also shown that America 2.0 is crumbling, and that we are in the midst of slow but wrenching transition to an emerging America 3.0. The first transition, from agrarian to industrial America was painful and protracted. This will certainly be true of the even bigger transition, from industrial to an individualized-and-networked economy that we are undergoing now.

For example, the entire concept of a "job" is going away. At the time of the Founding, most Americans did not have jobs. There is no reason to think most Americans in the future will have jobs, primarily working at the direction of others employing capital owned by others. Americans are not yet remotely prepared for this shift, either institutionally, or psychologically.

Our proposals for domestic policy are meant to reduce the difficulty of the transition, start the winding down process for our legacy institutions, or modify them as needed, and begin building the framework for the new America that is emerging.

Domestic and fiscal policies will have to deal with the towering legacy costs built up by the 2.0 institutions, whose founding assumptions are no longer are valid, and resolve the contentious political and social issues that have divided America so strikingly over the past half-century.

These policy dilemmas require neither a return to America 1.0 solutions, which is impossible, nor a doubling down on 2.0 solutions and mechanisms, which is futile and destructive. Rather, the 3.0 domestic policy structure will be a new synthesis incorporating some elements of both previous versions of America, including our Constitution, and some new elements.

Despite the major changes underway, driven mainly by technology, and the new structures that we will inevitably have, the American way of life will still be recognizably our own, part of the "changing same" that has continued for centuries. If we imagine Thomas Jefferson, Benjamin Franklin, or Alexander Hamilton magically restored to life a generation from now, they would recognize the country as the same at bottom, though certainly many details would be shocking. Further, our antici-pated world-to-come may have more congruence with the world of family farms and small businesses that these Founders knew than it will to mid-twentieth century America.

We will address five main areas of domestic policy where significant changes should be made to wind up the legacy state, and move us toward the future we foresee: (1) fiscal and regulatory policy, (2) law and justice, (3) employment, work and enterprise, (4) social services, and (5) consti-tutional and social issues and decentralization.

**Fiscal and Regulatory Policy.** The decline of America 2.0's institutions is being felt in many ways, but the fiscal pressure will probably be what brings them to an end. Franklin D. Roosevelt built the federal social safety net on the assumption that American families would continue to have on the order of three to four children, on average. They now have only two, and in recent years, fewer. Even with substantial immigration the United States is unlikely to regain the rates of population growth needed to sus-tain its pay-as-you-go intergenerational transfer programs.

At the same time, all levels of government have run up large debt obli-gations to pensioners, including retiring government workers, and bond-holders far beyond the Government's ability to pay them. At the time of this writing, America's government obligations, funded and unfunded, at all levels, are estimated to be various unfathomable numbers in the hun-dreds of trillions of dollars. Quibbling about which boulder is the correct one, when any of them will crush you, is an exercise for some other publi-cation. The point here is that all levels of American government have made promises that they cannot possibly keep, even if they confiscated all the existing wealth in the country. So, these governments are going to default on these obligations. That is inevitable. We propose that it be done transparently and openly, and preferably at once.

Any attempt to raise tax rates to the level needed to finance existing government obligations will be self-defeating. Taxes at such rates will suppress taxable economic activity, and will lead to less revenue. Very high tax rates will not generate large revenue streams. Further, very large rate increases will lead to a frenzy of political action to create further carve-outs, exceptions, and loopholes, making the system even more inefficient and less fair, and yet further reducing recovered revenue. An attempt to pay off the existing obligations of government by confiscatory levels of taxation cannot work, politically or practically.

Nor will hairshirt solutions that try to solve the fiscal problems on the back of the middle class be sufficient to fund the existing obligations. Austerity and fiscal retrenchment of programs millions of people rely on for their survival, without adopting pro-growth regulatory and tax reforms, will just make things worse, and will be politically unsustainable. The American people will not tolerate high taxes, low growth, and cuts in the government payments *all at the same time.*

Our government's promises are too big in total to ever be actually paid in full. This problem is structural and long-term. It requires a structural fix, including a one-time procedure to de-leverage the debt burden across all levels of government. We have dubbed this process "The Big Haircut."

**The Big Haircut – The Theory and Practice of National Bankruptcy.**
A central part of the strategy to transition to America 3.0 is a general reduction of America's public debt positions, which we suggest will be done through a mixture of reduction of entitlements, renegotiation of debts, and, where such renegotiation fails, unilateral rescheduling. In finance, a reduction of debt or other obligation (such as shareholdings) is called a "haircut"; we use the term Big Haircut to describe a resolution of America's debt position that is comprehensive – that reduces all categories of debt – and in which the losses borne by creditors is shared in equal proportion as widely as possible. Although the federal government cannot be placed into a formal state of bankruptcy, due to the lack of any higher power to authorize or supervise the process, the Big Haircut would be the effective equivalent of bankruptcy, reducing the debt of the US

government, the state, and local governments, and many corporations and individuals.

The Big Haircut is needed for several reasons. First, the debt levels of both federal and lower levels of government have grown to the level that merely servicing it going forward will take up an increasingly larger share of national income. If it is reduced merely by reducing outlays, many Americans would find themselves deprived of income they had been promised, and had been counting on their entire lives, with no means, at their advanced ages, or replacing the income. Ignoring whatever moral issues are raised by the breach of promise from government to citizen, it is a fact that placing such a level of hardship on such a substantial percentage of the population is politically impossible. If the debt were to be addressed by maintaining entitlements and raising taxes, the dead hand of taxation would depress business, ultimately drying up precisely the source of revenues on which the government depends. Although advocates of increased taxation point to European nations as models of higher taxation, it is also a fact that European taxation levels have been a powerful deterrent to new business starts and private sector job growth, hitting the young particularly hard. Such results would also be politically unpalatable.

One non-option would be to continue to borrow the money by selling federal bonds to finance the shortfall between revenue and expenditure. This will end sooner or later, and probably sooner, because international borrowers will eventually refuse to buy US bonds that carry an increasing risk of never getting repaid, or even getting serviced, at tolerable interest rates. Southern European states have already reached this point. At that point the government would likely turn to using the US Treasury to buy Federal Reserve Notes almost exclusively, as they already have been doing more and more. This is effectively printing money, which is to say expropriating money from America's creditors by inflation. It also has a stopping point, but one that may be pushed out well into the future because other countries' bonds are an even worse value than ours.

Another tactic we can expect is expropriation of America's domestic creditors by internal inflation. This could be done in a stealthy fashion by manipulating the definitions of inflation, and the measurements used in determining indexing of benefits for inflation, so that Social Security and Medicare payouts rise less than actual inflation, gradually cutting the value of benefits. Employed persons, businesses, and government entities can keep pace with inflation by negotiating for higher wages, raising prices, and raising taxes, although this process can be slow to respond. Entitlement recipients would find it difficult to organize and strike back against this relatively subtle form of income redistribution at their expense. Therefore, it is likely to be used.

There has also been discussion of expropriating 401(k) accounts and giving their owners some form of government-run "accounts," which would also permit the government to inflate any of its value away. This has already been done in Argentina during the financial crisis episode of the early 2000s, with unhappy results.

The likelihood of such tactics demonstrates why the basic principles of bankruptcy laws should be applied to resolving America's looming financial crisis. Specifically, if reform is undertaken piecemeal, it will almost certainly be the weakest and least powerful that will suffer expropriation. If any obligations are to be reneged on, all should have to suffer proportionally.

Perhaps the most sinister form of expropriation is the idea of rationing medical care through rationing of medical procedures in Medicare. There is an increasing drumbeat of battlespace preparation for the assault on the old in the form of lamentations that old people are being kept alive too long and consuming too many expensive procedures in the process.

The self-aggrandizing heiress Leona Helmsley, on being accused of tax evasion, famously remarked "paying taxes is for the little people," a category from which she considered herself to be excluded. This attitude has been demonstrated over and over again by members of America's current crony elite. Much of the lamentation over medical entitlements by the commentariat reduces, on examination, to an attitude that could be summarized as "dying sooner is for the little people." It is clear that both left-leaning commentators who clamor for (government-determined) health care for all, and right-leaning commentators who focus primarily, or entirely, on Medicare costs for solving the fiscal crisis, look forward to correcting this "problem" of old people living "too long."

Too often discussion of bankruptcy and moral hazard gets waylaid because there is too much discussion about what is fair, right, and just. But bankruptcy law does not address these abstractions. The essence of the bankruptcy procedure is that somebody has made agreements with multiple parties and is no longer able to fulfill all the agreements, and that he will escape without punishment for breaking the agreements so long as they weren't judged fraudulent from the start. Furthermore, the debtor escapes not only state punishment, but private punishment or redress as well; if any creditor harms the debtor, or takes some of the debtor's property in an attempt to gain redress, the creditor, not the debtor, is punished by the state and made to disgorge the property he took in fulfillment of an entirely valid debt.

Bankruptcy law is based entirely on predicting people's behavior. It prevents a rush to the exit by any individual creditor, avoiding a prisoner's dilemma situation, and permits the debtor to remain in business while negotiating the best possible settlement. It gives the creditor a strong incentive to realistically discount the debt, taking the bird of the voluntary settlement in hand rather than hoping for the two in the bush at the end of a bankruptcy proceeding. Thus it encourages realistic pricing of assets and keeps individual and corporate actors in the economic game (maximizing general social prosperity) rather than knocking them out for an extended period. If bankruptcy cannot be avoided, it gives each creditor something rather than nothing, and minimizing losses is an important component of business. It particularly protects the smaller creditors, because without bankruptcy the bigger ones would have moved first and grabbed all of the available assets, leaving the weaker claimants with nothing.

The reason this is relevant is that the Big Haircut operates on the same results-based principles as bankruptcy. Some, maybe many people, will get off the hook under the Big Haircut who, morally, don't deserve it, and some people will get treated unfairly who won't deserve it. The debate now warming up over who should take the brunt of the needed cuts is moralistic in tone. This is problematic, and very collectivist as it deals in broad classes of "guilty" people. The Big Haircut is about getting the country functional again, spreading the pain widely, and ending up with a new system that is less prone to the problems of the old.

The Big Haircut is needed because, although we object to the idea that the debt situation be resolved entirely at the cost of the middle class and the old, it is inevitable that part of the solution will involve sacrifices on the part of these classes of people. The problem is too big to be solved without it, and, additionally, no level of debt forgiveness through renegotiation will be adequate to merely keep the same system going forward. Social security will certainly require raising the eligibility age, a step that is happening slowly already but probably needs to be greatly accelerated. Medicare is more complex, because its reform requires not only changes in eligibility, but also changes in the way medical care is structured and delivered, as we will discuss further along.

Given these coming sacrifices, those who will bear the burden of them are right to insist that sacrifice be shared more widely. What is not generally realized is how much of the wealth of the US is currently wasted or misdirected. Those who paid into the Social Security and Medicare systems all their lives in expectation of promised benefits are entirely justified in demanding that no changes be made to these systems until other forms of waste and misdirection are placed on the cutting block. This includes (1) the direct waste of subsidies, such as those in agriculture, particularly ethanol subsidies, (2) indirect waste, such as the Davis-Bacon Act, which drives the actual cost of useful federal programs like highways far above the actual prevailing wage, and (3) government procurement procedures; and complete waste, such as expensive, anticompetitive, and useless regulations that drag the nation's economy down by an estimated $1.7 *trillion* per year.

Voters who are asked to accept delays or reductions in benefits should view their assent to such sacrifices as a bargaining chip to drive serious action to eliminate or greatly reduce such waste. Additionally, other large government commitments, such as pay and retirement benefits for federal, state, and local government employees should come under review as well. Both pay and benefits have risen well above their private sector equivalents in many if not most cases.

A large number of private pension beneficiaries have in the past several decades experienced bankruptcy of their former employers and default on pension obligations that had formed part of the compensation agreed to them in return for their lifetime service. In many cases, they had come to view this as an entitlement and were shocked to find that it was not forthcoming. Yet anybody dealing with a corporate entity is in effect an investor, and every investment, even one of labor alone, carries a risk. Every investor ultimately must rely on their own judgment of what the risk may be, and is responsible for their own actions to mitigate that risk as much as possible. Many employees did not take this responsibility, either in their own actions as employees or in their actions as union voters. Most unions in the United States took the attitude that their corporate employers were adversaries that would last forever and have effectively unlimited amounts of money at their disposal. These were wrong assumptions, and their members have frequently paid the price for those wrong assumptions. Japanese unions were frequently derided as "company unions" for their attitude that the health and competitiveness of their employers was in their direct interest as well, and the fruit of that attitude has been a much higher survival rate among large corporations, which has historically led to pension obligations being honored.

There is no reason to treat nonmilitary pensions differently. (We will make an exception for military pensions, particularly wartime ones, because they were paid for in blood, and thus are not subject to a purely economic calculus. Breaking promises to citizen-soldiers is a threat to national security.) This is particularly the case where state and local jurisdictions permitted collective bargaining, and where public-employee unions used their political clout to amass unreasonable and far above-market pension obligations. The Big Haircut must include a bankruptcy-like process that will revalue legacy pension obligations to a supportable level that neither crushes the taxpayers nor deprives them of a reasonable level of municipal services. Public employees who pressured jurisdictions to give unsustainable levels of pension obligations made the same investment decisions as did private employees – failing to take into account the long-term health of their employer in their demands, decisions, and behavior. They chose poorly, and the primary burden of the bad choices should in fairness fall upon them.

Even in the matter of federal pensions, which were not subject to collective bargaining, a similar logic is in play. Federal employees also mobilized lobbying power to raid the public treasury without regard to the sustainability of their obligations, and in doing so made a poor investment choice. In times where private employees paid their taxes and Social Security "contributions," and now must face reductions in the promised benefits, federal retirees should in fairness take pro rata reductions in their pensions – if Social Security benefits are taken at 70 or 73 rather than 65, that (assuming the standard life expectancy remains at 83) implies a reduction of around 25% in average lifetime benefit received. Reducing federal pensions by a similar amount would be a fair reduction, although there is some logic and fairness in making the cuts progressive; a retired letter carrier would be cut less, or not at all, whereas the senior administrator might take a heftier cut.

Finally, even the bond obligations of the federal government should not be immune from scrutiny. Default is a bad precedent to set and there are good reasons to avoid it if at all possible, if for no other reason than it would make future borrowing more costly. However, it is not impossible. The logic of the Big Haircut is that it is a package of reforms that must be presented as an all-or-nothing, "up-or-down" vote. Passage of the Big Haircut would trigger defaults on a variety of obligations. But the logic would be to leave the United States in a steady, sustainable condition, where the ratio of debt to GDP is modest, and above all does not rise. This would give international financial markets something they want and do not have: a borrower that is large enough to safely absorb very large amounts of money.

Currently, no such entity exists. The European Union was designed largely to offer an alternative world-class financial center, while its currency the euro was designed to be an alternative safe haven for parking capital. Yet the inherent flaws in the European model are tearing the European Monetary Union apart, and investors are currently nervously eyeing alternatives. Japan is stagnant; China has serious transparency and trust problems, and is probably on the verge of a bursting bubble, although because no information from them is trustworthy, it is hard to tell for sure. Canada and Australia are sound, but their economies are too small, individually or collectively, to absorb the amounts of funds needing placement. The USA is absorbing capital not because we are trusted to do the right thing, but because we are "the least dirty shirt," a bit less untrustworthy than anybody else.

Although nobody would be overjoyed about having their US Treasuries involuntarily rescheduled, if the accompanying package of reforms were seriously implemented and well designed, it would probably result in an increase in the attractiveness of the United States as a destination. Additionally, most intelligent observers know that the most likely alternative to the Big Haircut is not faithful repayment of the US's obligations in sound dollars, but repudiation by stealth in the form of severe inflation. A well-designed rescheduling would result in a predictable adjustment in expectations, and some guarantee that the Big Haircut would be a one-time, predictable event, and damages would be known quickly. A stealth repudiation by inflation has the problem that nobody would know how far it would go or where it would end, and if past precedents are relevant, it would have the threat of becoming a runaway inflation beyond the ability of those who started it to stop it, other than by wiping the slate clean. The Big Haircut is far preferable to that.

The Big Haircut would also include, via renegotiation or bankruptcy-equivalent processes, all unfunded or underfunded obligations of state and local governments to a realistic and sustainable level, based on existing levels of permanent taxation. In return for this renegotiation, the federal government will lend reasonable levels of funds to refinance states out of bankruptcy. These loans will be guaranteed by natural resource deposits under state control, whether currently being developed or not. If states fall behind on repayment, the pledged assets will fall under federal control as federal reservations exempt from state regulation, and be leased for development.

Given the temptation of government to abuse every exception and turn every convenient emergency measure into permanent institutions, we stress that for the Big Haircut to work, it must be structured so that it is impossible to do it again. Otherwise the temptation to go out and borrow to the hilt again, and hope to default a second time, will be naturally irresistible. The best way to ensure that the Big Haircut is a one-time event is to dismantle key parts of the mechanisms that allowed the government to drift into the situation in the first place. Such mechanisms include the particular "pay as you go" feature of Social Security and Medicare – the fiction that a trust fund existed in which payments were somehow sequestered for future needs, rather than being immediately lent to the Federal Reserve and receiving an IOU in return. Because it is almost impossible to achieve genuine sequestration in any institution under the direct control of the government, the only truly safe means of guarding assets for future generations is to transition retirement savings to private accounts under the control of their individual owners, particularly permitting them to be deposited abroad – beyond the ability of the government to confiscate them, as has been done recently in Argentina and Portugal.

Without the Big Haircut, it is unlikely that sufficient simultaneous reforms will be carried out before the United States becomes so stagnant that an entire generation, those coming of age between 2000 and 2020, finds their prospects so badly damaged by stunted economic opportunity that they will be unable follow a career direction adequate to their innate talents, or to start and maintain a functional family life. Most reform packages currently under discussion would merely reduce the rate of increase in spending. This is no more than whistling past the graveyard. It is not enough.

**Abolishing the Income Tax.** There is an excellent case for abolishing the federal income tax and replacing it with a national consumption tax of one variety or another. At the top end, the income tax is so riddled with loopholes and exemptions that many of the rich manage to avoid anything close to its top rates. At the bottom end, several key exemptions and deductions have the effect of shielding the bottom half of the population, in income terms, from any income tax at all, although all working income is still subject to the regressive 15 percent flat tax supposedly going to fund the Social Security and Medicare systems. The skewed incentives created by the loopholes in the income tax code misallocate resources in the economy, and the very large amount of time and expense needed to account for and comply with income tax disclosure requirements is not merely misallocated, but entirely wasted, as far as genuine economic productivity is concerned.

The required disclosure of personal economic information required in filing tax forms constitutes perhaps the largest single invasion of civil liberties in America, violating the spirit of the Fourth Amendment's guarantee against search and seizure of personal information without a judicial warrant. That it has been permitted by the Supreme Court is one of many examples where the highest court appears to have acted from expedience rather than following plain English. In a free society the government should not have the ability to know how much wealth a citizen has without sufficient probable cause to issue a search warrant. Ending income taxation will end this circumvention of the Bill of Rights, one which has been used again and again to political advantage by unscrupulous presidential administrations.

The fact that the intrusive power of the Internal Revenue Service (IRS) has not been cut back is a dangerous precedent for American liberties in other ways. The trends toward the abolition of the *mens rea* doctrine apply even more strongly to enforcement of the income tax code. *Mens rea* is Latin for "guilty mind," and it is one of the ancient Common Law requirements for a criminal conviction. The state had to show not only that the person in fact committed the crime, but that he intended to do so. Proof of intent is hard in an ordinary criminal prosecution. It would be nearly impossible in most tax cases. Two experienced tax accountants will rarely come up the exact same dollar amount owed to the IRS on anything more than the simplest return. The Tax Code is so convoluted that probably any American who files an income tax return could be prosecuted.

The income tax is perhaps the most typical of all America 2.0 institutions. As it fails it draws more resistance, but in response to this resistance it proposes to double down on the very features that cause resistance: its intrusion, its exemption from the protections of the Bill of Rights and due process, and its geometric growth of incomprehensible regulations that no two IRS offices, much less any two accountants or attorneys, can use to guide a taxpayer to the correct answer.

We propose abolishing the federal income tax in its entirety as soon as possible by repealing the Sixteenth Amendment, which authorizes it. With the Sixteenth Amendment gone, there would be no prospect of an income tax creeping back in.

The total elimination of the existing Tax Code would free up the resources wasted on compliance, make obsolete the large array of tax-avoidance mechanisms, and reduce part of the burden on the law enforcement, judicial, and prison systems. Destroying the files of the Internal Revenue Service would be the largest restoration of privacy since the destruction of the records of the East German Stasi and other Eastern European secret police services, possibly more so since the Stasi spied only on part of its population but the IRS is interested in everyone who makes any money at all.

That being said, it is not clear whether, in present circumstances, abolition of the federal income tax could be successfully pursued as a policy option. The distortions intentionally built into the tax code have also created the large and powerful lobbies for their continuation, and one that is well dispersed across the country. Further, every person and all institutions have sunk costs in mastering compliance with the Tax Code, and there would be a large cost to learning a new system. There would also be the simple and often well-founded fear that any big change is a risk with unknown consequences, and thus muddling along with tweaks is preferable to wholesale change.

The many interests, such as public-employee unions, that want and need large federal income streams would see their future on the line in any battle to abolish the existing Tax Code, and mobilize their considerable organizing strength to preserve it. Finally, the advocates of even the core functions of the federal government, ones that we would wish to see well funded even in a highly decentralized federation, would likely be concerned as to whether they could be adequately funded under alternative scenarios.

In any event, the Big Haircut reforms, as we mention below, would probably have to be well on the way to resolution before the federal government's debt will be sufficiently reduced to permit abolition of the income tax. Nonetheless abolition should be on the agenda, subject to certain conditions to be met. It is a goal to be worked toward.

Even if abolition of the income tax is a long time in coming, it will happen. As the 2.0 model of employment further erodes, the average 3.0 American will be deriving his or her income from a variety of sources, some of them global and accessed over the Internet, and paid via Internet cyber-currencies, and some will be local, perhaps mediated by on-line barter. The ordinary means that the IRS has used to track income will be less and less useful in these circumstances. W-2-type employment will continue to decline. Like other 2.0 organizations, the IRS will have to attempt to function through an increasingly intrusive surveillance capability, more strenuous enforcement tactics, tougher collection methods, and harsher penalties. The public reaction against such tactics will eventually overpower the interest groups that lobby for its preservation.

Several possible financing models remain. One is some form of the existing tax structure, where an assortment of federal taxes fund the core federal functions and continue to finance some portion of legacy programs and debt. This could include a federal sales tax (studies have suggested that supporting federal expenditures at their pre-2008 levels would require a 20 to 25 percent national sales tax, depending on precisely what approach is taken. This is basically the level of value-added tax (VAT) common in Europe; with no income tax it would not be excessively burdensome for most. Exemptions for necessary items (groceries, for example) could cushion its impact on everyday life for less affluent Americans.

Collecting a supplementary tax on greater wealth would also be an option. Provision for such a tax, with a mandatory cap on the percentage collected, could be included in the amendment repealing the Sixteenth Amendment. This supplementary tax would have to be substantially smaller than today's income tax (say, in the 15 to 20 percent range) so as to minimize the burden on wealth creation, and prevent the reintroduction of high marginal rates by inflating the currency. The costs of collection would be a smaller percentage of the total tax revenue recovered than is currently the case for middle-class and poor taxpayers. History has shown that most rich people are willing to pay a moderate percentage of their income as a price of remaining in their communities as respected members, but that they grow resistant, and lobby for exceptions and deductions, when they perceive rates to be confiscatory.

**Law and Justice.** The 2.0 model depended on uniform and universal national institutions and solutions. Many facets of human behavior that were previously of concern primarily to neighbors and clergymen now came under the view of government authorities. To ensure universality and uniformity in an individualistic country, institutions were made mandatory, and behavior was to be regulated by rules administered by panels of impartial technical experts. And, of course, to ensure people did what the experts decided, penalties were imposed for noncompliance. Congress delegated its lawmaking authority to these panels and regulations had the force of law. In many cases failure to comply was made a felony. Because there were a great many of these regulations, there were a great many federal felonies, and the number has increased steadily over time. The entire concept of federal regulatory agencies with the ability to create felonies through extra-legislative rulings is a 2.0, Progressive-era concept that has failed in practice. The original constitutional practice of requiring any federal felony to be created by an act of Congress should be restored.

States in parallel created their own regulatory regimes, and thus a great mass of state and local regulations also carried the force of law, and a great increase in the number and type of crimes occurred at the state level as well. Similar reforms are needed there as well.

The justice and penal system should be thoroughly reformed at both the state and federal levels. The federal penal code should be reviewed to eliminate duplicative offenses already covered by state laws. A review should be undertaken of the armed enforcement functions of federal agencies to determine which of them really need armed SWAT teams to inspect chickens or ensure honest weights and measures. Of course, reduction in the number of federal felonies will in itself reduce the number of federal agents needed to enforce them.

The Progressives' concern with public hygiene extended to mental health, which they dealt with by broad and vague involuntary commitment laws that permitted doctors to send persons to state mental institutions where they were kept, often for life, and either warehoused or given treatments of dubious effectiveness. The effect of these developments was to remove from everyday life a great many people whose behavior could be disturbing, annoying, or dangerous.

In the 1960s and 1970s criminal sentences were reduced, new psychiatric drugs allowed many state mental institutions to be emptied and closed, and the mental illness defense more frequently resulted in persons implicated in crimes being released into treatment that quickly returned them to the streets. Genuinely mentally ill patients often stopped taking their medication once free from supervision, which led to a highly visible increase in deranged and dangerous persons wandering public streets in city centers.

Personal crime, especially violent crime increased greatly in these decades. Americans showed their traditional propensity to safeguard their families and homes by harsh measures. Public reaction to this crime wave led to a new wave of mandatory sentencing, greatly lengthened sentences, curbing of the insanity defense, more discretion for prosecutors, and, ultimately, much larger prison populations. The escalating war on drugs, like all prohibitory laws, created lucrative unlawful markets. Hardened gangs appeared to service those markets. The response has been an increasing police power and increasing arrests and convictions, which in turn has swelled the prison population. The September 11, 2001 terror attack led to new categories of crimes and new enforcement and surveillance agencies with very broad powers. The result of these developments has been a historically and globally unprecedented population in incarceration, many of whom are imprisoned for nonviolent and victimless crimes. Traditional safeguards for suspects and the accused have decayed, yet prosecutors and the police often believe they are barely holding back an incoming tide of crime.

The much enlarged power of the government's law enforcement machinery has allowed it to pry more and more into the lives of ordinary Americans. These powers were developed primarily to wage the "War on Drugs" and the "War on Terrorism." But trial balloons are being floated for using these capabilities for persons whose only distinguishing characteristic is "distrust of government." This overt distrust and encroaching surveillance is becoming intolerable to an individualistic culture with a high regard for individual autonomy.

Rather than making Americans feel safer, this growing power to invade the privacy of American citizens has led to what strategic analyst Mark Safranski terms the "Creepy State." The Creepy State already has the capacity, and sometimes the will, to arbitrarily do any of the following:

Read your email

Track your movements on GPS

Track your online activity

Track your spending

Track your political activity

Read your medical records

Read your financial records

Scan your body

Scan your house

Scan your DNA

Keep you under video surveillance in public

Detain you at random in public places for security checks

Listen to your phone calls

Close off public spaces for private use

Seize private property for private use

Censor your speech

Block your access to judicial relief

Determine your educational and career path

Regulate your diet, place of residence, lifestyle and living standards

Charge you with secret crimes for breaking secret regulations

Share or leak information about you at will

The Creepy State is a symptom of a system in distress and, we believe, terminal distress.

America 2.0 began as a hopeful crusade carried forward by a group of bright young writers, thinkers, and government officials. They believed they had answers to the most vexing problems of the day, and they were seized by a religious fervor (sanctified by a generation of liberal Protestant ministers, who proclaimed the "Social Gospel"). Their intentions were usually good. The faced real problems of poverty, dirty and crowded cities, unsafe work conditions, adulterated food, unsafe railroads, monopolistic business practices, cyclic downturns that put millions of wage laborers out onto the street, illiterate children, and uneducated adults. They solved some problems, ameliorated others, and in other cases were ineffective.

Progressive reform often created unintended consequences, sometimes causing worse problems than they solved. A spectacular case of counterproductive policy was Prohibition. Alcoholism destroyed personal dignity and ruined families, and trapped people in poverty, and Progressives wanted to end the scourge. Progressives struggled to amend the Constitution to outlaw the sale of liquor, and their success was felt to be a triumph at the time. But perversely, it led to contempt for the law, rampant government corruption, and the appearance of organized crime on a scale never seen before in America, which operated large-scale illegal businesses to meet the demand, and fought bloody battles for turf.

Most importantly regulatory programs require coercion. When their solutions stopped working, or delivered undesirable results, the first solution at hand was not to rethink the goal but to double down on coercion. Today, the apparatus has gotten out of control. Regulatory machinery that treats masses of nonviolent Americans as criminals does not serve the public interest. In general, we need a leaner, less ambitious apparatus, bounded by the limitations on power embodied in the Constitution by the Founders.

**Employment, Work, and Enterprise.** One of the most visible effects of the transition from 2.0 America to 3.0 is the collapse of the corporate factory model of work. Since the rise of the Industrial Revolution, manufacturing enterprises needed to coordinate the actions of a large group of people operating machinery run by large sources of power: first water power, then steam, and subsequently electricity.

Three trends have combined to reduce the percentage of Americans working in classical factory environments. The first is automation and computer-aided manufacturing, which has reduced the number of people needed to make the same volume of products as before. The second has been the proliferation of regulation of productive activities, which has resulted in many former industrial activities being abandoned or curtailed in the United States. The third has been the trend toward offshore production, as the lower labor costs, lower regulatory requirements, and lower taxes of competing foreign areas have allowed corporations to produce offshore what was more expensive, more difficult, or impossible to produce any longer in the United States. The tendency of governments and unions alike to treat a job as an object that is owned, and that can be protected or guaranteed to an individual, has perversely made it more difficult for American companies to retain jobs domestically.

After factory work, the second great corporate job creator was the need for a vast administrative staff to run large corporations, to organize and process information. This need created a new middle class after World War II. The need for these jobs has eroded for many years because of the rise of computers. Many functions that once required an individual or a team to perform have now been automated.

In place of a corporate job, whether blue collar on the factory line or white collar in the office, we have seen the rise of the small company, the start-up, and the self-employed free agent.

The entrepreneurial companies of Silicon Valley are the most visible example of the new entrepreneurism made possible by the information revolution, but they are just a fraction of the new activity made possible by technology and deregulation. Transportation is relatively far cheaper than at the height of the 2.0 era, and communications have fallen to effective rates of zero, thanks to digital telephony and the Internet. This has made it possible for teams of people and companies to form task-based networks nationally and internationally to take on activities that formerly would have taken a corporation with hundreds or thousands of employees.

Manufacturing is on the verge of a similar revolution. What happened with electrons will soon happen with atoms. Potential breakthroughs include new methods of "3-D printing" or "additive manufacturing" that allow products to be manufactured in locally based machines. We are on the verge of a customized, localized, additive, distributed (CLAD) manufacturing revolution. Small items can be produced in devices the size of computer printers or microwaves, and costing no more than early consumer versions of those devices. Larger products can be produced in decentralized local shops with larger versions of 3-D printers, or with computer-controlled automated machines, essentially a more sophisticated version of today's numerically controlled lathes and milling machines. This will have the effect of making the economics of manufacturing many physical objects more like that of software, as the value will be primarily in the design and manufacturing-instruction software used to run the machines.

These developments will lead to a mixed model of production for a long time to come. Some items (e.g., ships) will not be amenable to this style of production and will continue to be made in traditional workplaces with relatively traditional workplace relations. Further, products that work only if the material has the proper processing history (e.g., jet engine fan blades) may be made for a long time with techniques similar to current practice.

However, a large portion, perhaps a majority, of the workforce will not be in shipyards or factories. It will consist of free agents, singly or combined in "virtual companies," small teams of agents who come together for a project or a series of projects. This will likely lead to the creation of many valuable public domain goods, produced via these automated techniques using free design software produced in a manner similar to today's free software products such as Linux.

For those who own 3-D printers large enough to produce an item, these goods will be available for the cost of the feedstock needed to make them. Many free agents and virtual companies will market proprietary improvements, or offer to service and troubleshoot public domain goods. Above that will be entirely new categories of customized products. Some producers will design specialized goods and services for a premium price.

These methods will coexist with traditional craft producers creating handmade items or items made in an archaic fashion, as luxury goods, or niche products. Marshall McLuhan observed that superseded technology has always survived as an art form, and a golden age of handcrafts could occur as most ordinary manufacturing requires far fewer hands.

In this emerging economy, there will be no need for crowding masses of people together in large areas as industrial workforces or masses of administrative headquarters staff. These old-style workplaces needed workers to be in close proximity to function. Networked, collaborative employment will allow the workforce to be increasingly dispersed, without losing efficiency. Housing costs will push a move to the periphery, especially if, as we expect, educational reforms lessen the intense demand to live in neighborhoods with good school systems. On the other hand, inertia and existing community ties will cause existing centers to retain a substantial percentage of their current populations, barring catastrophe, for many years. Plus, a lot of people just like living in cities.

Infrastructure items such as large airports with direct long-distance service will remain attractors for economically engaged populations. What is more likely than complete dispersal of population will be the rapid growth of far exurbs, so that the area within 90 to 120 minutes travel from major airports will see a medium-density development of their fringe areas with many village-style clusters for human gathering places or "third places." These will include many buffer areas and green belts, so that the area will not feel like one big megalopolis; green spaces will enhance property values around these new developments and will be guaranteed by covenant. Automated vehicle systems (of which the Google self-driving cars are a forerunner) have the potential, because of their superior speed, to expand the 90- to 120-minute travel time zone beyond the distance it currently covers.

These changes in technology and demographics will have a chicken-and-egg relationship with 3.0 political reform. Disintermediation of large institutional systems (i.e., removing the bureaucratic layers between service provider and service recipient), such as severing health insurance from permanent wage employment, is one such driver. Decentralization of power as the federal government becomes unable to sustain its overly centralized role, and states and localities growing more assertive, is another. All of the trends described above will have the effect of moving federal decisions to the state level, state decisions to the local level, and local decisions to the family and individual. As power decentralizes, the newer, more flexible modes of production become more possible, and the areas that are most receptive to them will gain an influx of productive people, enriching them and impoverishing the areas they leave. This will become a virtuous circle, promoting the constitutional and structural reforms we will describe below.

America's culture, historically based on Absolute Nuclear Families, makes us naturally receptive to 3.0 decentralization. The lack of attachment to place and its consequent openness to geographical mobility will accelerate the exodus to exurban work and housing currently in progress. The individualistic, contract orientation of the culture lends itself to the flexible, contract-based relationships of the free agent production mode. The disinclination to blind obedience leads to a desire for personal choices and an antipathy to authoritarian structures, which will also feed the movement toward decentralization and autonomy. The ability to uproot and move to new settings facilitated the movement from farms to big cities a century ago, and it will facilitate the new, more dispersed mode of living in the decades to come.

**Social Services: Health, Education, and Welfare.** Americans have tended to understand the word "socialism" primarily in terms of the form advocated by early twentieth-century Marxists, centering on state ownership and administration of heavy industry. Because for the most part the United States has avoided such a pattern, we have tended to think of America as a market economy and European mixed economies as socialist. For example, Britain under the Labour government elected after the end of the Second World War chose to nationalize its railways, coal mines, and steel mills, as well as the bulk of its health system, while in the United States all of those industries have remained private. Yet today, where the railways, mines, and mills all have been returned to private operation, the US and British health and education systems display an almost mirror image of operational modes. And in both cases, the problems in both sectors have been growing worse for years.

In the United States, education through the end of high school is overwhelmingly taxpayer-funded, publicly administered through elected school boards, and free at the point of delivery. Some parents choose to pay additional fees on top of taxes to send their children to private or religiously run schools that are entirely separate from the tax-paid school system. Nonetheless, primary and secondary education is mostly provided by government, and payment for them is mandatory, whether parents use the government schools or not.

Healthcare, on the other hand, is a complex mixture of private and public providers and payers; although most Americans under 65 pay either directly or as a work benefit for health-insurance policies, people over 65, military veterans, active-duty military and their families, and the lower-income brackets receive some or all healthcare paid for by government or from government agencies. The categories receiving all or most of their care on federal tax dollars amount to roughly half of the population.

In the United Kingdom, as a counterexample, health care is provided primarily by a government-administered, taxpayer-paid entity, the National Health Service, and is free at the point of delivery, whether it is a case of heartburn or a heart transplant. It might take forever, and you may not live until your doctor's appointment, but it is all free. Some patients choose to pay for care privately, on top of taxes, financed by private or employer-paid insurance. Education, on the other hand, is provided by a complex mixture of taxpayer-supported state schools, religious schools, and independent private schools, partly subsidized and partly charging fees. Just as Americans take for granted that medical care must be paid for and education will be free, British take the opposite for granted.

The contrast between Britain and America on education and health care shows that our approach is not carved in stone. Significant variations are possible, and the defects in the existing model are not inevitable and unchangeable, but amenable to reform, particularly where it is facilitated by technological change.

Education, health, and other public social services already have a substantial taxpayer-funded component, and have for a long time. This will likely continue in the future. As with transportation, there is a general public interest in having a healthy and well-educated population, and it makes sense for the better-off to subsidize to some extent the provision of these services for the less well-off.

General free public education had its roots in the Calvinist and Lutheran belief that all Christians, men and women alike, should be able to read the Bible for themselves. However, broad public education was confined mostly to parts of Germany, the Nethrlands, Scandinavia, Scotland, and New England until the nineteenth century and the era of mass armies initiated by the French Revolution. At that time it was realized that modern armies and navies required literate soldiers and sailors. After the effects of the early Industrial Revolution, the military found that the cities did not produce the robust, healthy recruits who were comfortable in the outdoors that an agricultural society had always taken for granted.

The British governing classes were appalled by the high rate of rejection for disease and illiteracy experienced in conscription intakes in the First and Second World Wars, especially compared with the stronger and healthier recruits arriving from Australia and New Zealand, whose smaller populations and steady revenue streams from their agricultural exports had made it easy to subsidize well-equipped schools and basic medical insurance. Americans also had unhealthy conscripts from the slums of New York and Boston in the Civil War, and they reached similar conclusions earlier. Progressives had a sense that improving national health and education was immediate and necessary, not only for the well-being of the American people, but also as an essential part of our national defense.

Thus, part of the Progressive agenda for American 2.0 was to institutionalize public schools and public health services for everyone, as part of the eugenic campaign to bring the country's population up to standard. Education leagues, the National Education Association, and the Parent–Teachers Associations became lobbies for tax increases and an ever-larger percentage of children funneled into not just elementary schools, but also high schools. A high school diploma was once considered to be reserved for only the top stratum of students. In fact the high school curriculum of the early twentieth century required mastering Latin and a modern language, if not classical Greek as well. Higher mathematics, and the physical sciences, as well as a thorough grounding in history, geography, and literature were also required. It was in many ways the equivalent of a bachelor's degree from an ordinary American university today, with the people of those earlier days being more literate than we are now.

However, like most 2.0 institutions founded on universality and taxpayer financing, educational institutions experienced a steady one-way pressure for expansion in all directions, including expanding the percentage of students taking higher-level diplomas. After World War I there was a steady increase in the expected school-leaving age, until graduation from high school became the norm for all social classes. After World War II the GI Bill created a vast expansion of the university population as well.

America 2.0 changed the nature of education. In the 1.0 era, it had been a handcrafted item in which learning was passed down from a professor to a handful of motivated students through a great deal of personal interaction. Jefferson thought of university education in terms of his relationship with William Small, his professor at the College of William and Mary, and a personal acquaintance and colleague of many of the great minds of the eighteenth century.

If education were to be turned into a universal product, however, it would have to be turned effectively into a mass-produced product, simplified, homogenized, and produced in identical lots in great numbers. Standards would have to be lowered. Larger and larger numbers of students swarmed into high schools and colleges, to the institutional and personal benefit of their administrators and staff. As public institutions they were subject to political pressure, and few parents wanted to be told their child was actually not suited to the higher education they had to offer. As education became universal, it also became lower in quality for the most part, and the need for more years of education to obtain a similarly trained young adult increased.

The family structure changes of the 1960s and 1970s and onward led to many families with absent fathers and working mothers unable to devote their time to their children. Schools, particularly in low-income urban areas, began to take on more and more responsibility for teaching things that were once part of the cultural heritage handed down by parents, peer children, and neighbors. In fact, schools began to take on more responsibility for feeding children and other basic parental responsibilities. At the same time, as opportunities opened up for women across the economy, the traditional pool of young women who would have gone into teaching went into more lucrative careers. On average, teacher quality suffered as a result.

There is now a wide range in the quality of public schools, from community to community and state to state. Many of the worst schools still receive large amounts of funding, despite abysmal results. Their unions, with their seniority rules which make it difficult to fire even the most incompetent teacher, and their underfunded pensions, remain powerful. These schools and their workforces are likely to find their power collapsing because of the increased financial pressure that is inevitable in the decades ahead. The question is, what kind of 3.0 solutions are likely to replace the existing model?

As with manufacturing, the 2.0 to 3.0 transition in education will include a greater diversity in the sources of supply and approaches they would embody, many small providers networked into several loose alliances that would be concerned with quality control, and a range of different funding sources and strategies. The voucher and charter movements already under way may serve as pathfinders for this process. Certainly the voucher system can be gamed by public authorities and co-opted by crony capitalists. The fundamental logic behind taxpayer support is nonetheless still valid. The costs of a generally ignorant population are so widely spread it is worth ensuring that all have access.

However, the entire model of a teacher holding lectures and discussion sessions to impart knowledge to a group of students, all sitting in a room, is only one model of learning. Children trooping into a schoolhouse and moving from class to class as bells ring is a model derived from the factory floor of a century ago. The diversity of approaches that are now developing, based on advancing technology, will permit other models to supplement or replace this activity. These new methods, like the new style of manufacturing, will allow mass customization, and a personalized education that was recently only within the grasp of a tiny handful of students at elite schools.

The core of the university experience at Oxford and Cambridge, still considered the highest-quality education available in the English language, consists of one-on-one interaction between the student and the full professor. This is supplemented with a great deal of lecturing in small group sessions, writing and critiquing of essays by a tutor, and assigned and self-chosen reading. But the personal access to high-level minds is the unique and critical component of this approach. Of course this model was abandoned elsewhere, because it was very resource-intensive and not replicable on an industrial scale.

Today, university education has become an indispensable credential for a wide variety of middle-class jobs. But many of these jobs should not need more than a high-school diploma, if that diploma had the rigor it once had when its graduates constituted only a few percent of the population. Many years are now spent on the college campus learning remedially, at great expense on borrowed money, what should have been taught for free in high school. For many students that time would be better spent apprenticing in a workplace learning real skills and real-world lessons.

The America 3.0 transition in education will likely parallel the reforms occurring in the workplace. Large, centralized learning-places built on industrial-style imparting of a standardized model of knowledge, adapted to the lowest common denominator of cognitive styles, will gradually fade away. In its place will be community-based schools using a wide variety of learning methods and materials, and a proliferation of other models of learning, including on-line learning and learning infused with making a livelihood. Federal and state aid to education, to the extent it is deemed desirable and affordable, should follow the child rather than follow the politician – that is, it should be targeted to the parent and, when older, the child, and spendable on a wide variety of learning opportunities.

Similarly, a combination of scientific-technical advances and changes in the structure of the field has the potential to transform the nature of the policy dilemmas we now face in medicine. To date, medical advances have tended to make treatment more expensive both through the need to provide more expensive machines and medications, and through the less-often-discussed fact that the longer a person is kept alive, the more future treatments he or she will need. But at some point treatments now being researched or projected have the potential to treat disorders radically and systemically, which is to say make a finite and definitive series of interventions that cure the disorder and restore the patient to functioning without need for further treatment, support, or palliative care.

Consider the case of polio. A forecast on future polio care needs written in the late 1940s might have tried to forecast the number of iron lungs needed, potential improvements in iron lung technology, and numbers of trained personnel needed to operate and maintain them. What it would not have foreseen is what actually happened, which is that a cheap and generally effective vaccine would be found within a few years, and that polio was on the way to becoming a thing of the past.

Or consider the case of stomach ulcers, where one scientist going against the settled science in the field proposed a new and radical theory that allowed stomach ulcers to be permanently cured with a simple antibiotic treatment of a sort that had been available for years.

Given the many promising leads now being followed up in research, it is likely that some, and possibly many of the expensive, life-shortening, and care-intensive conditions will be susceptible to one or another form of radical medical treatment. An effective treatment for Alzheimer's disease, or other forms of dementia, would restore decades of meaningful life to many millions, and at the same time greatly reduce the burden on Medicare and other medical plans by eliminating the need for long-term facility care for the former patients. Even additive manufacturing may contribute to medicine. 3-D printers using a slurry of the patient's own cells as feedstock have already been used to print skin and other biological materials to repair damage. Printing entire new organs with no rejection issues may be a commonplace thing in the future.

Although we have advocated reducing government expenditure in many areas, support of more aggressive research in advanced medicine is an area where an investment now may reap enormous dividends in the form of reduced medical support costs. Additionally, the regulatory reform agenda must include a thorough review of the FDA's current approach to approval of new drugs and treatments. Accelerating that process would save lives and, potentially, a great deal of money that would otherwise have to be raised through taxation.

**Constitutional and Social Issues: Restoring Decentralization.** A critically important reform for the transition to America 3.0 will be the decentralization of the economic and political systems of the country. Technological and demographic trends throughout the 2.0 period all drove centralization, as the old Jeffersonian ideal of a family farm sustaining independence at a competitive standard of living became more difficult to maintain. Rising standards of living in town and falling crop prices resulted in isolation from the many new opportunities and conveniences of modern life. Americans, and would-be Americans from across the globe, flocked into the swelling cities, creating new and unforeseen problems that resulted in new, centralized institutions and solutions.

Now the technology and demographics have changed, and life on the exurban fringes of America is more comfortable, more convenient, and more affordable than either rural or urban life. Meanwhile, the institutions that once addressed the problems of 2.0 urban America no longer can assume the preconditions that once allowed their programs to function. The crises of 2.0 corporations, unions, and governments, which have been rendered unworkable, threaten to swamp America financially while leaving many of the needed tasks of life done poorly or not at all.

Decentralizing decision-making and creating a more diverse set of government bodies will suit our future economy and society better than what we have today. But to adopt effective decentralizing will require humility on all sides, and giving up trying to compel the entire country to live by one set of rules.

Both political sides in the American cultural debate are still focused on promoting and ultimately imposing their vision of life on the country as a whole. We will use the shorthand "Left" and "Right" to mean the part of the population that, respectively, generally support what are called Liberal or Progressive policies, or tend to support what are known as Conservative or Libertarian or Traditionalist perspectives.

The Left and Democratic Party overlap closely, with only a fringe on the Left deeply alienated from the main leftward party. The aspiration of the American political Left is, very roughly, an updated version of the 2.0 model. Government, unions, and corporations will be restored to solvency. These revived institutions will provide a secure life for the general population through stable employment mediated by regulation and union borrowing power. A cash flow will be generated through taxes and union dues automatically deducted from regular paychecks. It is more or less an idealized version of the US economic structure of the 1950s with Progressive personal values and family relations added to the mix.

The political Right and Republican Party overlap less closely. Various factions on the Right in America often see the GOP as an adversary, a co-opted junior partner to the Democrats, joint custodians of Big Government. The term the "Combine," originated by John Kass of the *Chicago Tribune*, captures this idea, as does the labeling of many Republican politicians as RINOs ("Republicans in Name Only"). Recent populist efforts to depose established GOP officeholders have had only mixed success, sometimes losing "safe seats" when enthusiastic amateurs are nominated and eaten alive by Democratic professionals.

Nonetheless, there is something like a consensus vision on the Right and within the GOP. It is a vision of a robust entrepreneurial economy characterized by a lean, rationalized government restored to solvency by cutting back social transfers and privatizing their functions, the continued dwindling away of unions, a much diminished role for public sector unions, and new company formation providing general prosperity and resolution of poverty through economic growth. It is a vision of an eco-

nomic structure similar to that of the previous eras of technology innovation and growth, combined uneasily with religiously based conservative
personal values.

These visions point in opposite directions. There is something like a
30 percent segment of the American public on each side politically that
believes quite strongly that the other side is fundamentally wrong and
that any action toward realizing their agenda will be not only undesirable, but catastrophic. The acrimony is particularly strong on questions
of sexual morality. When one side wins electorally, or makes strides influ-
encing the culture in their direction, the opposing side does not embrace
their vision or even accept their loss as inevitable. Instead, they mobilize
all the more strongly to oppose and reverse the change, and in doing so
they utilize all the considerable levels of checks and balances that the
Founders' design, and historical circumstances, have embedded in the
American social and political system.

While America is viewed as a "winner's culture," there is a readily
accessible tradition and vocabulary of diehard intransigence and belief in
resistance leading to ultimate victory even following disaster. From the
starvation of Valley Forge, through the burning of the White House in
the War of 1812, to the Alamo, the "unreconstructed Rebel" of post–Civil
War song, to "Surrender Hell, we just got here," mere defeat in battle has
never been viewed as the end of a strongly held cause, and electoral
defeat, even less.

It is true that some of the tenets of both sides ultimately must face an
unhappy meeting with external reality. Progressive politicians, and the
voters who support them, cannot perpetually borrow, or inflate, or raise
tax rates, to keep their 2.0 institutions financially afloat forever. Unrealistic taxes and regulation drive capital from state to state, or to foreign
destinations; and ultimately smart, talented Americans will begin following that money even overseas if necessary. But just when crisis points
appear to be reached inescapably, it is often possible to kick the can even
further down the road, or plumb even deeper the limits of Adam Smith's
observation that there is a lot of ruin in a nation.

If the Left dreams of keeping things going as they have been, only
more so, the Right dreams of a board-clearing change that will make the
real, existing government falter sufficiently that common sense will
return spontaneously. Some of the more apocalyptic voices on the Right

seem to hope that America will drift into a sufficiently large catastrophe within the next administration or two to cause widespread social collapse and a massive reaction against the centralizing 2.0 institutions they despise. This is almost certainly overwrought. The existing government, for better or worse, will be able to stagger on for some time.

Most importantly, the US government's capacity to borrow at comparatively low interest is not likely to disappear any time soon. If the United States had a sufficiently large and dynamic competitor such a catastrophe might occur. But there is no visible alternative to the United States on the horizon as a political, military, or financial leader of the world. This is not because the USA is currently a raging success, but because all the other possible alternatives are even further down the path to paralysis than America. Europe as an entity is fundamentally dysfunctional, fiscally, socially, and demographically. It is now consuming its own seed corn. China has grown old before it grew prosperous, no matter how glittering its coastal trading cities have gotten by selling the discounted labor of the interior for Federal Reserve Notes. Russia is in a demographic death spiral, with devastating public health problems. The Japanese have become old and stagnant. All others are just too small to fill America's shoes.

If the United States ends up repudiating its debt by inflating it away, as it will do by default if the current stalemate continues, US Treasury debt will become one of the worst trades in history since the Manhattan Indians sold what they thought were hunting rights in their backyard to the Dutch. But as long as America is comparatively a haven of safety, capital will continue to come here. As a result, it is entirely possible that the current stalemate can stagger on for another one to two decades with no basic resolution.

During this time government debt would continue to grow. In the event that government debt becomes unattractive to third parties, substantial inflation will result, which in turn will substantially deepen the stagnation of the economy and the sclerosis of the system. These effects will be somewhat offset by the development of domestic energy resources, as union and pension-recipient pressures overwhelm green and NIMBY (Not In My Back Yard) objections to energy development. When most energy was imported, inflation threatened to lead oil exporters to price oil in other currencies, like the euro. An inflating dollar and a large oil import bill priced in other more stable currencies (if there were any) would quickly explode the remainder of the US economy, as runaway inflation has done in nations like Argentina. However, a United States that continued to run large debts and continued to experience low or negative growth, as would result from increased taxation and regulation, would more resemble the struggling economy Japan has suffered with over the past two decades.

Therefore, it appears unlikely that the American Right, or for that matter the American Left, will be able to implement its agenda consistently and thoroughly at the federal level over the coming decades. It is also likely that although the credit situation of the federal government and the state and local governments will continue to deteriorate, it may be possible, and in fact is the most likely outcome, that a series of partial (and ultimately inadequate) fixes will prevent the full implementation of the financial reforms – the "Big Haircut" – recommended in this book. On the other hand, it may be the case that partial reforms implemented piecemeal may relieve enough pressure to develop a consensus for further reform. We can envision a series of "little haircuts" at the state level, with perhaps the initial ones being imposed as the price of federal bailouts, and subsequent ones negotiated voluntarily between parties as the credibility of the threat of an imposed settlement is established. But the vision of a general crisis creating the environment for a large-scale imposition of either the Right or the Left's agenda may not come to pass in the foreseeable future.

Neither a decisive triumph nor a general crisis may resolve the national standoff in the foreseeable future. The question then becomes whether there is a better use of the considerable political power of the existing blocs than vainly striving for the final triumph that is almost certainly out of reach. In the wake of the 2012 electoral defeat, and an apparent long-term senescence of the GOP, there is much stocktaking and introspection on the American Right. Political defeat has a way of increasing willingness to reconsider assumptions, but perhaps not yet deeply enough.

The first step in responding to a defeat, and to reverse the apparent slow decay of one's position, is to assess honestly the remaining assets you hold. In the case of the Right, those assets, although obviously inadequate to dominate the political sphere, are still very substantial, including an undisputed veto over the policy and platform of the Republican

Party, and the adherence of a substantial percentage of the American people, spread widely but not uniformly across the country. The precise estimate of this strength is somewhat dependent on the definition of Right. The American Right is a highly diverse community including traditionalists and social conservatives, religious conservatives, economic conservatives, libertarian conservatives, classical liberals, and pure libertarians. There are significant subdivisions within each category, and the categories are in flux and subject to change. And they all fight among themselves.

From the 1980s through the end of the 2000s, a category called "neoconservatives" was prominent, centering around a group of intellectuals who had originally been on the Left, and who had moved Rightward originally out of a concern that the Democratic Party had become too unrealistic about the threat of the Soviet Union, and later out of concern about the effect of liberal policy on social cohesion, particularly with minorities and working-class families. Mostly Democrats and Socialists originally, the neoconservatives continued to believe in a role for a substantial federal government, but abandoning specific liberal ideas about what and how its programs should act to improve the general welfare. However, post–Cold War neoconservatism became primarily identified with the advocacy of large-scale armed intervention in the Middle East with the goal of substantially transforming the areas from which Islamist terrorism has originated. With the general disillusionment that has set in with regard to the Iraqi and Afghan interventions, this form of neoconservatism has declined in influence, although it still has important proponents at think tanks and publications.

The particularly strong point of neoconservatism, which has not been repudiated in practice, is its insight on domestic policy. They work from a realistic understanding of how large the US government actually is, how difficult it is to reduce its functions, and to what extent the size of government is a result of genuine popular demand for particular services. This type of dispassionate assessment of proper size and role of government is valuable in understanding of the current situation.

But most of the American Right does not have the patience, the time, or the innate wonkishness to engage in debates that get too far into the weeds of how the government actually works, let alone into the minutiæ in tens of thousands of pages in the Code of Federal Regulations. Most of the American Right converges on a well-justified distrust and dislike of a government as large as ours today, and strongly opposes the use of the apparatus of government to impose the social agenda of the Left on the population at large. Because they share this consensus, the various factions of the Right are often more effective at exercising a veto over government actions and Leftist policy proposals than at generating a positive platform of their own. As a result, they can rarely muster a firm national backing sufficient to overcome the Left's similar veto ability. It is this veto that explains much of the American exceptionalism that has resulted, for example, in the United States having (so far) no government-mandated universal health system, or the United States having retained the old "Imperial" measure system, rejecting the metric system.

The question then is whether the Right can use electoral and cultural strength to impose a general political solution on America as a whole. Is it possible to use such strength more productively than merely exercising a veto? This is particularly important from the standpoint of communication as the Left still enjoys a fundamental dominance in the established legacy media, including the daily press, broadcast and most cable/satellite television, and almost all of Hollywood. Even if the formal political system remains effectively deadlocked for decades, the Left's dominance of the formal cultural apparatus of the country will result in continual leftward creep. Therefore, the idea of continuing to resist structural change through the generally (but not consistently) effective political veto while hoping to grow the percentage share of the conservative and libertarian American communities is likely to be futile.

## A Social Settlement, Not a Social Truce

The realities of American culture and politics suggest using the core political strength of the Right to move away from struggling to take over the federal government, and instead push for a long-term, structural decentralization away from Washington, moving most of the political decisions affecting everyday life, economic and social, to the state and community level. This agenda will necessarily require, as a practical matter, de-prioritizing other important issues at the national level. We are not advocating social truce, but a social settlement. We are advocating that this political focus be worked out first within the party and broad-based organizations on the Right, and then advocated to the nation.

Of course, under the banner of "states' rights," "tenth amendment advocacy," and "federalism" decentralization of power and decision-making have long been part of the verbal repertoire of the Right. But it has never been front and center in the agenda, and it has tended to be trotted out as an auxiliary argument in support of other issues, but seldom as a general principle. There is an inevitable concern that any reference to "states rights" – a legal misnomer in any case – will adversely impact African Americans. Our proposals, detailed below, specifically address these concerns.

The Right has never aggressively sought allies beyond its own circles when it has advocated decentralization. Nor has it been consistent about decentralization when federal power could be used to advance its own agenda. All this has led moderates and single-issue activists to suspect, and reasonably so, that any concession from the Right is entirely temporary, and that as soon as politics permit, the Right will seek to override local decision-making and impose their solution by federal power. Yet these are the people whose support must be gained for the Right to go above the 50 percent (at which it appears to be permanently stuck) to achieve any part of its agenda.

This distrust of the Right has several bad effects. The most obvious one is that it stands in the way of potentially useful alliances. The second is that it also leaves moderates vulnerable to a slippery slope argument from the hard Left, as there is no obvious stopping point between small, sensible Burkean steps and radical Jacobin solutions. The third is that by preventing any sort of social settlement, the Left is able to achieve its goals by judicial activism. Such victories are by their nature shaky and require constant vigilance to ensure the retention of a sympathetic bench. Therefore, the last thing the Left or the Democratic leadership wants is a firm social settlement that no longer makes the choice of a Supreme Court justice a high-stakes event that allows them to mobilize and motivate millions on election day.

If the Right could overcome this distrust, it would have the effect of allowing a coalition for decentralization to separate moderates from the Left. The fear and constant anxiety that the Left requires to keep its moderate allies onside could be turned against the Left, as moderates and people with localized interests discern that secure guarantees for local autonomy are ultimately a better prize than depending continually on the victory of one party. The only way this distrust can be overcome will be by adopting specific proposed reforms and persisting in promoting them.

Let us be quite clear about what an alliance for decentralization requires. Various voices on the Right, notably Indiana Governor Mitch Daniels, called for a "social truce" between social conservatives and libertarians before the 2012 elections. For the most part, the various factions of the Right complied with this call. However, their opponents on the Left did not, and very assiduously dragged up every possible quote designed to reopen social issue battles that were tangential to the real issues that needed to be discussed. This proved a distraction and almost certainly contributed to the mobilization of some components of the Left's winning coalition.

What is needed is not a social truce, for that is ineffective, as was demonstrated. What is needed is a social settlement: a general acceptance on the Right of a plank that takes social issues off the federal political agenda for at least two decades and puts an end to the Left's ability to play on slippery slope fears. The way to do that is to promote a constitutional amendment that clearly places the main set of contentious social issues, including abortion, the definition of marriage, and in general the police powers of the state beyond the reach of the federal government and the court system entirely, leaving them squarely in the hands of state legislators and voters. This would mean that the large set of voters concerned with such issues would never again have such a strong stake in the exact views of Supreme Court nominees, nor have to fear every case that might wind its way up to the Courts.

In pursuit of such an amendment, the Right would be forced to reach out to elements with whom it did not agree on the specific outcomes of issues, but who would prefer to see the prospect of total defeat permanently placed out of their concerns. In other words, be the first to firmly occupy the center of the spectrum, force the opponents of the amendment to the extremes, and drive a wedge between moderates and extremes in all camps.

\* \* \*

## AN AGENDA FOR DECENTRALIZATION

What would an agenda for domestic decentralization look like, how would it achieve its goals, and how would it prioritize its targets? Certain core functions would remain at the federal level, especially common defense and preserving free and open trade throughout the national territory. Further, the federal government would continue basic civil rights to all citizens. However, with these basic safeguards, the goal would to devolve as many other functions as possible to states and localities, with the possibility that states would form compacts to work cooperatively. The purpose would be to set up a competitive environment between the states, and minimizing the cost of people moving freely out of poorly managed states to those with superior public policies. Secession would not be allowed, but breaking up some of the larger states, while difficult, would have positive effects.

## WHICH FUNCTIONS SHOULD BE DECENTRALIZED?

The first question in decentralization is always what functions should reside at the federal level and which ones should reside at the state and the local levels. One way to look at the question is similar to the one Founders faced at Philadelphia, not to write the Constitution, but to write the initial Articles of Confederation. At that point each former colony was, for all intents and purposes, an independent nation. The first question the drafters faced was, why should we federate at all? Why not just remain thirteen independent nations trading and cooperating with each other as the occasion demanded?

The same question has been asked at multiple junctures in American history, most recently in the days after the presidential elections of 2012 and 2004. America's tradition of decentralism is linked to the recurring temptation to secession. This is not surprising since our founding document, the Declaration of Independence is, among other things, a philosophical justification for secession. Two of America's current states, Texas and Hawaii, have had substantial histories as generally recognized independent nations participating in the international system of states. Fifteen others (the thirteen original states, plus Vermont and California) had at least de jure independence and some level of dealing with foreign powers as such. And of course the Confederacy, each of whose member states also claimed the right to separate independence if they so chose, had at least partial international recognition as a belligerent power under international law.

America is actually quite exceptional in being flatly opposed to secession of its subunits and openly stating its right and intent to use force to prevent secession. Canada's Supreme Court has ruled that if a province votes unambiguously in referendum for secession, its federal government has an obligation to negotiate in good faith on the matter. The British government has placidly accepted Scotland's demand for a secession referendum in 2014 and has pledged to negotiate a separation agreement if they vote to leave the United Kingdom, which was originally united by the union of England and Scotland in 1707.

The failure of the Articles of Confederation provided justification for a single "federal" government – literally the government of a "federation" of states. There are two main reasons. The first was to provide for the common defense. America has perceived itself under foreign threat from the beginning of its settlement, with the geopolitical threats of the French in Quebec and the Spanish in Florida, not to mention the tribal cultures of the Native Americans. Americans knew that political union allowed it to muster the army and navy based on all available resources, which would be needed to defeat foreign enemies. It also need a strong enough financial system to afford the forts, dockyards, and ships, and roads and canals that a strong navy and army required. The American perception that it faces foreign threats has never gone away, and correctly so.

As defense became more high-tech, and America itself became the world's maritime, and later aerial and space-faring, commons-keeper, the need for a single, powerful military has only grown more acute. In the age of nuclear weapons, a single, legally defined custodian of all of America's arsenal of warheads and bombs is absolutely imperative. We want to decentralize many things, but having fifty or more states each with nuclear weapons, or even any ambiguity about who owns these weapons and is authorized to use them, will never be on our agenda.

The second reason the Founders created a strong federal government was to assure the largest possible unified internal area for the movement of people, goods, services, information, and capital. Fresh in the minds of the Founders was the example of Britain and France whereby France, with three times as many people as Britain, was yet financially weaker. France had failed to create an efficient taxing body, and it had a poor record of paying its public obligations, and could borrow only at high interest rates. Thus hobbled, France had trouble supporting a navy competitive with Britain's, because a world-class navy requires permanent, high levels of expenditure. Britain maintained a moderate but predictable and consistently enforced level of taxation, and a competently run financial system, which made its bonds reliable, and its interest rates for borrowing very low.

France was also economically weaker than Britain, despite its much larger size and natural wealth. France divided its internal space into many small jurisdictions that were allowed to prey upon traders and travelers with taxes and tolls, inconsistent and corrupted weights and measures, and arbitrary and inconsistent rules and regulations. One consequence was that although France had plentiful timber supplies, these internal barriers made it uneconomic to move the timber from inland to the seaports where its warships were built. Instead, they imported supplies from the Baltic countries, a supply that was easily blockaded and cut off by the Royal Navy in wartime. Britain, to the contrary, kept the entire island of Great Britain a single internal market with free flows of goods and capital.

The Founders saw that internal barriers were growing up between the states under the Articles of Confederation. That was the French road, not the English one, and it would inevitably lead to a weakened and impoverished new country, which would not only make us poorer but subject to attack and intimidation by foreign powers.

These security concerns led to the Annapolis Convention, which was convened to discuss improving the Articles. This then led to the call for a Constitutional Convention in Philadelphia. Alexander Hamilton was the leading actor at the Convention. Hamilton's particular contribution to America was more than anything else to understand how the English system worked. He saw that there was an "Anglosphere financial toolkit" – as we, not he, would call it – of internal free movement, low but competently administered taxes, and financial institutions like banks and bond markets that allowed a government to borrow at low interest and finance needed defense and transportation investments without ruinous levels of taxation, or allowing local crony capitalists to protect themselves from competition.

All of these strengths at the federal level would be maintained under the decentralizing model we propose, and assurances on this score will be an important part of promoting the approach.

**Guarantees of Civil Rights.** Any decentralizing proposal, to be effective and to have any moral authority, must guarantee an agreed-upon level of civil rights and liberties to all within the federation.

In drafting the American Constitution, many originally thought that the states, being closest to the people would be the best guardian of rights, but others foresaw that the federal government, no matter how carefully its powers were circumscribed, needed specific curbs on its ability to use its power. Thus as part of the compromises needed to get the Constitution ratified, federalist forces agreed to pass the ten first amendments, known as the Bill of Rights, to entrench certain basic liberties, copied in many parts from the English Bill of Rights and, harking back to Magna Carta. Still, these rights were only guaranteed in reference to the powers of the federal government. Even more problematically, they sidestepped the growing disagreement over chattel slavery.

The existence of slavery in the United States, under the original Constitution, illustrates most forcefully the fundamental tension between the desire to permit local self-government (including, ultimately, the freedom to leave a federation) and the obligations of the federal level to defend the rights of its citizens when they are abused by local authority. The federal government's capacity and will to enforce such guarantees is one of the main reasons for it to exist at all. The question of what rights belong to which members of a community, and to what degree the democratic will of a local majority can bind the minority's rights can never be discussed in the United States without reference to slavery, the Civil War, and the subsequent political battles over civil rights.

To be specific, our proposals for federalism and decentralization will not in any way impact the rights of African Americans or other minorities. The Constitution, including the Civil War Amendments, are essential guarantees for all citizens and are not subject to local control. The Civil Rights Act and Voting Rights Act will continue to be enforced by the federal government and be binding on all the states. Our proposed decentralization will not touch these protections. Guaranteeing the civil rights of all citizens will remain a responsibility of the national government and the federal courts.

We also oppose secession, especially unilateral secession, which is not within the scope of the decentralization we propose. The seceding states of 1860, in large measure, were motivated by the desire to maintain and expand slavery. In other words, America's only major episode of attempted secession was meant to perpetuate what we would now call a human rights abuse. Even without this precedent, any unilateral secession would likely violate too many minority rights. Do citizens of a particular federation have the right to stay in their homes and continue to enjoy the government of that federation? Many Americans would say yes, particularly black residents of southern states today, who would undoubtedly view any secession attempt supported conspicuously by the local white majority, with justified suspicion and resistance.

It is the legacy of slavery and racial-based community division in America that makes any proposed decentralization of power, even far short of unilateral secession by one or more states, an emotionally fraught subject. As we noted, Canadians and Britons have generally indicated that they would not expect or approve of the use of force to prevent Quebec or Scotland from seceding. In those cases, complications would arise if a part of either seceding entity, say the Cree Indian ("First Nations" in Canadian parlance) and Inuit lands of northern Quebec, or the Shetland Islands, unilaterally resisted leaving their present federations, or even resorted to arms to remain Canadian or British. The national government would have to protect those minority communities, who are its citizens. This has already happened in the United States. The northwestern counties of Virginia refused to participate in Virginia's secession, and they formed a new state of West Virginia and stayed in the Union.

The prospect of such "sub-secessions" illustrates why secession cannot be a part of any decentralization.

**Voice and Exit.** How should we determine which rules should be enforced across the "federation" and which should be determined locally? Here it is useful to use the distinction made by Albert Hirschman between "Voice" and "Exit" in his 1970 treatise "Exit, Voice, and Loyalty." Hirschman observed that a participant in a human system, whether as a consumer in a marketplace or a citizen in a political system, typically has two choices if he is unhappy with the state of the system. "Exit" is to leave the system and find another, more satisfactory one; "Voice" is to seek to use available tools (including threat of exit) to improve the quality of the system. "Loyalty" enters the picture as a reminder that, humans being humans, the two options are not always equal, as the emotion of loyalty may tip the scales toward voice and against exit.

Typically, exit is the solution used by consumers (and employees) in a market situation, and voice is the solution used by citizens in a political system. Exit usually has a higher costs in political systems than in market systems. The cost of exit in a market situation may be as trivial as a slightly higher price for a competing product, or the non-market costs of getting used to the new characteristics of a somewhat different product. The costs of exit in a political system are usually substantial – physically moving one's household, arranging new employment or moving a business, perhaps gaining recognition for professional credentials, resettling children in a new school system, and above all the issues of gaining entry and work permits, and ultimately citizenship in the new jurisdiction. Exit from one sovereign state to another, even if both have the same language and similar cultures, has become a major, and often impossible task in the era of America 2.0 and its many bureaucratic requirements. Exit to a country with a different language, legal and political system, and substantially different culture is even more daunting. It is little wonder that most people unhappy with a political system seek to exercise voice instead.

In recent years, however, advocates of decentralism have returned to Hirschman's distinctions with renewed interest. His original emphasis was on the limitations of exit as a strategy for consumers. It was previously taken for granted that voice is a much more important tool than exit in political systems, except perhaps in very abnormal totalitarian systems, such as the Soviet bloc, where exit and the need to guard against exit became a major pressure on the system, and in 1989 actually became the point of its unraveling.

Looking back on the last fifty years, we have seen examples of exit in the American migration from the Northeast to the Sunbelt, and the current flight from the high-tax, high-regulation states like California to low-tax, low-regulation states like Texas. This has suggested that exit as a strategy within a federation has been a successful strategy not only for individuals and businesses, but it has also helped shift political power. In other words, exit also becomes a sort of voice ("voting with the feet"), and the threat of exit makes voice more convincing.

In fact exit even between countries with common languages and legal systems has been an effective phenomenon in past eras. Americans and Canadians freely moved back and forth across the border throughout the nineteenth century, with many families "double-dipping" homesteading by claiming one in the USA, selling the property when title was obtained, and then crossing the border and homesteading on the other side. Although this practice was technically illegal under both nations' laws, authorities not only tolerated but encouraged it. Canada lowered its time of probation before granting title from five years, matching the United States, to three years.

Furthermore, Canadian authorities realized that many homesteaders (one in five, by official estimate) didn't bother to check in at customs, but merely drove their wagons and livestock cross-country directly to their new homesteads. Rather than erecting walls or patrolling the border, they merely adjusted their census figures to account for this phenomenon. This free and easy attitude toward nationality lasted until World War I, when the increasing bureaucracy of everyday life then and in the subsequent Depression increased the transaction costs of exit.

This historical example suggests that the optimum degree of decentralization in a federation, is where the transaction costs of physical exit within the federation is minimized. Since the Civil War, concern for individual rights has been focused primarily on voice – rights of political participation, and rules for access to participation in society. The Thirteenth, Fourteenth, and Twentieth Amendments have all been about access to voice and formal political rights, as has legislation like the Civil Rights Act and Voting Rights Act of 1965. Arguably, however, the greatest immediate benefit of the Thirteenth Amendment, aside from the flat prohibition of chattel slavery, was the granting of unquestioned citizenship to the emancipated slaves and their children.

Even though the "Redeemer" movement in the South repealed Reconstruction and made the "voice" provisions of the Thirteenth and Fourteenth Amendments a dead letter for decades to come, the national citizenship provisions made exit a real possibility for Southern blacks for the first time. At first there were movements like the "Exodusters," in the late 1870s and 1880s, that led freed blacks from the South to Kansas and other parts of the West. Then there was the Great Migration that began during World War I, with its great demand for labor in northern and midwestern factory towns, and then in World War II and afterward, the demise of sharecropping segued into a northern and midwestern urban industrial population of black Americans. As voice led to exit, exit then led to new and stronger voice as northern blacks voted, joined unions, published newspapers, and began to undermine the old order of the South politically from secure new bases.

Nobody has less voice than an enslaved person. Therefore, exit was everywhere the primary strategy of liberation. Slave-owning society maintained a large apparatus of coercion – the network of militia patrols that policed the prewar South, and the apparatus of bounty-hunter slave-catchers to track down and recover runaway slaves. In counting the cost of slavery, it is not just the differential between the room and board given the slave and the salary that might have been needed to hire a free man for the same job, but the value of the exit that was kept from the slave. The value of that exit can be seen in the number of sharecroppers who chose to use it once the word had reached them that there was a better world to exit to.

America was built on the value the people fleeing Europe and Asia and the rest of the world brought here by using their ability to exit. Internal exit has changed America many times over, and that process continues today. Our strategy should be to push as many contentious issues as possible to the most local level possible, and then reducing the transaction costs of exit as low as possible. This will allows as many people as possible to choose communities to their liking, and reduce the number of items to be fought over in stalemate trench politics. To some extent this also provides a visible means by which alternative solutions can be tried and evaluated locally, and if successful can be spread by adopting them elsewhere, rather than becoming subject to national contention.

**Getting to "Exit."** The initial steps toward a decentralization of maximum exit within the United States should be those achievable by legislation and executive order. The original Constitution was intended to be highly decentralized, and indeed it would be hard to improve on the wording of the Tenth Amendment, if only it were kept: "The powers not delegated to the United States by the Constitution, nor prohibited by it to the States, are reserved to the States respectively, or to the people." And the Tenth Amendment does nothing more than restate what is obvious from the construction of the enumerated powers. It is equivalent to stating "And we mean it." Nevertheless there has been a long train of circumventions around the elegant Enlightenment structure of the Constitution, and unpacking two centuries of complex workarounds will be a matter of some time and effort.

One approach to restoring the Founders' intent would be to reduce the federal role to near the classical limited-state definition, primarily defense, justice, and foreign affairs, and offload almost all social functions to the states, or to regional compacts of states created for that purpose. New England, or at least New England minus New Hampshire, might well form such a compact or regional confederation. These states might choose to fund substantially more in the way of social services, perhaps even a public health service on the Canadian or British models. So long as their citizens are free to move and quit their home states without penalty, there is no reason not to.

In fact, social-democratic solutions on the European model have always succeeded the best when undertaken on a small scale. Denmark and Sweden are often-cited models of successful social democracy; it is useful to remember that they are quite small; Sweden at 9.5 million is smaller than North Carolina, at 9.6 million, and would only be the eleventh largest US state, ahead of New Jersey. Denmark, at 5.5 million, is smaller than Wisconsin and would rate twenty-first in size, ahead of Minnesota. When governments run day-to-day functions that are critical to life, it is better than they be run in smaller, more transparent jurisdictions that are more easily kept under the eye of the people. Smaller states could easily band together with like-minded jurisdictions and run programs jointly where economies of scale mattered.

Such multistate compacts would require no constitutional amendment, and in fact were foreseen by the Founders. It is perhaps a result of the rapid growth of the federal level as the Progressive 2.0 program took hold that federal actions pre-empted multi-state compacts from arising as the Founders had envisioned.

In a future America, where almost all of the domestic functions of the federal government had been handed back down to states, or multistate compacts, federal revenue needs might be met at least in part by giving states funding contribution quotas and letting each state, or multistate compacts, decide how best to make them. States adamantly opposed to income taxation might choose higher sales or property taxes as the means to making their quotas; states whose populations believed in more progressive taxation might choose to use state income taxes as their primary means. Yet other states might choose a mix of the various methods. Frankly, so long as productive people choose of their own free will to live in a particular jurisdiction and comply with its tax rules, the jurisdiction will be a success. This will be a powerful incentive for states to improve the transparency and effectiveness of their governments.

Another tool that is overdue for use is the division of large or conflicted states into several smaller states. This state-level secession is not to be confused with secession of a state from the United States. Any such division of existing states would not be unilateral, but it would be negotiated. It is perfectly constitutional and has been done twice in US history, the first time in 1820 when the state of Massachusetts divided peacefully into present-day Massachusetts and Maine. The second time was hotly contested, in 1863, when West Virginians formed a separate state and gained admission as such into the Union when Virginia seceded. As these precedents demonstrate, dividing an existing state into two or more states is a remedy that can be pursued without any constitutional amendment, by state legislative action, although new states would require the approval of Congress before admission. The one exception is Texas, which has an automatic right to subdivide into as many as five states pursuant to the terms under which it first joined the Union.

The benefits of subdivision of certain large states would be several. To begin with, very few governing entities in the modern industrialized world are unitary governments as large as the larger American states. California (37.7 million) and New York (19.4 million) are larger than any OECD unitary state except four (Italy, Britain, France, and Japan). The span of administrative control is wide enough that governance tends to be extremely bureaucratized. It is not a coincidence that most of the worst-governed, most highly taxed, most-indebted, and least well-served states are among the larger ones. Texas is an exception, partly because the voters of Texas have always preferred lower taxes and fewer services, while

Rhode Island is small but poorly governed, showing that size isn't everything. But the preponderance of evidence favors smaller states.

Dividing the larger or more contentiously varied states has the potential to increase the coherence of the wider community that each state constitutes, and in doing so, makes it more likely that the policies determined at the state level more accurately give their inhabitants the governmental policies they desire. If decentralization is pursued to remove the deadlock of government, and to allow each community to determine much of their policy locally, it will likely make sense to subdivide some of the existing states. Locking divergent communities into a single state framework will merely reproduces locally the gridlock that now prevails at the federal level.

Although compromise may be the lifeblood of constitutional government, there are many issues where compromise is not practical, and one or another policy simply must prevail. Perhaps the paradigmatic example is whether traffic should keep to the left or right side of the road. There is no moral or ethical reason to prefer the right or the left, but it is essential that one prevail, and prevail entirely. Given the relative ease of relocation within a federation with free movement of people and capital within it, a solution with a variety of local outcomes and easy exit may give more people effective choice than the limited voice of overly large democratic systems has managed. Reducing the size and increasing the number of fundamental jurisdictions increases the ease and opportunity of exit while improving the quality of voice in the smaller polities remaining.

Additionally, increasing the number and reducing the size of states reduces the exaggerated inequalities that have arisen between states over the history of the Union. Although we are constitutional republicans, and thus do not believe that the mathematical perfection of the process of democracy necessarily improves outcomes. Nonetheless, democratically elected government should be at least broadly representative.

Since the division of West Virginia, there have been a great many proposals to divide various states, and for that matter to unite various pieces into new composite states. It was revived in modern political discourse by William F. Buckley's provocative proposal, in his 1965 candidacy for mayor of New York City, that the city should become a separate state, to the benefit of both itself and the rest of the state. None of these proposals have prevailed, because in every case various local interests that stand to lose by such divisions have managed to block the efforts.

The coming era of financial crises over state finances may offer a historical opportunity to override these obstacles. If we view the workout of the states as an equivalent of a Chapter 11 bankruptcy, which is to say one in which the previous management continues to operate but reorganizes the business under the guidance of the courts and the creditors, one measure always considered by the supervisors of the process is whether the business would make more sense being divided into several smaller, more focused, and more easily managed corporations. The same logic would apply in the case of an effectively bankrupt state. Federal funds for reorganization, which will certainly be needed, should be conditioned on a pledge to hold a division referendum, with the proviso that a majority for division in either side (or any side, if the division would be into more than two) would place the process in motion.

Division of a state in modern times would be a complex process, but clear guidelines can be imposed, and the process will be manageable. Precedents exist for division of state debt, and state assets, and this could be negotiated as part of the general debt workout. Creative solutions might include the creation of an interstate compact between the two (or more) new states to continue joint operation, either temporarily or permanently, of some state institutions or facilities that could not readily be divided. In fact, most financial and institutional matters might be handled in that matter temporarily, while still allowing each new state its own Senate and Electoral College representation, and, most importantly, to begin resolving taxation and social issues according to local majority will. From the beginning of the Union, new states have been admitted in pairs, to maintain the partisan balance in Congress. The practice of negotiating the entry of new states based on such political considerations will certainly be revived.

The theoretically easier way to achieve many of these goals without breaking up states, or in addition to doing so, would be to introduce a more federal element into state constitutions. This approach has been prevented by the key "one man one vote" decisions of the Supreme Court, notably *Wesberry v. Sanders*, *Reynolds v. Sims*, and *Baker v. Carr*. Nonetheless, either creative state constitutional design, or amendment of the federal Constitution, could possibly serve the goals of decentralization without violating the dictates of the courts. The key is, again, the devolution of key social decisions, and decisions regarding the levels and mechanisms of taxation, and these could be decentralized without creating unequal representation in state legislatures. Ultimately a combination of state division and decentralization of decision-making within states could serve the goal of creating many competing jurisdiction with local voice while upholding many choices for exit.

Regional differences in the United States, as with other English-speaking countries, can be very enduring. The degree to which state and other key jurisdictional lines conform to the actual differences among Americans will make the Union work better in the long run. The United States is fundamentally made up of a number of cultural building blocks, traceable in some cases back to the 1600s. These are the areas, whether states or parts of states, that have some feeling of likeness or coherence. They share many of the same media. They have common professional or state university sports teams that are community passions. They have local foods, accents, and customs. And they often have social and policy preferences. These should be the fundamental political building blocks wherever practical, and in America 3.0 these will tend to emerge.

**The Magnitude of the Task.** Reform will be hellishly difficult. Many people benefit from the current regime and will fight to retain the benefits they get from it. They will truly believe that they are right to do so, and that the status quo, which happens to benefit them, is the best of all possible worlds. People who theoretically believe the system should be changed nonetheless have trouble accepting the severity of the consequences if no changes are actually made. People keep on in the old ways, and even though more problems seem to be arising, they can't imagine that the things they have taken for granted all their lives may come to an end, whether suddenly or by slow erosion.

However, America has had a remarkable capacity for reinvention. Our people have a "can do" spirit and are unlikely to wait passively while the sky falls. More likely we will have a cacophony of disparate reform plans, which are enacted in bits and pieces.

Our hope is that the process of changing from America 2.0 to America 3.0 will be as painless as possible, and timely reforms will ease the transition. Even if reforms are insufficient, even if the process is traumatic, we are going to arrive at a different and better state of affairs. The strength of our underlying culture, the ongoing value of many of our institutions, not least our Constitution, and most importantly ongoing technological progress all point toward a successful transition. It is just a matter of how long and hard the road will be.

# Chapter 9
# Defense and Foreign Policy

**The Foreign Policy of an Individualist Nation.** It is not difficult to understand how the American way of life, with its emphasis on freedom and individualism, expresses itself in our domestic preferences and policies. As we have discussed, America has a long-standing bias toward decentralized solutions that maximize individual choice and freedom. Even during the 2.0 period, the greater emphasis on centralization and large organizations was justified as a means of giving individuals more practical freedom. Indeed, if America had enjoyed the luxury of being immune from war and the consequences of foreign powers' policies, we probably would have never seen the government become as large and intrusive as it has become.

Although Americans like to think of themselves as a peaceful people who have avoided a culture of militarism, in fact war and concern about war have been major influences shaping American history. Americans established themselves as permanent residents of the continent by driving the prior inhabitants off of their land, often by armed force. They did so by emigrating away from religious persecution or dire economic circumstances in Europe. The Founding generation formed the United States by prevailing against the Crown's forces in an extended war. We passed the Constitution partly to provide for an adequate defense against the foreign powers scheming to break up the United States. Step by step, we built small but effective armed forces and a defense industry to guard our independence.

Immediately after independence we discovered how much protection Britain had been providing our merchants and sailors. The Barbary Coast pirates of North Africa descended on our merchant ships like

locusts, and we built a small but effective navy to begin protecting ourselves. The War of 1812 is little remembered, but the difficulty of moving
defense supplies to the Great Lakes to build Commodore Perry's fleet
spurred determination to fund and build the Erie Canal three years later,
after being debated for the previous century and a half. We created West
Point not as a war academy on the German model but as America's first
engineering school, so that we would always have the talent in country to
build the fortifications, roads, and bridges needed for our defense. In fact,
many of our first railroads were designed by West Point graduates lent by
the government to the railroad companies – which the Army was happy
to do because they knew how essential their transport capabilities would
be in wartime. Within a few decades, the Civil War would prove them right.

During the Civil War, Confederate troops penetrated as far west as
Arizona. The Confederate threat to California and the prospect of British
intervention brought home the truth that many of America's rich new
possessions on the Pacific Coast were effectively unprotected from foreign invasion. In 1862, in the midst of a war that was not going well, Congress had the foresight to authorize the construction of a railroad to the
Pacific, primarily out of strategic considerations.

For the remainder of the century, the United States and Canada
engaged in a strategic contest to fill the un-farmed lands on the Great
Plains and the areas to their west through railway construction and
aggressive recruitment of settlers. Although the border had been set at
the 49th parallel by treaty, both sides knew that if lands on the other side
of the line were settled primarily by pioneers from their own side, political control could follow the plow, not the treaty.

**A Nation Shaped by War.** Far from being isolated from foreign policy
considerations, America was shaped by such concerns in its most basic
decisions. Every step it has taken had, somewhere, a concern about gaining or preserving national independence and prosperity. Once America
was shaped by the Treaty of Paris at the end of the Revolution, giving it
territory up to the Mississippi River, the United States had a critical foreign policy interest in gaining and maintaining the control of the mouth
of the river, as the entire product of the middle of the country could at first
reach world markets cost effectively only through New Orleans. The interior of North America constitutes the largest piece of fertile land connected

to the global marketplace by a unified transportation system on the face of the globe. Abraham Lincoln, having grown up along the Ohio and Mississippi valleys, knew this as a fundamental truth, and understood that any military price would have to be paid to avoid having New Orleans and the mouth of the Mississippi under the control of a separate nation. Generations of Americans similarly wanted Cuba to be either American territory, or a friendly independent republic, so it could not be used as a military base by hostile powers to threaten exports via New Orleans.

Even though the USA has not been traditionally face-to-face with large hostile powers planning immanent invasion, as was the case with France and Germany, it has been far more aware of military realities than is generally assumed. America has been a global trading nation from its initial colonization, dependent on its agricultural and manufactured exports across the Atlantic. For the first part of its existence, within the British Empire, it was able to rely on the Royal Navy to keep the ocean trading routes open to its ships. For the second phase, from independence through the early twentieth century, it continued to rely on Britain's power as guardian of the freedom of navigation. The US Navy served first as a junior partner in policing the world's ocean, gradually becoming a regional power, then an equal partner, and then, finally, after World War II, becoming the senior power. Guarding the freedom of the seas and our ability to trade unhindered is still the primary task of the US Navy, and there is no effective replacement for that role in sight.

The structure of the United States defense system, its choice of weapons and tactics, and the United States' foreign policy all bear the mark of the previous century and its three great struggles, first with German ambition for European hegemony, secondly with German National Socialism and Japanese Imperialism and their hegemonic ambitions, and finally the protracted struggle with Soviet communism. Each of these historical struggles drove a large and deep mobilization of American strength and the attendant centralization of the American economy and political systems. The whole story of the rise of America 2.0 and its institutions, as we have seen, is inextricably tied up in the mass mobilizations for the two World Wars and the subsequent Cold War.

Since the end of the Cold War, Americans have been suspended between two competing desires. On the one hand, to continue the familiar mobilizations, but oriented toward a new enemy, whether it be China,

Islamic radicalism, or a resurgent Russia. On the other hand, to demobilize and retreat either into an isolationist regime that never deploys a soldier beyond our borders in peacetime, and turns the task of world order over to a (largely illusionary) mechanism of international governance.

At first, the September 11, 2001 attacks seemed to demonstrate that retreat was impossible. The sources of the attack would have to be tracked down and confronted abroad. We looked on our successful history of leading a grand alliance to destroy totalitarian regimes and replace them with prosperous, peaceful allies, and hoped to "drain the swamp" of the impoverished, volatile Mideast and its violent, aggressive regimes. The quick success in toppling the loathsome Taliban regime in Afghanistan led to the hopes of a similar quick decapitation of the Saddam Hussein regime in Iraq, followed by a patient but inexorable construction of a viable, democratic model state that would provide a contagious example for the Mideast.

Over a decade later, with a very substantial sacrifice of lives and fortune, these efforts, although not totally unsuccessful, have produced little that would encourage any American or other nation to repeat the experience. The results probably will serve as a deterrent to a similar effort for at least a generation. The fundamental reason for efforts by America and other industrialized nations to remake unfree societies in the mold of a free society (as we know it) comes from the value of freedom. The limited success in actually fulfilling that vision, however, is based on the differences between our understanding of the nature of freedom and that of other peoples. These differences are real, and set real limits on what can be accomplished in intervening in other nations' affairs, and also suggest which means are more likely to succeed, and which less so. These limits also have consequences for the sorts of alliances the USA should and should not enter into, the sorts of military actions that we should prepare ourselves to fight, and thus the forces and force structures we should prefer.

**Individualism and the Limits of Universalism.** The classic Chinese strategist Sun Tzu famously said, "If you know both yourself and your enemy, you may win a hundred battles without jeopardy." America has too often failed to understand either itself or its enemy, for to think that there is no real difference between the two is to know neither.

The truth about ourselves we must understand is that we have a strong preference for individual freedom and autonomy, and are reluctant to compromise it. We are indifferent to inequality of outcome so long as we think it has been achieved fairly, and we are not even willing to compromise autonomy very much to give members of society an equal start. The idea of fraternity or solidarity with other members of our society is weak relative to that of other cultures, although we are willing to extend a helping hand to those we consider deserving, and are more generous with individual charity than many other cultures. The truth about other cultures that we are reluctant to understand is that the great majority of cultures on this planet order their preferences differently, and have no desire to change their cultures to more closely resemble ours, although many of them would like to enjoy its benefits if they could do so without otherwise changing.

This means that our ability to accomplish "nation-building" and change other cultures is much weaker than the more idealistic among us believe. The impact Americans may have also varies from culture to culture. Some historical cases that appear to have been successful nation-building actually had little to do with our own efforts.

The classic example of this is the US experience with rebuilding Western Europe and northeast Asia after World War II, compared with more recent "nation-building" exercises. When we began these tasks in 1944 and 1945, as areas were liberated, the task seemed daunting. Much of the physical infrastructure had been flattened by bombing and artillery. Large numbers of people were homeless, and many were displaced persons, including millions of Germans expelled from Eastern Europe, many of whom were premodern peasants who had never seen Germany before. Many nations had no civil government, or ones in which many officeholders and civil servants had been badly tainted by collaboration with the Nazi or Japanese occupiers.

Starting from these unpromising circumstances, the Allied Military Government in Europe, and Occupation authorities in Asia, rapidly reestablished communications, transport, and manufacturing. The Marshall Plan loaned money that rebuilt smashed infrastructure, restarted factories, and thus gave ordinary people jobs and homes. In the occupied countries, governments in exile returned, and new elections were held, reestablishing legitimate self-government. Restored courts gave accused collaborators fair trials, the worst were hanged, and the lower-level ones punished and rehabilitated.

Even in Germany and Japan, democratic self-government was gradually restored as political figures were found who had resisted or remained apart from the totalitarian government apparatus. American political ideas were popular, as the German and Japanese constitutions were rewritten with substantial American input. And the local economies and political systems responded vigorously once the immediate postwar problems were overcome. Germany's *Wirtschaftswunder* (Economic Miracle), and France's *Trente Glorieuses* (Thirty Glorious Years) became watchwords for a general postwar boom of restored free trade and expanding economies.

A combination of ready American credit and rapid growth in the restored democracies seemed to demonstrate that the American model was exportable both by military and political power. The rapid recovery of the "Asian Tiger," Japan and, slightly later, the "Four Little Tigers" (Taiwan, South Korea, Hong Kong, and Singapore) also seemed to indicate that the model did not depend on white skin, Western culture, or Christianity. We seemed to have found a universal formula for freedom, democracy, and prosperity (of which the 2.0 model was the particular American flavor), and it began to seem like bringing the rest of the world to similar freedom and prosperity would be a mere mopping-up operation.

**First Flaws Appear in the Model.** The Oil Shock and the stagflation of the 1970s cast doubt on this cheerful and rosy scenario. Suddenly the old policies no longer brought automatic growth and much of the developed world went into a decade-long slump. But by the early 1980s, things seemed to get back on track, at least for some nations and segments of populations. In America and Britain, Reagan and Thatcher cut taxes, trimmed back regulation and privatized some government functions. On the European continent, the "social-market" model was further refined, with elaborate subsidies and protections preserving jobs or subsidizing those out of work so they did not suffer. Japan streamlined its industries and became an even more aggressive exporter. But unlike previous decades, tax cuts in the English-speaking nations, and more elaborate subsidies and welfare benefits on the Continent were not paid out of economic and population growth. The advanced industrial nations had begun to experience a fertility decline of unexpected proportions that had undercut all the assumptions of the modern welfare state.

It was at this point that the advanced nations of the West and developed East Asia began to diverge more visibly in their paths. The English-speaking democracies in general chose to stop subsidizing uncompetitive industries and encourage innovation and new company starts. They accepted the decline of classical blue-collar manufacturing employment but saw the creation of many new jobs, new business sectors, and new companies. They saw regions dominated by traditional manufacturing employment decline and lose population as many moved to areas with cheaper housing and nontraditional employment: Florida and the Southwest in the United States, Alberta in Canada, Western Australia in Australia, and the far exurbs of London in the United Kingdom. In the social democracies of continental Europe, the governments began to borrow heavily to subsidize existing manufacturing jobs and support the unemployed at high levels of income rather than accept their decline. Nations with high-value industries like Japan and Germany poured more effort into exporting more and more valuable goods, climbing the value ladder as they came under more and more competition at the lower end of the marketplace.

For several decades, all of these strategies more or less worked. The model was even able to accommodate the entry of China into the world marketplace in a big way, as they began to undercut every other low-cost exporter. The Soviet Union collapsed after their elite classes began to realize that they could benefit far more from taking their copious natural resources and selling them on the global marketplace, pocketing the profits, than they could by the old system of using the same resources in grossly inefficient factories turning out junk that nobody would voluntarily buy. Economists typically calculate industrial output in terms of value added, which is to say the difference between the cost of the resources and labor that went into making a good or service, and the market price that good or service can fetch. In studying the former Soviet Union and its satellites, they discovered that most manufacturing actually subtracted value – the raw materials alone being worth more on the world market than the products of the factory. Once the leaders realized they could personally pocket the difference, the Soviet system was assured of collapse. The Chinese, who had fewer natural resources relative to population, were able to adjust their manufacturing to ensure that their factory outputs could actually be sold at a profit provided the labor was cheap enough. So far, the Chinese have been successful through that strategy, though the impending end of cheap labor and an aging population are going to present China with serious challenges.

By the 1990s the international system had restabilized and seemed to be adjusting to these profound changes. Prosperity and constitutional government seemed to be spreading as well, as the Mediterranean nations like Greece, Spain, and Portugal had thrown off dictatorships in the 1970s, joined what became the European Union and NATO, and began to share in modern prosperity. Similarly, many of the post-Soviet states of Eastern Europe enjoyed a return to democracy, although the Balkans and many former Soviet republics failed in many ways. Even Latin America, which had been sunk into military dictatorship, populist demagoguery, and political crony capitalism for many decades, began to reform itself as Chile, Argentina, and Brazil returned to functioning democracy, currency stability, and reforming market economies, and experienced a boom in consequence. The toolkit of liberal democracy and market reform, after a number of misadventures and detours, seemed to be on track toward global prosperity once again. Only Africa and the Mideast seemed to be stuck in poverty, and there were hopeful signs of reform there as well.

**The Current World Crisis as a Global Collapse of the 2.0 Model.** However, the subsequent decade has brought to the surface serious problems with the model of universal development. These problems have begun to call into question whether it is in fact a model that works for everyone, everywhere, given enough time, or whether the social transitions of modernity are highly culture-dependent, with some cultures adapting to modernity readily, some only with great difficulty, and others not at all. This, if true, would have great implications for the foreign and defense policy the United States has been following since the end of World War Two, and particularly since 1990.

These problems included Japan's entry into a prolonged slump in the early 1990s, from which it has not yet recovered. Ominously, the ongoing collapse in Japan's fertility rate, which is on the verge of beginning a permanent and accelerating reduction in Japan's population, appears to be a major driver of this slump. Toward the end of the 1990s, a series of melt-downs of emerging economies, first in Asia, and then in Argentina and other Latin American reforming economies, began to call into doubt the idea of steady forward progress in emerging economies. The Argentine default and abandonment of its hard-currency peg was particularly cata-strophic and has resulted in the return of demagogic politics, which is once again, as in the 1980s, beginning to express itself in military threats in its region.

The largest problems, however, have been the September 11 attacks on the United States and the subsequent wars they triggered, the failure of the United States to regain a sustained growth economy, and the fall-out of the global meltdown of October 2008. It is one thing for an eco-nomic model to encounter problems in extending itself to dissimilar cultures; it is another thing to see dysfunctionality in the heartlands of these models. What is actually going on here, and how does it affect the world of America 3.0?

It is important to realize that the global financial crisis that reached a crisis inflection point has deep roots reaching back many decades, and that all was not wonderful with the United States through either the sec-ond Bush or Clinton administrations, despite the partisan claims of vari-ous flavors. The institutions of America 2.0 had been growing increasingly unworkable over previous decades, and it was only by a combination of the deep reserve strengths of America (the culture, not the government) and a series of one-time tricks pulled by various administrations that had allowed prosperity to continue, at least in fits and starts.

The institutions of America 2.0, as we discussed in Chapter 6, emerged in response to a series of real problems, and for the most part managed to fix or at least alleviate those problems. Yet in solving them, they created new ones, in many cases problems that would not show themselves fully for decades, often under conditions never anticipated during the Pro-gressive era. The Progressives and New Dealers believed that business was consolidating itself into fewer and fewer large corporations, who among themselves would plan the future of technology and lead the economy permanently. So long as this corporate structure could be regu-lated and steered by the government, and so long as the individual workers could be given security and stability through membership in government-approved labor unions, this was all fine with Progressives.

They believed this was the natural direction of social evolution, and that the main problems they faced were those of stabilizing this economy and making it fairer. Almost all social and economic legislation and regulation under both the Wilson and Roosevelt-Truman administrations was guided by this philosophy.

Internationally, following World War II, Progressives saw an opportunity to spread this enlightened pattern globally, working with European Social Democrats and Christian Democrats, who had similar visions, to install variants of this system wherever they had influence. American Progressives and their European colleagues set up a series of international organizations based on the ideal of free trade among regulated market economies, which would naturally become dominated by large benevolent regulated corporations, aided by progressive political parties and their labor union allies.

The United States and its allies created a system of international organizations to impose what they hoped would be an increasingly comprehensive international regulation and policing of this order. The Bretton Woods international financial system (and its operational components, the IMF, the World Bank, and the General Agreement on Trade and Tariffs), the European cooperative mechanisms that eventually became the European Union and the Organization for Economic Cooperation and Development, and in security, NATO and its less successful knockoffs SEATO and CENTO. These all connected the USA, its Western European allies, and various sympathetic states in Asia and Latin America. The postwar planners also had high hopes for a wider, more inclusive set of organizations, flowing downward from what they had hoped would be the crown of the new international system, the United Nations.

Unfortunately for their hopes, the UN was based on the idea that the Soviet Union would continue its wartime cooperation with the United States and its Western allies, gradually mellowing its totalitarian system as the West gradually widened the centralized, directive element in its systems, until all of the powers converged on a single, benign, administrative social model. This "convergence theory," as it was known, was fundamentally wrong. Communism had established itself in a series of cultures that had no liberal roots, as Westerners understood them. Those cultures were communitarian and authoritarian by nature and, in fact, were hostile to Western assumptions even without the incessant propaganda of their governments. Thus, there were no internal forces driving toward fundamental liberalization as we know it.

However, there was in each country a particular historical set of institutions, practices, and customs that were in contradiction to the peculiarly Western religion of Marxism. Marxism, in this story, is best understood as a sort of Christian heresy, driving like Christian theology to an End Times beyond which lay Heaven, but rather than being driven by God and his Grace, it was driven by a sort of depersonalized god named History, and which would, through an Armageddon named The Proletarian Revolution, led by an elect known as the Vanguard, bring about Heaven on Earth. It was easy for a restless minority of Western intellectuals to adopt this religion.

It was even easier for students from the premodern lands of Russia and China, eager to learn and copy the secrets of Western success, to adopt this religion as well, which seemed to offer a relatively easy and accessible salvation to their own peoples. After all, Western nations had had to go through a lengthy process of Bourgeois Revolution, and still needed to undergo Proletarian Revolution as well. Lenin, Trotsky, and Mao fell in love with the idea that their lands might be able to compress these steps, which had required centuries in the West, into a single quick step. Furthermore, they believed that bourgeois individualism (which they mistakenly thought was a recent development in Europe) was needed for the bourgeois revolution, but became an impediment to the proletarian revolution. They reasoned that it was therefore possible to arrive at the final destination of communism more rapidly that the West, if only the vestiges of (what they thought of as) feudalism, superstition, and tradition could be thrown off under the leadership of enlightened elite, namely them.

**The Free World: Some Countries Were Freer Than Others.** The period between 1917 and 1992 was not a binary opposition between the Free World and Communism. It was actually a three-sided contest. In one corner were a relatively small group of nations that had cultures that lent themselves to modern democratic market societies with relative ease. Most of the rest of the world had substantial cultural barriers to the full toolkit of modernity, democracy, and market economies. Several large nations – Russia and China, noticeably – had such premodern cultures, but had come under the control of elites who had converted to the Marxism in its Leninist form. Leninist leaders were able to use the communitarian and authoritarian elements of their cultures to form strong states with effective military and police services and enough industrial base to equip themselves for modern warfare. The Soviet Communists brought under their control a group of neighboring nations, some of which had similarly communitarian and authoritarian systems, but others of which did not. The latter were occupied militarily and ruled through a system of collaborators and opportunists.

Most of the rest of the cultures of the world were not modern, not democratic, and had only partially instituted a market economy. However, they also tended to adhere to religious, social, and cultural customs and institutions that found the Marxist religion uncongenial at a minimum, and often abhorrent. Although small groups of intellectuals might convert to Marxist beliefs, usually while studying abroad, few Marxist mass movements formed. First local elites, and eventually Western intelligence services, learned to recruit various sectors of these traditional societies and strike deals with indigenous movements and entities to ally themselves with the West against the Marxist powers, in return for being permitted to run their states consistent with their various values and goals. Often the deal required they adopt at least pro forma certain modern forms and institutions, such as legislatures and elections, but rarely was any attempt made to genuinely implement modernity. Often the Western nations settled for what amounted to planting seeds of reform – starting schools and universities; bringing promising students or young military officers to the West for education and implementing some rural or labor reform, in the hopes that it might help push those nations eventually toward modernity.

Part of the deal was terminating any outright colonial rule from European powers and setting up local elites as rulers of independent states treated equally to long-existing nation-states under the Westphalian system. This often created a minuscule layer of Western-educated local elites living a superficially modern lifestyle in local capital cities, raking off profits from the former colonial export industries (often still owned by corporations in the former colonial power, happy to pay off the local elites). One of the perquisites of elite status was membership in the international organizations of the UN, which provided many well-paid jobs for the proliferating children of this elite. However, any pretense that the resulting international system constituted a modern world was an illusion. Most of these new nations were entirely dependent on Western government patronage and support, including military support. Below the surface a third of the world's population lived in the deepest form of poverty, enjoying few if any modern services, even basic ones such as clean water to drink, suppression of common infectious diseases, or even civil order, and subject to plague and famine at the slightest provocation.

After World War II the West felt threatened by the presence of huge, well-armed Soviet and Chinese armies on the borders of Western Europe and Japan. Though there was constant Communist propaganda and subversion activities domestically and internationally, the Communist powers found themselves insecure and frustrated by the refusal of the god of history to grant them their final reward. The West had a stubborn ability to thrive and organize resistance to them throughout the rest of the world. The Communists had conquered Russia and China comparatively easily. The bulk of the population, after some initial resistance from traditional forces, had accepted rule from the center and provided the masses of soldiers and police who did not hesitate to apply force as ordered.

Once beyond these culture areas already predisposed to collectivism and authoritarianism, however, nobody was similarly cooperative, and many groups were incredibly stubborn in their resistance. The Ukrainians, even though close cultural cousins of the Russians, were adamant in clinging to their little private farms, and had to be starved into joining the collectives. Poles held fast to their Catholicism. Hungarians, incredibly, did not hesitate to pick up their guns and fight against overwhelming odds. The Eastern Germans, despite the best standard of living in the Soviet bloc, kept deserting to the West whenever their watchdogs turned their backs.

When the first generations of Marxist true believers died off in Russia and China the next generations were primarily concerned about their own personal benefits within the system. The Party stopped being the vanguard of revolution. The nomenklatura was an oligarchy, a set of privileged families working together to preserve their privileges. They abandoned any real expectation of converting nations beyond their immediate culture area to anything like their real domestic systems.

The Soviets began to acquire proxies in the premodern areas in roughly the same way the Western powers had, by striking an alliance with some sector of the local elite (typically, young military officers) and seizing state control. These nations would be aligned into the outer circle of the Soviet international system, but no attempt would be made to genuinely Sovietize the countries, or, say, integrate them into the Warsaw Pact alliance system. The Soviets acquired these puppet states to deny them to the West, to provide military and intelligence advantages, and to support Soviet positions in international fora like the UN. This had the effect of supporting some rather nasty proxy regimes throughout the premodern world, but other than some marginal military and diplomatic advantages, this tactic did nothing to help the collectivist states keep their heads above water.

**The Communist Systems Falter.** The Soviet and Chinese systems suited their local cultures sufficiently well to function day by day, though with stagnating economies, and to maintain internal security. But they were unable compete in weaponry or military power projection with the West, and particularly with the United States. The United States modernized its forces not just once in the Cold War, but, in effect, conducted a revolution in military affairs at least once every generation. The Soviets had to extract more and more scarce capital from their faltering economy. The Cold War arms race sucked them dry of capital for any other purpose, and limited the self-enrichment of the elites. In the 1980s and 1990s the military systems of the West and the Soviet Bloc were tested in a series of small- to medium-sized wars: The Falkland Islands (1982), the Israeli destruction of a Soviet surface to air missile network in the Bekaa Valley in Lebanon (1982), and the first Gulf War (1991–92). These conflicts demonstrated that even small Western forces using new weapons could rapidly overcome even quite recently armed, sizable, and plentifully equipped forces using previous-generation technologies. Using the electronics of ten years ago was no better than using stone axes, it seemed.

The general stagnation, after a period of initial gains, of technology and economic growth made each successive generation of new military technology harder for the Soviets to match, and used up more and more of the available capacity of the economy. Finally, in the late 1980s, Reagan's Strategic Defense Initiative threatened the deterrent power of Soviet missiles. Whatever the ultimate practicality of SDI may have been, new weapons would be developed which the Soviets would never be able to match. Meanwhile the Soviet bloc's gradual economic integration into the global economy both made it increasingly difficult to alienate international capital sources, while making Soviet elites more and more aware of the value of the raw materials the Soviet Union was wasting internally.

Mikhail Gorbachev took power intending to carry out sufficient reforms to restore some semblance of economic and military self-sufficiency to the Soviet Union. Part of his plan was an intelligent retrenchment of Soviet international exposures. Gorbachev abandoned the costly and unrewarding Third World adventurism of the Brezhnev years, most particularly the Afghan war. He signaled that the Soviet Union could live with less submissive governments in its Eastern European satellites. And he began to placate restive nationalities inside the USSR, attempting to give the pro-forma federalism of the Soviet constitution enough substance to appease at least moderate nationalists. In all cases the Gorbachev program proved too little, too late. The Soviet empire fell apart in two years, leaving a variety of now-independent former satellites, a Russian successor state, and a swarm of independent republics in various degrees of democracy and prosperity.

China's transformation took a different course, with the Chinese Communist Party still intact and in charge of the same one-party state, but having almost entirely abandoned Marxist religion. Instead, without becoming democratic, China reverted to something like its traditional version of a market economy, in which family ties and state influence played a large role. In fact, the numerous state-owned and military-owned enterprises and the large role of state-owned banks have blurred the line between private and state ownership, with the common thread of oligarchy the key element.

Although this oligarchy has resulted in an unequal and often unfair society, it has been tolerated and to some extent welcomed by large sectors of the Chinese population because it has delivered, and has continued to deliver, a rapidly growing prosperity to broad but not universal sectors of the Chinese population. China has captured a large part of the world market for manufactures, and has continually expanded the breadth of its export sectors. It has become a voracious consumer of raw materials and energy resources, creating demand and driving prices up globally.

China has also upgraded its military and raised its regional and global profile. Although its capabilities are inferior to those of US forces, it is not so far behind that it would be possible for the US to militarily dominate China, short of absolute destruction, considering the size of China's forces and the extent of Chinese territory. China also continues to upgrade its forces and weapons technologies, including through industrial espionage, and is narrowing the capability gap with the United States.

**The End of History: The Failure of Universalism in the Post–Cold War Era.** The foreign policy and defense situation of the United States has entered a new era. It is not merely beyond the Cold War. It is beyond the hopeful post-war decade of the 1990s, in which it was possible to imagine the swift democratization of both Russia and China. And it is beyond the post–September 11 decade, in which there was both the fear of repeated or worsening urban mass terrorism attacks and a global jihadist insurrection, and a hope of a reconstructed and democratized Middle East, a drained swamp turned into a flowering meadow, by a new liberating US-led alliance.

None of these things happened. More than anything else, the past two decades have been an illustration of the limits of universalism. Russia today is a somewhat better place than the Soviet Union. Wealth is spread more widely, and people are freer in several important ways, particularly in being free to travel and emigrate. They are also freer to receive information from the rest of the world, thanks to the Internet. Their political and economic freedoms are only partial and under threat from a grasping oligarchy allied to a widespread criminal underground. China, similarly, although it is now much more open to the world, has made very few moves toward political liberalization, much less democracy. Both Russia and China remain obstructive in the United Nations, and often aid repellent regimes in the Third World. It is often the only card they have to play. They can act as "spoiler" in any international forum but clearly understand that the larger economic decisions and financial arrangements in the global economy will be made with or without their cooperation.

The other post-Communist states have had mixed results. Their post-Soviet progress toward liberal market democracy has reflected very closely the various strength of civil society in each country before they came under totalitarian control in the twentieth century. What is now the Czech Republic, the Baltic states, and to a lesser degree Poland and Hungary had thriving liberal civil societies prior to Nazi and Communist invasion. They have recovered the best today. The former East Germany, a special case, continues to lag its fellow citizens to the West, partly because it was crippled by a premature currency union. Bulgaria and Romania had poor records historically, and struggle today. The Muslim republics of Central Asia, which never had a history of democracy or civil society, do not have democratic governments today.

The hoped-for transformation in the Middle East has not happened. There were great hopes that the Palestinian Authority enabled by the Camp David accords would establish a functional civil society on the West Bank and Gaza that would gradually evolve into a Palestinian state in a peaceful relationship with Israel. Instead, the Palestinian Authority has lost legitimacy, and Gaza has been taken over by the Islamicist Hamas that acts as a proxy for Iran and rejects the very idea of a peaceful two-state solution.

The Bush administration and its neoconservative advisors had hoped that a liberated Iraq would serve as a model of a democratic and liberal Islamic republic that could accommodate Sunni, Shia, and Kurdish populations in a modernizing Iraqi state. Similar dreams were offered for the Pashtun and other ethnic groups of Afghanistan, in a modernizing state. Instead, after a great investment of money and combat casualties, Iraq has achieved a fragile peace still interrupted by jihadist bombings. The country is heavily manipulated through Iranian influence in the Shia population, as well as other external actors. Meanwhile in Afghanistan the Taliban have not been beaten, and neither peace nor much progress in social reconstruction has occurred. By many metrics Afghanistan has not even gotten back to the level of the monarchy that was overthrown by a Soviet-backed coup in 1975.

Most recently, the so-called Arab Spring of 2012 has seen the overthrow of a series of Arab-nationalist authoritarian governments throughout the Middle East and their replacement with Islamist parties of various (and yet to be fully disclosed) degrees of radicalism. If the invasion and attempted reconstruction of Iraq was an example of universalist optimism of the Right, support of the Arab Spring has been an example of universalist optimism of the Left.

Americans, typically on the political Left, have sometimes mistaken the essence of democracy as its mechanisms of participation, such as universal suffrage, multiparty elections, and majority rule. Although all of these things are good, they are effects, rather than causes of democracy. The essence of democracy actually lies in making all citizens of a nation stakeholders in that society, and all stakeholders, citizens. Historically, this has been done by two principal means. One is by extending the franchise to all who paid taxes, and by all who pay taxes demanding the vote. The other is by extending the franchise to all who are called on to fight for the country, and by all who fight demanding the vote. Each of these paths has ancient roots; for the first, it goes back, directly, to the municipal corporations of the self-governing cities of the Middle Ages, which any tax-paying property above a certain minimum value carried with it the right to vote in the corporation's elections. The other lay in the tribal councils of the European tribes, where every armed man voted in an annual assembly, a process that can still be seen in the smaller cantons of Switzerland today.

Democracy arose from communities in which the great majority of citizens felt connected to the society in which they lived, and the great majority of voters knew that their vote would have consequences: a tax they would have to pay, or a war in which they would have to fight. At the same time, they knew, unlike subjects of despotic nations or empires, that they had some control over negative consequences of government: If taxes grew too high, they could elect governments that would lower them, and if a war proved foolish or poorly conducted, they could elect a government that would make peace, or correct errors in the war's conduct. As a result of these policies being at least roughly honored over time, democratic societies also developed a shared belief that government's actions would benefit all, rather than one group at the expense of another. Even when some actions clearly benefited some sections more, as when, for example, rich regions saw their taxes used disproportionately to build roads in poorer regions, this was accepted on the basis that (as in this example) a national road network made the whole country richer over time, and easier to defend.

Despotic countries, on the other hand, have few if any of these traditions and little or no experience of state power, like taxation or conscription, being used for the general good. Their experience was precisely the opposite: the group that controlled the government used it to take from other sectors and give to themselves. Having democratic elections did not change this pattern. The elected officials used their power to enrich themselves, their families, or their ethnic and/or religious groups at the expense of others, and to use the state to rig all future elections so that their group would remain on top. This is sometimes described as corruption, but that is a bit of a misnomer. Corruption implies that a system has been distorted to work in a way other than it was intended to work. In these nations, the point of the system is to enrich those in power, so when it does so, it is functioning precisely as intended. Nor should officials in such a system be seen as immoral people, at least by their own understanding. In such countries, the family systems ideologies typically hold that the primary ethical duty of a person is to help his own family first, and a judge who (for example) awarded possession of a piece of disputed property to a stranger over a member of his own family would be seen as a bad person who had failed his primary ethical duty.

The consequence of these realities is not that democracy is bad, or even that democracy can never work outside of a minority of nations. There are examples of functional democracy in a wide variety of places, some of which would have seemed at first glance unlikely to succeed. However, it is a reality that democracy is not a certain solution, and cannot be airlifted into place without preconditions being present and automatically expected to work. A foreign policy based primarily on "democracy-promotion" and "nation-building" is one that will fail more times than not, and will fair to deliver other important goods that foreign policies should pursue, such as peace, stability, and friendliness toward America. Imperfections can be deplored, and the United States can encourage progress toward democracy, particularly in things like widespread access to education and more stable property rights for all. But we should recognize that our ability to affect distant and very different nations is limited, and the inability to make much progress in directions we find desirable should not be a reason to avoid trade and cooperation with such nations.

## AFTER UNIVERSALISM: WHAT TO CHANGE, WHAT TO KEEP

The foreign and defense policy of the United States is an enormous subject, with many contending schools composed of full-time experts who have mastery of the details. We cannot get to that level in this book. We will not discuss military doctrine, force structure, or particular platforms. We will not advocate any particular strictly military strategy for employment of US military power, let alone tactics to be used. Nor will we discuss the division of labor between the various branches of the military in executing the broad policies we advocate. We also refrain speculating about game-changing technological breakthroughs, which are highly likely in the years ahead.

We also do not need to discuss the US nuclear deterrent force. We strongly believe that the United States should maintain a strong and credible nuclear deterrent. The existence of this capacity has brought an unexpected measure of peace to the world, so far, and has pushed conflict away from large-scale conventional war. This is a top defense priority now and it should not change.

What, then, does a foreign and defense policy for America 3.0 look like? Some aspects of the new policy are not too different from what we have been doing since the end of the Second World War. For one thing, the United States has invested an enormous amount of money, human effort, and political capital to create capabilities and relationships around the world, many of which are useful now and would continue to be useful in the future. It costs much less to maintain them in place that it did to create them originally, and it will certainly cost less to maintain them than to recreate something like them in the future if we were to abandon them now.

For example, we are not convinced that America's large aircraft carriers are obsolete. If anti-ballistic weapons will soon be feasible, then having these big hulls will provide the massive power generation needed to run a battery of lasers or railguns at sea. History shows that sea power always seesaws back and forth between big hulls and small, fast ships. It would make little sense to abandon these platforms now without a high degree of certainty they would not be needed again, and in a world likely to undergo substantial change in the next two decades, there can be no such certainty.

In addition to technical capabilities, the USA is blessed with a valuable set of critical defense alliances and structures: NATO, the US–Japan Security Treaty, ANZUS, UKUSA, and NORAD. These, especially NATO, may require restructuring and repurposing to take into account new realities, but the basic structures are valuable and would be difficult to replace.

It took a great deal of effort to standardize military systems across NATO; it does not cost much to continue to maintain those systems and standards, but if they were allowed to diverge again, it would be expensive to re-standardize them.

At present, much of NATO is still oriented around defending Western and Central Europe against a land invasion from the East. This is a far less likely scenario now than it was for the majority of the organization's existence. At the same time, new threats outside of the European area are far more likely. NATO should continue to guarantee the defense of its members' territories. However, to the extent that NATO members are willing and able do so, they should assist the USA as a guarantor of the world's maritime and aviation commons, the high seas and the international air lanes above them.

The United States, as a global trading nation, has an irreducible interest in seeing these commons remain open. The first thing any enemy wishing to hurt us has always done is to strike at our trade. We could abandon any other foreign-policy goal before we could abandon this one. Our NATO allies have a similar interest, and they could possibly be of some use if they chose to do so. It would mean steering some of their defense investment, as well as ours, away from land warfare, and more toward sea and air war. This would be a significant shift, but it would complement their desires to remain competitive in the sorts of high technology needed to dominate in those areas. The recent examples of war in Libya and Mali highlight the harsh constraints on European military deployments. They are years, and hundreds of millions of euros, from providing adequate logistical and reconnaissance capabilities for their own troops.

The second, related change would be to expand NATO's formal operating area beyond Europe to include the high seas globally, and to consider adding compatible partners outside of NATO's traditional area, most particularly Australia and Japan, and probably Singapore and New Zealand. This would also give the alliance a worldwide chain of bases, taking into account British and French insular possessions around the globe as well, making it easier for the alliance to shift to its new global role without dependence on basing rights in less stable and less closely aligned nations on the Eurasian mainland. This strategy could be made more attractive to some partners by including a NATO guarantee of territorial integrity for their insular possessions, freeing their resources from the sometimes-considerable expense of preparing to defend them unilaterally, as is the case of the British with the Falklands, or the French with their Pacific Islands.

Existing defense ties with Israel should be maintained, particularly in the field of advanced technology such as missile defense and in intelligence sharing regarding terrorist threats. The political impetus to support Israel is strong in the United States, it is broadly based, and there is little sign that it will diminish in the future. The highly competent Israeli Defense Force, as well as Israel's nuclear deterrent, allows the United States to serve as a backstop without needing to commit its own forces. Nonetheless, America's security guarantee to Israel enhances stability in the region.

**Bloc Theory: Another Geopolitical Fad.** Beyond guaranteeing the freedom of the seas and air lanes, US foreign policy should aim at an open world system, economically and in opposition to any attempts to construct alliances against the United States, or to divide the world into aligned, competitive blocs. Over the past two decades, there has been an intellectual fad based on the idea that the post–Cold War world is forming into a series of regional blocs. In this analysis, the European Union is the first and most advanced of these blocs, but rival blocs along similar lines are forming in North America, East Asia, and elsewhere. Countries will follow the European path and eventually form a North American Union under US leadership, and an East Asian Union, which initially was predicted to be under Japanese leadership, but now is typically described as being under Chinese leadership.

This bloc theory is elegant and seems plausible, but it has a notable flaw: there is no evidence that this is actually happening. There is considerable evidence that something other is emerging instead. In fact, the principal evidence that other blocs are forming outside of Europe consists of proposals for such blocs from academics who themselves are promoting bloc theory; thus, it has the characteristics of a completely circular argument. The only actual example of a free-trade area growing into a customs union and then a political union is the European Union itself, and in that instance, its founders had intended the final outcome all along, and had designed built-in accelerators of the process in the founding agreements.

Bloc theorists had pointed to the signing of the North American Free Trade Agreement (NAFTA), which came into effect in 1994 between the United States, Canada, and Mexico as a parallel step that would be followed in relatively quick order by the formation of a North American Union (NAU) on the EU model. But this ignores a number of realities. To begin with, even the earliest precursor of the EU, the European Coal and Steel Community (1952) was from the beginning more ambitious than NAFTA. NAFTA is a trade agreement, pure and simple: three sovereign nations agree that if the others lower their trade barriers to them, they will lower their own trade barriers reciprocally. There are some details, and several arbitration mechanisms to deal with details of implementation that might not be anticipated or spelled out in detail in the agreement.

There is no separate NAFTA bureaucracy or organization, unlike the European Union and its precursors, which deliberately created as large a bureaucracy as possible dedicated to expanding their scope, authority, and budget. Most importantly, there is no North American Unionist "movement" on the model of the Europeanist movement, and few if any politicians in any of the three member states are advocating such a Union. On the contrary, to the extent the public in the three countries is aware of the idea, they are vigorously opposed to any deepening of NAFTA or movement toward a North American Union. The concept, in fact, is the subject of various conspiracy theories who maintain that such a project is secretly further along than is publicly known. There is no indication that such concerns are correct; it appears to be part of a circular form of reasoning on the part of bloc theorists. "The world is forming into regional blocs. Therefore the North American states should form one of their own. What is the proof the world is forming into these blocs? Why, there is discussion of turning NAFTA into a North America Union. Discussion among whom?" When you get down to it, the only people discussing a North American Union are the bloc theorists themselves.

East Asia, the other potential "bloc" candidate, not only shows no movement toward becoming a bloc of its own, but in fact represents a history of movement in the opposite direction. Until 1945, Japan, Korea, Taiwan, and Manchuria were in effect a unified, highly integrated economic bloc under the Japanese Empire. At the end of the war, the Allies broke up the Empire. Manchuria became part of China, and after 1948 Taiwan, North Korea, South Korea, and Japan became entirely separate independent states. Except for North Korea, every one of these states became prosperous and advanced as independent states. There is today a Trans-Pacific Partnership of democratic nations, APEC, and an organization, the Association of Southeast Asian Nations, ASEAN, that has sponsored a preferential tariff agreement (AFTA) that reduces but does not eliminate tariffs among its members. There is no active proposal to form a comprehensive trade agreement on the scope of NAFTA, and even less for an analogue to the European Union.

The Shanghai Cooperation Organization (SCO) consisting of China, Russia, Kazakhstan, Kyrgyzstan, Tajikistan, and Uzbekistan has strengthened defense and economic ties between China and Russia. The SCO incorporates the "stans," former Soviet republics of Central Asia, with their energy and mineral resources, into a joint Russian-Chinese led entity. Neighboring states, including India are Observer members, and taken together the SCO contains half of humanity. The members have engaged in joint counterterrorism exercises, and may have a major impact in denying Central Asia as a base for Islamic extremism. China has provided development aid for the Central Asian members, and may come to dominate the region by "yuan diplomacy." It has pushed for a United States withdrawal of all forces from Central Asia. Whether this enormous aggregation can even form a bloc remains to be seen. The potential for disputes and conflict between Russia and China may prevent the SCO from acting as a coherent bloc. It is too early to say what role the SCO will play, but it certainly has the resources and potential to be a major actor in the future.

None of the other regional associations or free trade areas forming globally is showing signs of cohering into EU-type supernational organizations either. MERCOSUR, the South American free-trade area of Brazil, Argentina, Uruguay, and Paraguay (now including Venezuela, with Paraguay suspended) is successful as a free-trade area. It is now implementing a common market, but the pace of movement toward unification, particularly as Argentina struggles to maintain basic economic stability, remains open to question. South American nations have also created a process to create a Union of South American Nations, on the EU model, but this remains largely a statement of intent at present. Similarly, the African Union is an intergovernmental organization with a stated goal of closer union, but few signs of actually implementing it.

To some extent, the proliferation of would-be EU look-alikes is life imitating art, a self-fulfilling prophecy of the advocates of the regional bloc theory. Whereas the EU started as a concrete, functional organization for integration of the Western European coal and steel industries, and only gradually, over decades, acquired the state-like trappings of symbols and permanent bureaucracies, the African and Latin American organizations went for symbolism first, substance later. It is more likely that the European Union will remain a one-off organization, born of a particular and unique set of historical circumstances, than it will represent a template whose substance will become the form of the world to come. And should it come to economic harm in coming years, its impact on the unifying aspirations of other regions of the world will be substantial. Just as America 2.0 is showing its age, the international appetite for big bureaucracies and multilateral agreements may run up against the limits of national budgets.

**Language, Culture, and Cooperation.** If regional blocs are not to be the building blocks of this century's world, what will be? It may not be any one single pattern. At least some of the current members of the European Union will probably continue to cooperate closely in some organization, whether the EU itself or some successor organization. Other patterns of cooperation will also emerge. We have written before of an emerging phenomenon we call the "Network Commonwealth," which is an alignment of nations, not necessarily nearby geographical neighbors, who share common ties that may include language, culture, and common legal systems. It would be linked together with trade agreements, defense communities, and an increasingly seamless web of modern electronic communications. Destined to never become a state, but linking like states together more closely than mere allies of convenience, the Anglosphere, composed mainly of the English-speaking nations, has come a long way along this path without particularly intending to travel it, or even noticing, until recently, that it had. Other linguistic communities, such as those of Spanish-speakers, French-speakers, and even Portuguese-speakers have seen similar tendencies emerge, forming a nascent "Francosphere," "Hispanosphere" and "Lusosphere."

In a world where English is the primary commercial, scientific, and academic language, why does the fact that a nation have English as its native language mean that it should be closer to America for trade or alliance purposes? Language per se is not of primary importance. Cheap translator software is eroding strictly linguisitc barriers. Rather, language is a marker for culture, including the important things we have discussed as underpinning the American way of life and its values. The American family is in fact the ancient family system of the English-speaking world, and it is something we share with other native English-speaking nations and only a handful of others; for example, parts of the Netherlands and Denmark. These family systems in turn influence issues like radius of trust, parental expectations of independence and self-reliance in children, and children's expectations of independence from the control of their parents, coupled with a lack of a firm sense of entitlement to family wealth. Students who travel to the English-speaking world for education or career opportunities are exposed to the absolute nuclear family model just as they are forming their own families, often far from the obligations of clan, tribe or patriarch in their home country. Whether they stay in an Anglosphere country or return home, they may well find the ANF type of marriage personally compelling.

Such things in turn influence attitudes toward government and citizens' expectations of independence from government. It drives a "transactional" view of society in which the basic unit is the individual, and the basic relationship is the voluntary contract. This social model has been labeled "Lockean," after John Locke, the British philosopher whose work was the basis of the philosophy Jefferson laid out in the Declaration of Independence. But Locke did not invent the model, he merely articulated the deep-seated historical values that had shaped English, and then American society for centuries. (Locke was also directly involved in the shaping of America; he wrote the original constitution of the colony of Georgia, the first ever to ban slavery.)

Most importantly, the individualist culture of America values fair dealing with strangers under an impartial code of law. Unlike many countries, successful dealing does not require paying off officials or having the judge's cousin as your lawyer. Americans trade best and most successfully, and create joint ventures most freely when dealing with individuals from cultures with similar expectations. Not surprisingly, Britain and America are each other's largest financial partners, while the United

States and Canada are each others' largest trading partners. Most large businesses in the United States start their first foreign ventures in either Britain or Canada. England has been America's largest foreign source of capital from the founding of Virginia onward, and remains so today.

Despite the fact that Americans, British, and Canadians fought what was effectively a series of civil wars within the English-speaking world between 1775 and 1814, we have now been fighting side by side for a century since 1917, as allies in the long series of wars against totalitarianism. The United States has treaties of alliance with many nations today. However, if one defines an ally as somebody who, if you are fighting, shows up with men, guns, ships, and planes. America's allies have been, most consistently, Britain, Australia, and Canada. We believe this is not coincidence, but rather stems from the fact that we see many issues in the world similarly because we share the same fundamental values. As individuals and military units, the people from these four countries have common expectations about how they will deal with strangers and then establish trust on the way to personal friendship. What starts as a temporary obligation between countries often ends up as a dense and enduring web of relationships between professional colleagues that may last for decades.

The English-speaking alliance has been strained in the twenty-first century due to the mismanaged and misconceived wars in Afghanistan and Iraq. Britain, Canada, and to a lesser extent Australia and New Zealand willingly committed forces to these conflicts, but then found that both the American and British commands had unrealistic expectations of what might be achieved by these interventions, and how best to go about it. Neither the initial American interventions in central Iraq nor the "light footprint" tactics of the British forces in Basra worked as hoped. It was only after the coalition forces backed off severely from their initial expectations, made realistic agreements and understandings with local clan heads (frankly, bribing their loyalty, as the Ottomans, the old-time British administrators, and Saddam Hussein had done previously) that things turned around. Surging forces to ensure security, and waiting for the jihadist forces to discredit themselves with the Iraqi populations, was the new approach. The alliance managed to secure an exit without an immediate takeover by overtly hostile forces. At the time of publication, Iraq's long-term future is an open question.

The adventure has illustrated that direct military interventions in cultures with very different understandings and expectations may occasionally be justified for strategic reasons. However, it is unrealistic to expect us to be able to transplant anything like our democracy or liberal order in a short period of time. Nor can we expect the local populations to automatically be enthusiastic about our ideals or goals.

**Between Isolation and Intervention: Force Structure for the Keeper of the Global Commons.** As explained previously, we had been badly misled by our relatively successful experiences in restoring democracy after World War II when we tried to apply those lessons to a very different set of societies. Our failure to adequately understand the limits of transformation in Afghanistan and Iraq, and to limit our objectives in intervening in those countries, in the end strained America's armed forces, those of our allies of conviction, and strained as well the willingness of the public in the allied nations to act in concert with the United States in any future actions that appear to turn out the same way.

The United States must now reorient its national strategy to a primary emphasis on maintaining the freedom of the global commons of air, sea, and space. Secondarily, we must defend the nation and our close allies. Third, we must be capable of intervening when needed, primarily to inhibit the formation of dangerous and aggressive totalitarian powers globally. This more limited set of tasks is less likely to enmesh ourselves and our allies in extended foreign interventions with a large land component. In such conflicts our enemies do not contest ground but rather inflict steady casualties, expecting the Americans to weary of the effort and go home.

A shift to a global commons strategy also increases the likelihood that other current allies, such as continental European nations and Japan, will be useful participants. The quiet and very substantial antipiracy cooperation of OECD navies off the coast of Somalia is a case in point. Some of these nations have good quality sea and air forces, although limited in number. Their populations and political systems have been extremely reluctant to commit ground forces to combat in the various interventions in which they have contributed. Given the chance to participate in international activities which dramatically improve the skills of their military, with minimal diplomatic fuss, most of America's allies will respond positively.

In the case of Germany and Japan many of their neighboring nations also have unpleasant memories of those nations' forces occupying them in World War II, memories that create lingering unease at seeing them deployed beyond national borders again. The use of sea and air forces in international airspace and waters is less problematic. NATO and other alliances continue to be useful vehicles for coordinating such activities. America 3.0 should seek to keep such alliances in being, but at the same time examining whether further forces could be withdrawn from bases in continental Europe, and otherwise reduce our footprint and costs. The so-called "lily pad" approach to force deployment (pre-deployed logistics and training units with almost no combat units) has many benefits.

We expect the world for the foreseeable future to no longer be divided into the two great camps as it was during the Cold War. As a result, the United States has, for the time being, the capacity to return to a more traditional Anglospheric role as a primarily maritime power – or a maritime, air, space, and Internet power. In the event that an imminent threat emerges of a hostile, Eurasian hegemonic challenger, the United States would most likely have to participate in a coalition against it, as it did in the conflicts of the twentieth century. But we appear to be facing a reprieve from that duty in the immediate future, though a China challenge may yet arise.

With the Cold War now two decades behind us, there is no further need to maintain the fiction that the traditional authoritarian states with which we maintained alliances of mutual convenience are also democracies, and part of the "Free World." We should strive for nothing more than normal, friendly trade and international relations with such states. We can hope that they evolve into genuinely liberal societies, and take such actions short of force as may hasten that transition, such as assisting improved education. But we should expect that such reform would be gradual and "home grown," if it occurs at all. In the meantime, America will benefit immensely by the immigration of exceptional individuals from those same countries. As we described above, people respond positively, perhaps even instinctively, to its individualistic culture and family structure. America attracts many a poor person with only the shirt on his back, looking for work. Most of us are descended from someone just like that. But the United States also attracts exceptional scientists, artists, and businesspeople. The positive aspects of American life are communicated back to the "old country" through these channels. If America is genuinely worth imitating, that will be the best form of "nation building."

If the world is neither in a standoff between two contending global coalitions, as it was during the Cold War, nor in the process of coalescing into jostling geographical blocs, as bloc theory suggested, what is the shape of the world to come? How should it affect the defense and diplomatic policies of America 3.0? As we have suggested, the global networks of affinity based on characteristics such as culture, language, and religion will likely be a major component of international relations. But that does not mean these networks will directly confront each other in a new Cold War, or even a new era of great power rivalry. Rather, we expect that it will be an era of shifting coalitions formed and dissolved as events dictate, and of global "frenemies" – countries that we trade and cooperate with on some levels while maintaining a rivalry on others.

We are also entering an era where hostile rivals will have means at their disposal to cause damage and distraction without any party clearly being identifiable as the cause. Modern terrorist tactics already tend in that direction. New tools taking advantage of microminiaturization, ubiquitous surveillance, and geolocation and information technology have the potential to do damage without leaving identifiable traces. We are likely to be in a paradoxical world where such technical capabilities may mean a lot, even as much as infantry and tanks. Although it may be a world without the sort of visible, large-scale war of the type that marked the world wars of the twentieth century, it will almost certainly not be a peaceful and settled world either. As the local versions of the Blue Model fail across the globe, it is likely that there will be a great deal of disruption, and some of it is bound to overflow into civil and nation-to-nation conflict before a new model emerges and becomes settled generally. As a result, the United States will still necessarily maintain well-equipped ground formations, preserve its competency in all aspects of land power, but it will use those capabilities more prudently.

**A 3.0 Military Establishment and Defense Industry: Affording Global Defense with a Constrained Government.** Some savings will occur form reorienting the armed forces of America 3.0 away from nation-building intervention and pulling back land forces currently stationed in Europe and other places not immediately threatened by mass ground invasion. Nonetheless, maintaining naval and air forces capable of keeping control of the global maritime commons will not be cheap. In an era in which the federal government's ability to raise money will be limited compared to today, it is fair to ask how the USA would be able to afford these forces.

There is no single answer to that question. It must be resolved by a multiple attack on current cost levels.

The first part of the attack lies in reform of the Blue Model in general. The procurement of defense and aerospace equipment (i.e., including NASA) at present is one of the worst examples of the America 2.0 bureaucratic system. Some of the rising costs of defense items such as ships and aircraft come from the enormous increase in their individual capabilities. But it is also the case that the procurement system of the US Department of Defense has become so cumbersome that it had added huge and unnecessary cost increases onto such items.

The problems of the defense industry are a stark illustration of why the Blue Model is in crisis. The US defense industry is in effect a victim of its past successes. In particular, the United States astounded the world in World War II by scaling up its defense industry enormously in an unbelievably short period of time. In the years leading up to the war, the European states measured aircraft production in the low hundreds per month, as Britain slowly and painfully rearmed to face Germany. As the United States entered the war, they declared their intent to produce aircraft by the thousands, setting and meeting the ultimate goal of producing ten thousand per month. In meeting these goals, the US government took the attitude that time and numbers of output were far more important than cost, and the industry became structured on that assumption.

During the war, many public complaints led to the creation of a Senate committee to investigate allegations of fraud and incompetence in the defense industry. The committee was led by then-Senator Harry S. Truman. The Truman Committee imposed stricter accounting and more reporting requirements for industries. These practices survived after the war. Over time, this striving for all the virtues of the 2.0 model – uniformity, statistical control, efficiency, and good regulation – led to unintended results that have saddled the defense procurement system with massive and costly inefficiencies.

These come in several forms. Perhaps the most ironic of these causes is the result of these past attempts to control waste and fraud through additional documentation. The Department of Defense requires that the labor time and materials used in building defense items which are priced on a "time and materials" basis, which is the great majority of all such items, be documented in excruciating detail. The costs of doing this are themselves allowed as expenses, so that the government ultimately pays for the costs of this proof. Therefore, when lurid accounts of $600 hammers procured by the Pentagon surface in the press, what is actually happening is a hammer whose functional equivalent might cost $20 in a hardware store is purchased in the Pentagon system, the actual time and materials cost of the hammer might be $60, with an additional $540 in documentation costs to ensure that the government is not being overcharged for the item. (In fairness, many of these examples occur when items usually procured in large quantities are occasionally purchased in small lots, and an arbitrary allocation of overhead costs is added to the price. Items purchased in larger lots would cost less per item. Still, the price would be substantially more than the equivalent civilian item.)

A second major cause is the bureaucracy of the procuring agency itself, which has stretched out the time scales of the average procurement by years compared to previous eras, and typically causes the requirements of the item to be changed, sometimes many times, over the history of the design and development process. Defense contractors have learned to bid relatively simple systems at relatively low costs, knowing that the procuring agency will not be able to resist changing the performance specifications or other aspects of the system before it has finished development. Each requested change runs the cost up and stretches the time to deployment out, at great expense to the government. The delay in deployment then encourages further changes to the system, in response to changing perceptions of need and interim advances in technology. It is often the case that the government would be better off finishing the original system as proposed, and then go on to design and build a replacement system a few years later. (In reality, such a strategy would probably create a crisis for the contractor, because they typically underbid the original proposal with certainty that the government will add expensive changes after the initial award.) But the high cost of the previous system then acts as a deterrent to retiring it too soon.

Finally, the high cost of operating in this system, combined with the difficulty of assembling teams with the highly specialized skills needed to design and build these esoteric technologies, and the substantial investment in accounting departments able to comply with the arcane minutiæ of the Defense Contract Accounting Standards, tends to limit the number of companies in any field qualified to bid on defense contracts. On top of these inherent barriers, the established companies maintain large lobbying divisions in Washington, hiring former Congressmen, former key Congressional staffers, and former generals and admirals, whose very presence on the lucrative corporate payrolls is a tacit promise of financial rewards for those who steer contracts to the right company. No explicit promises need be made for this to have its effect.

The result is a narrow circle of highly capable but expensive companies who dominate their markets. These companies compete for the prime contractor role, but it is understood that the losers will get lucrative consolation prizes in the form of large subcontracts. Skilled engineers and workers are "rebadged" frequently – moved from company to company as contracts change. The armed forces work hard to preserve at least two competitors for every key capability they need, but they are aware of the costs that this system lays on them. Yet it is such a complex system that nobody really knows how to begin to reform it. In the short term, it is easier to lobby for increased appropriations than it is to change the system.

What would defense products cost if the system could be reformed to bring costs into line with commercial, civilian development of items with comparable complexity and performance demands? The best examples come from aerospace, where even civilian airliners and space launchers have such complexity and demands. Large airliner development is a multibillion dollar effort, and today, only two firms worldwide are able to produce a major globally competitive airliner. Each such project is a multibillion dollar gamble. In space, almost every launch system built to date has been a government project produced under the military system of specifications and documentation, as NASA, the European Space Agency, and other national space agencies use the same method, if not identical paperwork.

Only recently have entirely private companies been capitalized sufficiently to produce launch systems using more commercial approaches. One company, Space Exploration Technologies, Inc. (SpaceX), launched a supply capsule to the International Space Station in 2012 and returned it safely to Earth, using its newly developed Falcon 9 rocket. It was developed without traditional cost-plus contracting or the massive documentation required in such contracts. Rather, the government purchased the flight the way they purchase other commercial items in the marketplace, paying only advance deposits as the company demonstrated its capabilities with real-world performance. After the company demonstrated its capabilities in three launches, NASA examined the program and tried to estimate how much it would have cost to produce the identical capability with the government's usual cost-plus contract approaches. It estimated that it would have been over three times the cost, or over a billion dollars for what SpaceX accomplished with three hundred million. Other aerospace engineers believe, on the basis of NASA's recent performance on its now-cancelled Constellation system, that this is an underestimate.

t's important to specify that the engineers of NASA, the Department of Defense, and the big contractor companies are generally honest and competent. It is the system that makes their work slow and expensive. It is more likely that had Falcon 9 been a rocket built under the traditional system, it would rapidly have had its design modified. NASA would have been forced to substitute some components chosen for engineering reasons, but with others less well suited, chosen because their suppliers were in a powerful chairman's home district. These changes would require further expensive modifications to the rocket design and would lengthen the amount of time needed to build the rocket. The entire workforce would be maintained at taxpayers' expense for a much longer period of time, again raising costs. The project would soon be way overbudget and overschedule. It might be halted by Congress, and then restarted after the program was again changed to "save money" by lowering its capabilities (requiring yet more expensive engineering changes) or ordering fewer vehicles built. The restart would itself be costly as many of the original engineers would now be unavailable, being on other projects or having entered other fields, and new staff would have to be familiarized with the project. Such a government-developed rocket could easily have cost ten times as much as Falcon 9, if not even more.

**Reforming Defense Procurement.** These deep-seated structural problems with the US defense and aerospace procurement systems permeate the defense industry. What can be done to ensure that a renewed and reoriented US military can maintain technological superiority while keeping defense costs within limits? A reduced federal budget and re-scoped federal government will be able to afford the mission we have outlined on a sustained basis. This will not be easy, of course. Every system has its advocates and supporters. Every district that enjoys jobs from a contract constitutes a lobby in Congress for the system's continuation. Entire categories of weapons systems – horse cavalry, big-gun battleships – become obsolete through technological change, but it is often not clear when it is time to put these once-critical weapons away for good. Further, obsolete systems often retain some value in particular situations. Once the specialized knowledge needed to maintain and operate a system is dispersed, it becomes very expensive and time-consuming to recreate it again. Military leaders are reluctant to give up a system that took so long and cost so much (often, costly in human life) to acquire. Yet as budgets grow tighter, and taxpayer resistance rises, change must come. Several approaches should be used:

1. Bottom-up capabilities reviews and a base-closure methodology for reducing capabilities. This approach would list the tasks that are essential for the US military to be able to perform, specify the systems and capabilities needed to perform them, and identify systems, units, and personnel to be retired. This should be done on an all-service basis, creating a one-time inclusive list of such actions, which would be subject to a single yes-or-no vote in Congress, with no amendments permitted. This approach was used at the end of the Cold War to close unneeded military bases, and the process, known as the Base Realignment and Closure process, or BRAC, has generally been considered a success, and in fact is one of the better achievements in public administration in recent decades. Serious consideration should be given to applying its methodology to further force reduction and realignment.

2. A thorough rethinking of defense procurement practices. Repeal of the Davis-Bacon Act (which we have advocated already for other issues) would reduce costs in some areas, although in much defense procurement the skills needed would require high wages in any event. Repeal of the Anti-Deficiency Act (which precludes the US government from executing binding multiyear contracts) would be much more to the point. Almost every defense contract is more expensive than it needs to be because the contractor cannot count on it being funded for more than one year, and consequently must

pad the contract (and write in high termination contingencies) to make up for it.

3. Require that the contractor build functioning hardware to bid for competitive contracts whenever feasible. This means, for example, when two or more competing concepts for a fighter aircraft are being evaluated, the proposing companies must build and fly a prototype in a "flyoff" evaluation. This reduces the temptation to grossly underbid a contract by using unrealistic assumptions, and demonstrates at least a minimal capability of building real hardware. This also helps newcomers, because if there is no hardware demonstration, the contract evaluators are more motivated to fall back on a past track record as a guarantee of capability. Even if the government is paying for the flyoff entries, as it should, it will still be far ahead in the calculus.

4. Rethink the entire assumption that strict documentation of time and materials as a basis for contract payment is a cost-effective approach except in production of systems that seriously test the limits of technology. Shift contracting to commercial procurement or firm-fixed-price bidding whenever feasible. Create higher barriers to change orders, and freeze customer requirements early in the contract unless there is strong demonstrated need, such as proof of technological obsolescence of a technology or approach.

5. Encourage commercial spinoffs of defense products, use allied technological capabilities more, and relax technology export rules among close trusted allies to bring in more technological expertise and capital from such allies.

We have ended up with two distinct profiles of high-technology companies. One, the competitive world of commercial high technology, produces large numbers of innovative products at continuously falling prices and increasing capabilities. They are made by networks of companies functioning worldwide, taking advantage of the best talents and capabilities of many nations. They are funded by international markets and venture funds. There is constant churn among these companies as they are continually challenged by new emerging companies with different ideas and approaches, and only those established companies that are able to adapt and reinvent themselves survive.

The other is the world of defense contractors. For the most part, they are distinct from commercial companies, or, like Boeing, have rigid internal divisions between their commercial and contracting sides. They produce small amounts of highly expensive items, and the cost of these items has been steeply rising over the years, although their capabilities have been expanding as well. Developing each new product takes a long time and the development cycles continue to lengthen. One major weapons system still used in combat, the B-52 bomber, is now flown in some cases by the grandchildren of the original pilots. The workforce of these companies is confined by security requirements to US citizens, and almost all such companies are US companies, financed by US capital. There are severe technology export laws making it difficult to sell almost any defense or aerospace product to foreign customers, except for a handful of trusted allied armed forces. The ranks of defense contractor corporations is dominated by a small number of prime contractors who have dominated the field since World War II, if not before. The number of such firms is shrinking as such prime contractors merge, with no new firms arising to challenge them except in a few specialized fields such as software.

Before World War II there were relatively few differences between defense contractors and non-defense contractors, and it was relatively easy for new companies to establish themselves. The Douglas Aircraft Company was started in 1933 as a civilian airliner builder, but by 1942 its principal product, the DC-3 airliner, was being built by the thousands for military use. During the war the entire industrial base was rapidly converted to defense production, with companies like the St. Louis Streetcar Company producing fighter aircraft and the Rock-ola Jukebox Company producing combat rifles.

Yet after the war the line between defense contracting and commercial production calcified, with the two developing into separate worlds. Each regulation that aided this calcification was added for some reason that seemed valid at the time. Some cutting-edge products truly couldn't have been produced in the needed time unless the government guaranteed to pay for the time and materials used, plus a reasonable profit, plus guaranteed termination costs in the event that the program was abruptly cancelled, as they often were. Of course, the companies' bills for time and materials came into question, so it was reasonable to demand documentation of those costs. Then companies found clever ways to circumvent those requirements, so still more documentation was required. It was not desirable to have adversary nations be able to access the latest developments of our defense industry. So it was logical to classify sensitive materials and restrict the number of people who could have access to that technology, and to restrict the export of those technologies. Because the mere written description of a technology was adequate to allow foreigners to copy it in many cases, even open publication of some information became forbidden, slowing down the necessary cross-fertilization that makes technological progress flourish.

Of course, each of these measures bred more unintended consequences. "Cost-plus" contracts (time and materials plus profit) figured profit as a percentage of total costs. This created an incentive to make costs as high as possible, which increased the total profit. Larger total contract size also helped justify higher managerial pay, and shareholders didn't object because the government paid the higher salaries. Meanwhile, the classification system became a convenient means for government managers and contractors alike to bury their mistakes, knowing that the higher a classification was given to a project, the fewer eyes would be examining it, especially eyes from the media. Restrictions on foreign competition and barriers to entry of new companies lessened competitive threats to jobs and contracts. The system of giving consolation prize subcontracts to competition losers and "rebadging" employees for losing companies to the winners meant that so long as a minimum level of competence was assured, a comfortable standard of living with many perquisites was virtually guaranteed. Of course, this way of life had its own frustrations, including particularly arrogant management, mandatory overtime, and disregard for employees' personal lives. In some companies, there is frequent mandatory relocation, and a culture of extreme conformity, all of which further self-select the employee pool and serve to insulate contractor industries from commercial ones.

Breaking down these barriers to cost-effective innovation and development of new generations of defense technology will not be simple or easy. It is also likely that reform will not occur merely because somebody has demonstrated that it would be desirable to do so. There are generations of blue-ribbon commissions and task forces that have studied these problems and have come to the same analysis presented here. Many reform agendas have been drawn up advocating reduction of paperwork, increasing commercial-style procurement, reducing the use of classification, reforming technology export and foreign-capital rules, and repealing perverse legislation such as the Anti-Deficiency Act and the Davis-Bacon Act. Each attempt has come up against the opposition of inertia, corporate and agency self-interest, and a hysterical media ready to take any incident that might be attributed to reform and turn it into a would-be muckraker case, ignoring the much larger problems currently accepted as part of the cost of doing business. It is likely that these barriers to reform will continue until the systemic crisis of America 2.0 comes to a head and military managers are faced with the choice of reforming their procurement radically or having no procurement at all.

**Making America Resilient.** During the Cold War, with the advent of thermonuclear weapons, civil defense came to be perceived as irrelevant. Whether or not that view was correct in the 1960s, we live in a very different world today, and civil defense, in a modernized form, should be part of America's defense profile in the years ahead. We now face decentralized threats from an increasingly diffuse group of potential enemies. The prospect of a single ten-kiloton explosion, or the release of poison gas or bioagents, in a single American city is now a more plausible scenario than an open attack by a foreign state.

The American tradition of voluntary, localized military units was extinguished by the mass mobilizations of the twentieth century, which turned the National Guard into an adjunct of the army. The older Anglo-American tradition should be revived, primarily as a precaution against terrorist attacks. These local units would rapidly report and work in cooperation with law enforcement in the event of domestic attack. They would also be skilled in responding to physical damage and casualties after the fact. These same skills and organization would also be useful for disaster relief.

State and local governments should build a "nation of first-responders" sharing training and best practices. These groups would work with advice and instruction from the military where needed, and plan to act in cooperation, but not be incorporated into the national military. This would provide an additional layer of defense in the regrettably likely event of future, large-scale terrorist attacks inside the United States. A reconfigured National Guard in each state might be part of this program. This effort would probably be inexpensive in comparison to modern weapon platforms, and may be of greater utility in the face of likely threats, including catastrophic but localized attacks.

**Fighting for Reform.** Defense and foreign policy reform will likely have several components.

The first component is to accomplish a reexamination of our foreign policy goals and strategies in light of what is achievable globally, what is beneficial to the United States, and what can serve as the binding principles of a narrower but deeper set of alliances that are maintained more consistently. We conclude that our core interest is preservation of the global commons for use by us and our allies, and that we should preserve our existing alliance structure to do it.

The second component will consist of a reexamination of the force structures, doctrine, training, and weapons systems that are necessary to accomplish the objectives of this foreign policy. The systems must be sufficient to permit the United States to deter aggression by their threat, to prevail in the event of conflict and affordable in the more constrained financial environment of the America 3.0 era. This level of analysis we do not undertake here, other than to point out that defense procurement is in desperate need of reform. Our proposed reforms are in line with the general thrust of our proposals for America 3.0.

The third component will consist of significant reform of the defense industry and weapons procurement systems of the United States and its close allies. We must save the many unique capabilities and skill sets that have emerged over our history, while addressing new threats emerging as new technology empowers it. These threats include space warfare, cyber-warfare, new biological and nanotechnological threats, and the new environment of pervasive communications and surveillance, micromachines and microdrones, and a panoply of threats barely conceivable at this moment.

The fourth component is increasing the resilience of the United States domestically to respond to and recover from disasters and attacks, including catastrophic attacks with weapons of mass destruction, or sustained campaigns of terrorism occurring within US territory. This will require local and state action as much or more than federal action.

We can sketch only the bare outlines of what an America 3.0 defense and foreign policy might be like in reality. But those policies must be consistent with what can actually be achieved by American power, with a renewed focus on securing the global commons for trade, maintaining our alliances, and defending the American free and prosperous way of life.

The one unchanging element across all iterations of America is the skill and courage of the American men and women who serve in our military. They are the ultimate shield of our freedom and prosperity.

# Bibliographic Essay

We have found only one writer who makes an argument similar to ours regarding the primacy of family structure. The first chapter of David Willetts's, *The Pinch: How the Baby Boomers Took Their Children's Future – And Why They Should Give It Back* (2010) closely tracks the argument made in this book regarding family structure and the deep roots of English and American culture, and their economic and political consequences. Mr. Willetts is one of a tiny minority who has read both Todd and Macfarlane. He is connecting the same dots we do. The authors hope that many others will soon join us in this exploration. We also note that Douglas Carswell in *The End of Politics and the Birth of iDemocracy* (2012) makes arguments and predictions regarding the rise of a new politico-economic order that are similar to our discussion of the forthcoming America 3.0.

The classic work on the problem of government in the face of the new world of big cities in the nineteenth century is James Bryce, *The American Commonwealth* (1888) (2 vols.). The best book on the rise of Chicago is by William Cronon, *Nature's Metropolis: Chicago and the Great West* (1991).

One example of a Democratic think tank admitting that entitlement spending is unsustainable is "Now or Never: The Moment for Democrats to Get a Grand Bargain" (June, 2012), published by Third Way.

The decline and destruction of the Austro-Hungarian Empire provoked an extraordinary literary response. Outstanding examples that capture the era include the memoirs of Stefan Zweig, *The World of Yesterday*, and Gregor von Rezzori, *The Snows of Yesteryear*, and the novels of Joseph Roth, *The Radetzky March,* and Robert Musil, *The Man Without*

*Qualities.* Our assertion that if World War I had not happened, or not happened when it did, the Empire might have survived is based in part on Joachim Remak, "The Healthy Invalid: How Doomed the Habsburg Empire?," *The Journal of Modern History*, Vol. 41, No 2 (Jun., 1969). Remak shows that memoirs after the fact claim that "everyone knew" the Empire was doomed. But the same authors made no such statements at the time. By 2040 people will claim that "everyone knew" in 2013 that America 2.0 was falling apart, even though very few are saying so now.

## AMERICA 2040

Our picture of 2040 is highly conservative if you believe, as we do, that Moore's Law will remain in effect. Moore's Law was first articulated by Gordon E. Moore, in 1965. "Cramming more components onto integrated circuits," *Electronics*, Vol. 38, No. 8, April 19, 1965. Available at http://download.intel.com/museum/Moores_Law/Articles-Press_Releases/Gordon_Moore_1965_Article.pdf. Moore found that the the number of transistors per square inch on integrated circuits was roughly doubling every year. Since that time, the long-term rate has been 18 months to double the capablity of integrated circuits. As a result, the cost of computational power has collapsed, as has its physical volume. Moore's Law has downstream effects on all aspects of the economy. *See* Philip Ball, "Moore's law is not just for computers," *Nature*, March 5, 2013. http://www.nature.com/news/moore-s-law-is-not-just-for-computers-1.12548 For a more aggressive depiction of the world of the future, see the works of Ray Kurzweil, *e.g. The Singularity is Near: When Humans Transcend Biology* (2006).

Works that have influenced our thinking about the future include Joel Garreau, *Edge City: Life on the New Frontier* (1988), *Radical Evolution: The Promise and Peril of Enhancing Our Minds, Our Bodies – and What It Means to Be Human* (2006), and "The Santa Fe-ing of the World," *New Geography*, May 24, 2010; Joel Kotkin, *New Geography: The New Geography: How the Digital Revolution is Reshaping the American Landscape* (2001) and his *The Next Hundred-Million: America in 2050* (2010). Joel Kotkin's blog is one of the best sources of insight about current issues and the direction the country is going, http://www.joelkotkin.com. John Robb, in his book *Brave New War: The Next Stage of Terrorism and the End of Globalization*

(2008) (Foreword by James Fallows) and on his blogs *Global Guerillas*, http://globalguerrillas.typepad.com, and *Resilient Communities*, http://www.resilientcommunities.com, has provided many valuable insights, sometimes hopeful, sometimes dystopian, but always keenly aware that the future will be very different from the world we now know. Bruce Sterling, *Tomorrow Now: Envisioning the Next Fifty Years* (2002) has interesting insights, though Sterling imagines a future quite different from our speculation. As Sterling himself put it, "nothing obsolesces like the future." And there will certainly be many surprises between now and 2040.

Glenn Reynolds, *An Army of Davids: How Markets and Technology Empower Ordinary People to Beat Big Media, Big Government, and Other Goliaths* (2007) depicts the power of network technology to create a new economic order. We agree with his conclusions and share his belief that improvements are on the way.

The term "the Big Sort" comes from Bill Bishop, *The Big Sort: Why the Clustering of Like-Minded America is Tearing Us Apart* (2009). Unlike Mr. Bishop, we do not see sorting as necessarily bad. His concern about the impossibility of finding a middle ground politically because people all live in a political and cultural echo chamber becomes less important as the role of the national government is scaled back massively. Disagreements are tolerable where diversity is tolerated.

Jonathan V. Last, "Amanda Marcotte and Making Babies," *Jonathan Last Online*, February 5, 2013, http://jonathanlast.com/2013/02/05/7699/, argues that the ideal fertility desired by Americans is well above replacement, 2.5 children per couple. The reason Americans reproduce below their preferred rate is the various burdens on parenthood, which are mainly caused by the failing 2.0 state. Last suggests reforms in "America's Baby Bust," *The Wall Street Journal* (February 2, 2013), which are consistent with our depiction of the American future, which would allow American couples to achieve their (average) ideal fertility, raising the United States once again above replacement levels of fertility, including facilitating the growth of exurban communities. Regrettably, Last's book *What to Expect When No One's Expecting: America's Coming Demographic Disaster* (2013) came out as this book was being completed.

A critically important influence on the authors' thinking about the future is Neal Stephenson's science fiction novel, *The Diamond Age, or A Young Lady's Illustrated Primer* (1995).

On the transition to self-employment from traditional jobs, *see* Ying Lowrey, "Estimating Entrepreneurial Jobs: Business Creation is Job Creation," American Economic Association Annual Meeting, 2011.


## THE AMERICAN FAMILY

Our analysis of the roots of American family life is based primarily on two related schools of historical and anthropological thought. The French school of family systems analysis is represented most recently and most thoroughly by Emmanuel Todd. His key works include: *The Explanation of Ideology: Family Structures and Social Systems* (1985) and *The Causes of Progress: Culture, Authority and Change* (1987). Todd has recently published the first of two volumes entitled *L'Origine des systèmes familiaux* (*The Origins of Family Systems*) (2011), which is currently available only in French, though the authors were able to scratch its surface with the help of Google Translate and a Francophone friend. The term "nonegalitarian" is derived from this book. Todd's work rests on older French scholars like Frédéric le Play and his successors. Todd uses the technical anthropological term Absolute Nuclear Family, which describes the family type we discuss in this book. Todd's map showing the geographical distribution of the Absolute Nuclear Family is in *Explanation of Ideology.* A remarkable later map, confirming Todd's findings, is in "Family Types and the Persistence of Regional Disparities in Europe," Gilles Duranton, Andrés Rodríguez-Poseb, and Richard Sandall, Bruges European Economic Research Paper No. 10 (2007), which is available online. The following publications employ Todd's family framework: Vicenzo Galasso and Paola Profeta, "When the State Mirrors the Family: The Design of Pension System," CESifo Working Paper No. 3191, Category 1: Public Finance, September 2010; Virginie Mamadouh, "A Political-Cultural Map of Europe: Family Structures and the Origins of Differencs Between National Political Cultures in the European Union," *GeoJournal* 47: 447–486, 1999; Konstantin Lalenis, Martin De Jong and Virginie Mamadouh, "Families of Nations and Institutional Transplantation," in De Jong, Lalenis and Mamadouth, eds. *The Theory and Practice of Institutional Transplantation* (2002); Alberto Alesina, Yann Algan, Pierre Cahuc, Paolo

Giuliano, "Family Values and the Regulation of Labor," NBER Working Paper No. 15747, Februray 2010. The findings in these papers are consistent with our analysis in this book. Avaluable essay contrasting Le Play and Alexis de Tocqueville is Pascal Tripier-Constantin, "Alexis de Tocqueville et Frédéric Le Play, les Origines d'une société libre et prospère," Institut Coppet, Paris, Arpil, 2011.

The primary British anthropologist we rely upon is Alan Macfarlane. His key works, for the purposes of this book, include: *The Origins of English Individualism* (1978), *The Culture of Capitalism* (1987), *Marriage and Love in England, 1300–1840* (1986), *The Riddle of the Modern World* (2000), *The Making of the Modern World* (2002), and *The Savage Wars of Peace: England, Japan and the Malthusian Trap* (2003). Prof. Macfarlane's most recent work, *The Invention of the Modern World* was published online as a serial by the *Fortnightly Review*, spring–summer 2012. It is not yet compiled into book form at the time of this writing. Professor Macfarlane published an essay that may be found on his website (www.alanmacfarlane.com), which is in effect a short version of his seminal work, *The Origins of English Individualism*. "The Origins of English Individualism: Some Surprises," *Theory and Society*, Volume 6, Issue 2 (Sep., 1978) is available on his website. It is a good, short primer of his thought. The historical, record-based evidence of a unique form of English individualism has been argued convincingly by Macfarlane, in the face of often harsh opposition. A response to his critics can be found in *The Culture of Capitalism* (1987). *Origins* and *Culture* show that the English were "capitalists" as far back as we have written records.

The more indirect, archeological evidence regarding the Anglo-Saxons is by Macfarlane's former professor at Oxford, James Campbell, whose key work is *The Anglo-Saxon State* (2000). We also drew on James Campbell, ed., *The Anglo-Saxons* (1982). This contains a good, short discussion of Roman Britain and its abandonment in Chapter 1. Of course, much is speculative, and the exact details of the end of Roman rule are lost to history. We also referred to Campbell's *Essays on Anglo-Saxon History* (1986). One of many sources on the contested issue of whether the Saxons physically displaced the Britons is Charlotte Russell, "The Anglo-Saxon Influence on Romano-Britain: Research Past and Present," *Durham Anthropology Journal*, Vol. 13(1) (2005), and her later-published Ph.D. thesis. Anglo-

Saxon kinship terminology emphasizing the nuclear family rather than clans is noted in John Hines, ed., *The Anglo-Saxons from the Migration Period to the Eighth Century: an Ethnographic Perspective* (1997), p. 137.

The case for English-speaking exceptionalism has been made, by comparison with the Spanish-speaking world, by Chilean-Australian historian Claudio Véliz, in *The New World of the Gothic Fox* (1994). *Gothic Fox* is a work of extraordinary erudition, handled with a deft and often humorous touch, and is really a neglected masterwork. Professor Veliz is currently working on a book provisionally entitled "The Englishness of Modernity," which we eagerly await.

For our claim that "Surveys prove that Americans have a uniquely powerful commitment to individual liberty, which they share only with the other English speaking peoples," *see* the World Values Survey, http://www.worldvaluessurvey.org, especially the "WVS Cultural Map of the World," written by Ronald Inglehard and Chris Weizel, on this site.

On American exceptionalism as embedded in cultural practices, *see* Joseph Henrich, Steven J. Heine and Ara Norenzayan, "The Weirdest People in the World?," *Behavioral and Brain Sciences* (2010) 33, 61–135, and the working paper of the same title, published by the German Data Forum (RatSWD) (April, 2010). "Americans stand out relative to Westerners on phenomena that are associated with independent self-concepts and individualism. A number of analyses, using a diverse range of methods, reveal that Americans are, on average, the most individualistic people in the world." *Id.* at 74.

James C. Bennett's *The Anglosphere Challenge: Why the English-Speaking Nations Will Lead the Way in the Twenty-First Century* (2004) and *The Third Anglosphere Century: The English-Speaking World in an Era of Transition* (2007) make arguments for English and American exceptionalism similar to this book. However, both of these works precede the authors' discovery of Emmanuel Todd. The Annotated Bibliography in *Anglosphere Challenge* supplements this one.

On the subject of the extended family in other cultures and its impact on economic development, *see* Douglass North, *Violence and Social Orders: A Conceptual Framework for Interpreting Recorded Human History* (2009). On the American "hustling" spirit, *see* Walter A. McDougall, *Freedom Just Around the Corner: A New American History, 1585–1828* (2004). On personal trust and free association, *see* Francis Fukuyama, *Trust: The Social*

*Virtues and The Creation of Prosperity* (1996). For a portrait of a society with minimal trust *see* Edward Banfield, *The Moral Basis of a Backward Society* (1958).

On the the roots of government power to regulate the economy in America, *see* Jonathan R. T. Hughes, *The Governmental Habit Redux: Economic Controls from Colonial Times to the Present* (1991). On the traditional police power of states and localities, *see* Richard Epstein, *How Progressives Rewrote the Constitution* (2007) for a summary. For an exhaustive compendium, *see* Ernst Freund, *The Police Power: Public Policy and Constitutional Rights* (1904).

The quote from George Stigler is from his essay "Director's Law of Public Income Distribution," *Journal of Law and Economics*, 13 (1970).

On animosity toward suburban life, *see* Robert Bruegemann, *Sprawl: A Compact History* (2006), which provides a historical background for suburban-type growth, and a more favorable picture of the American variant. A valuable short discussion of the rise of American suburbia, and European disdain for them, may be found in Witold Rybczynski, *City Life: Urban Expectations in a New World* (1995), with good bibliographic endnotes. The anecdote regarding Le Corbusier is in Chapter 2, from his *When the Cathedrals Were White: A Journey to the Country of Timid People* (1947). Rybczynski apparently does not see the cultural underpinnings of American suburbs, believing they arose by coincidence because of the availability of cheap land, which is only partially correct. *See also* John Archer, *Architecture and Suburbia: From English Villa to American Dream House, 1690–2000* (2006), though we place the origins of individualism and the aspiration for a single-family home about a thousand years earlier than Archer does. *See also* Joel Kotkin "The War Against Suburbia," *The American*, January 21, 2010. Also of interest is Lisa McGirr, *Suburban Warriors: The Origins of the New American Right* (2002), which shows the beginning of resistance to the A2.0 state arising in the new postwar suburbs, in this case in California.

A description of the impact of changing transportation technology on cities and the growth of suburbs may be found in Peter J. Hugill, *World Trade Since 1431: Geography, Technology, Capitalism* (1993). This book contains novel revelations on virtually every page and is highly recommended.

Regarding the features of the American character we list in our chapter on the American Family, a significant contribution has been made by Walter Russell Mead. Of particular importance is his essay "The Jacksonian Tradition" published in the Winter 1999/2000 issue of *The National Interest*. This essay became a chapter on "Jacksonian America" in his book *Special Providence: American Foreign Policy and How it Changed the World* (2002). Mead offered a short and fascinating discussion of how the Jacksonian mindset became in effect the default ideology of the American suburbs, what he calls "Crabgrass Jacksonianism." The depiction of the American suburban dweller Mead offers is similar to ours. We note also that the term "Blue Model" apparently originated with Mead. Mead's thinking, in his books and on his blog *Via Meadia*, is similar to the authors' on many points.

The Gunnar Myrdal quote is from David Hackett Fischer, *Albion's Seed: Four British Folkways in America* (1989), quoting from Gunnar Myrdal and Sissela Bok, *An American Dilemma: The Negro Problem and Modern Democracy*, Volume 1 (1954).

Our description of Americans as "non-egalitarian" is taken from Emmanuel Todd.

> England is a country with nuclear families, like Northern France, but its rules of inheritance are hazy. Since at least the sixteenth century, property has been divided freely, allocated in portions when children marry and set up house elsewhere, or distributed freely by will on the parents' death. The underlying English ideology is thus *liberal* and *non-egalitarian:* Brothers are different, as are men and peoples. The absence of *inegalitarianism*, strictly speaking, prevented the emergence in England and the Anglo-Saxon world in general of violent and absolute doctrines (e.g., Fascism) in the transition period.

This is still true.

One of the great themes in American life and literature is the immigrant family that moves to the United States, seeking a better life, and finds its children slipping away and becoming American. The novel and films of *The Godfather* by Mario Puzo are exemplary in showing this process at work.

## OUR GERMANIC INHERITANCE

A critical work in the development of the authors' thinking on the subject of cultural continuity is Fischer's *Albion's Seed*. This book was jarring to many critics, who perceived correctly that it undermined many politically correct ideas, particularly the prospect of making rapid and basic changes in American culture. Fischer responded to some of his critics in "Albion and The Critics: Further Evidence and Reflection," *William and Mary Quarterly* 48 (1991). *Albion's Seed* is truly a "must read" for anyone wishing to understand the United States, and how it got to be the way it is. A book making a similar argument to Fischer's regarding cultural continuity from an initial settlement is Wilbur Zielinsky, *Cultural Geography of the United States* (1972), which articulates a doctrine of "first effective settlement." On regional cultural differences in the United States *see* Joel Garreau, *The Nine Nations of North America* (1991). A very good book covering a later period that focuses on the cultural underpinnings of American politics is Kevin P. Phillips's *The Emerging Republican Majority* (1969), which was amazingly prescient in its day. Michael Barone's *Our Country: The Shaping of America from Roosevelt to Reagan* (1990) also focuses on regional, ethnic, and religious identity as key factors in voting behavior.

On the long-term persistence of "social capital" and its impact on economic performance in a setting outside the United States, *see* Robert D. Putnam, Robert Leonardi and Raffaella Y. Nannetti, *Making Democracy Work: Civic Traditions in Modern Italy* (1994) and Luigi Guiso, Paola Sapienza, and Luigi Zingales, "Long Term Persistence," Center on Economic Policy Research Discussion Paper 6981 (2008). Putnam et al., and Guiso et al. show that the civic life of free Italian cities centuries ago materially impact economic performance to this day. Sascha O. Becker and Ludger Woessmann, show the long-term influence of the Habsburg Empire, specifically regarding trust in government, a century after it ended, in their post "How the long-gone Habsburg Empire is still visible in Eastern European bureaucracies today," http://www.voxeu.org/article/habsburg-empire-and-long-half-life-economic-institutions (May 31, 2011).

Edward Augustus Freeman's "The English People in its Three Homes" from his book *Lectures to American Audiences* (1882) is recommended for its style and relative brevity, and as a statement of the older Victorian era view of cultural continuity. To experience Freeman in full-throated non-brevity, *see History of the Norman Conquest* (1867–1876). The quote regarding the assimilation of the Normans is from this book.

Thomas Jefferson's reference to Saxon liberties can be found in *Summary View of the Rights of British America*, 1774, and it is quoted in numerous places. Jefferson's suggestion that Hengist and Horsa be depicted on the national seal is noted in a letter from John Adams to Abigail Adams dated August 14, 1776, which is available online.

Montesquieu's *Spirit of the Laws* and Tocqueville's *Democracy in America* are canonical and need no further endorsement here. Tocqueville's lesser known later writings compiled in *Journeys to England and Ireland* are enlightening and consistent with our thesis. Alan Macfarlane has written about both Montesquieu and Tocqueville as part of his *Modern World* series, which we highly recommend.

One of many sources showing the academic repudiation of racialist Anglo-Saxonism, and throwing out the baby with the bathwater at the same time, is Hugh A. MacDougall, *Racial Myth in English History: Trojans, Teutons and Anglo-Saxons* (1982). It is typical of the thinking from a generation or two ago.

Perhaps the exemplary figure from the Victorian era is William Stubbs, an Anglican bishop as well as a historian, who wrote the massive three-volume *Constitutional History of England* (1873). While some of Stubbs' claims have not survived subsequent research, his picture of institutional continuity over many centuries has not been rebutted, and is consistent with our case. For an assessment of the merit of his work and its impact, *see* Helen Cam, "Stubbs Seventy Years After," in *Law-Finders and Law-Makers in Medieval England: Collected Studies in Legal and Constitutional History* (1962). *See also* F. W. Maitland, "William Stubbs, Bishop of Oxford," *English Historical Review*, July 1901, included in *The Collected Papers of Frederic William Maitland*, Vol. 3 (1911).

Frederic W. Maitland is generally regarded as the greatest scholar of English law. He studied the law not for its own sake, but to discover the English society revealed by its laws. As Maitland put it:

Think for a moment what lies concealed within the hard rind of legal history. Legal documents, documents of the most technical kind, are the best, often the only evidence that we have for social and economic history, for the history of morality, for the history of practical religion. Take a broad subject – the condition of the great mass of Englishmen in the later middle ages, the condition of the villagers. That might be pictured for us in all truthful detail; its political, social, economic, moral aspects might all be brought out; every tendency of progress or degradation might be traced; our supply of evidence is inexhaustible.

Maitland's writings are often highly technical, referring to terms that the uninitiated reader would have to plow through. His most famous work is the two-volume *History of English Law before the Time of Edward I* (1985), written with Sir Frederic Pollock and referred to as simply "Pollock and Maitland." A series of early lectures were compiled into *The Constitutional History of England* and published after his death. For anyone who is fascinated with the American Constitution, Maitland's deep delve back before the beginning is eye-opening and truly a "must read." Maitland's essay "A Sketch of English Legal History" is a short masterpiece and is relatively nontechnical and available in several places on the Internet. Similarly useful, and nontechnical, is Maitland's "Outlines of English Legal History, 560–1600." A good compendium of his essays is *Historical Essays*, Helen Cam, ed. (1957). Alan Macfarlane, as part of his *Modern World* series, has a short book on Maitland, entitled *F. W. Maitland and the Making of the Modern World*, which is not only a building block of Macfarlane's larger story, but also includes an excellent explanation of Maitland's life and work and its significance. The importance of Maitland's work to the history, really the pre-history, of American freedom is virtually unknown today. This situation cries out to be rectified.

In addition to the above-cited works on the Saxons, we note the following. A good, short discussion of Roman Britain and its abandonment is Chapter 1, "The End of Roman Britain," in *The Anglo-Saxons*, James Campbell, ed. (1982). An older, standard history of the Anglo-Saxons, which served as background, was Sir Frank Stenton, *Anglo-Saxon England*, 3d ed. (1971), part of *The Oxford History of England* series. There are many sources for St. Bede's writing, including *Ecclesiastical History of England*, A. M. Sellar, trans. (1907).

The quote from Frédéric le Play is from his *The Organization Labor in Accordance with Custom and the Law of the Decalogue* (1871). It is typical of European, and especially French, dislike of English culture and its style of family life. Todd's own book *After the Empire: The Breakdown of American Order* (2001) contains much of this long-standing French animus. Todd's reference to the Absolute Nuclear Family arising in opposition to Norman-imposed primogeniture is from his *L'Origine*.

The quote from François Guizot is from his *History of Civilization in Europe* (1911), from a series of lectures originally given in 1828. A different translation is available online at the Online Library of Liberty. Guizot was an excellent scholar and writer who is almost forgotten. This book and other writings by him merit a revisit, particularly regarding the decline of liberty from the medieval to the modern period.

On the "Jutes, Angles and Saxons" the only writer we have discovered who attempted to make a distinction between the different settling peoples is the nineteenth-century French anthropologist, Henri de Tourville. Tourville's book *The Growth of Modern Nations: A History of the Particularist Form of Society* (1907). Tourville provides a detailed discussion that purports to explain the origin of the English nuclear family. Tourville cites to no authority, or at least the American translation of the book does not, and we have not succeeded in obtaining a copy of the French original. Much of Tourville's writing seems frankly imaginary and even fantastical. Further, Tourville purveys racialist explanations that are obviously wrong. Nonetheless, his claim that English individualism is strictly Saxon, and originated in the lands around the fjords of Norway, is fascinating, though of course unprovable. The authors have found no other writer who claims to make a meaningful distinction between the Germanic groups that conquered England. Author Lotus, in his now-blown guise as Lexington Green, discusses Tourville in a post entitled "Do we really owe it all to the geography of the Norwegians fjords?" at http://chicagoboyz.net/archives/4725.html. This post examines Tourville's idea and related themes. Without regard to the fjords, Tourville is 100 percent correct about the critical importance of what he called the "particularist family," which is identical to the Absolute Nuclear Family.

## OUR ENGLISH INHERITANCE

The quote from Alan Macfarlane regarding the four "spheres" of life is from his *Maitland*. On the English origins of Modernity, *see also* Veliz, *Gothic Fox*. The discussion of English fertility is derived from, *inter alia*, Alan Macfarlane, *The Savage Wars of Peace: England, Japan and the Malthusian Trap* (2003). Macfarlane's *Thomas Malthus and the Making of the Modern World* (2007) is available as an e-book on his website, and it contains a detailed discussion of demographic aspects of English history.

On the "Hajnal Line," *see* John Hajnal "European Marriage Patterns in Historical Perspective," in D. V. Glass and D.E.C. Eversley, eds., *Population in History* (1965). On English people varying their fertility:

Wrigley and Schofield in their recent fundamental and revolutionary reconstruction of English demographic history from 151 to 1871, have presented a picture of substantial variation over time in rate of population growth due to variations in marriage rate, which reflected changes in age at marriage and proportions marrying. Wrigley and Schofield interpret these changes in marriage rate as a lagged response (the lag is on the order of 25–30 years) to economic changes as shown in an index of real wages.

John Hajnal, "Two Kinds of Preindustrial Household Formation Systems," *Population and Development Review*, Vol. 8, No. 3 (Sep. 1982), citing E. A. Wrigley and R. S. Schofield, *The Population History of England, 1541–1871* (1981).

On the military revolution and the survival of medieval limits on government power in England, *see* Brian M. Downing, *The Military Revolution and Political Change: Origins of Democracy and Autocracy in Early Modern Europe* (1992). On the politically correct suppression of knowledge about the medieval inheritance of freedom, and its Germanic roots, *see* David Gress, *From Plato To NATO: The Idea of the West and Its Opponents* (1998). The James Madison quote on government power is from his letter to Thomas Jefferson dated October 17, 1788. *See also* Alexander Hamilton's Federalist Paper No. 8, which tersely explains the effect of a standing army on liberty.

A good discussion of civil-military relations, especially civilian control of the military, including its English roots, is Arthur A. Ekirch, Jr., *The Civilian and the Military* (1956). Ekirch shows the long-standing American opposition to militarism, conscription, and a militarized government and economy. On the theory and practice of conscription in US history, *see* Eliot A. Cohen, *Citizens and Soldiers: The Dilemmas of Military Service* (1985).

A popular treatment of Lord Coke's life is Catherine Drinker Bowen, *The Lion and the Throne: The Life and Times of Sir Edward Coke* (1957). A brilliant but very technical discussion of the medieval limitations on royal authority is Charles Howard McIlwain, *Constitutionalism Ancient and Modern* (1947), Chapter IV, "Constitutionalism in the Middle Ages." For any reader who enjoys the "detective story" of tracing the thread of freedom back through time, this chapter is a revelation. Could the medieval legal writer Henry de Bracton have made an intentional mistranslation of a key passage in Justinian's Code, thus providing a legal basis for limitations on the king's power?

The quote from Sir Paul Vinogradoff is from his *Roman Law in Medieval Europe* (1909).

On the importance of Magna Carta and the lawyerly use of it in later political argument, *see* John Phillip Reid, *The Ancient Constitution and the Origins of Anglo-American Liberty* (2005). The quote from Leonard W. Levy is from *The Origin of the Bill of Rights* (1999). On the English legal and constitutional inheritance *see* Joyce Lee Malcolm, "Freedom and the Rule of Law: The Ingenious British Legacy" in Anthony A. Peacock, ed., *Freedom and the Rule of Law* (2010).

On local government in England *see* Edward Potts Cheyney, *The European Background of American History* (1966), chapters XIII through XVI. The reference to a county as a "country" is from Helen Cam, *Law-Finders*, chapter IX, "The Theory and Practice of Representation in Medieval England."

On the decline of local government in Europe, Guizot, in his *History of Civilization in Europe*, has this vivid passage in which he imagines a citizen of a medieval town appearing in the same town at the time of the French Revolution in 1789:

> he inquires how things are going on, what is the nature of its government, and the character of its inhabitants. He learns that there

is an authority not resident within its walls, which imposes whatever taxes it pleases to levy upon them without their consent;
which requires them to keep up a militia, and to serve in the army
without their inclination being consulted. They talk to him about
the magistrates, about the mayor and aldermen, and he is obliged
to hear that the burgesses have nothing to do with their nomination. He learns that the municipal government is not conducted
by the burgesses, but that a servant of the king, a steward living at
a distance, has the sole management of their affairs. In addition to
this, he is informed that they are prohibited from assembling to
take into consideration matters immediately concerning themselves, that the church bells have ceased to announce public meetings for such purposes.

This free and independent civic life of the towns and shires (counties) of
England, in contrast, survived.

On the Bill of Rights of 1688, *see* Maitland, *Constitutional History*. *See
also* Michael Barone, *Our First Revolution: The Remarkable British
Upheaval That Inspired America's Founding Fathers* (2007), which is a good
discussion of the Glorious Revolution and the Bill of Rights of 1688
viewed in light of the downstream impact on the USA. The recent
Supreme Court opinions referred to are *District of Columbia v. Heller*, 554
U.S. 570 (2008) and *McDonald v. Chicago*, 561 U.S. 3025 (2010). They
contain a good discussion of the attempts by the Southerners to disarm
freed slaves after the Civil War.

The subject of representative government is so immense that we cannot do much beyond point in its general direction. One excellent book on
the medieval inheritance as the source of freedom in England and American, including representative government, is M. Stanton Evans, *The
Theme is Freedom: Religion, Politics and the American Tradition* (1994).
Evans's book is too little known, and is virtually an encyclopedia on the
historical foundations of American freedom, with an excellent bibliography. It should be on the short list of books that every American conservative, and libertarian, ought to read. Maitland's *Constitutional History* is
also invaluable. A good overview of the subject is included in the text-
book by Colin Rhys Lovell, *English Constitutional and Legal History: A Survey* (1962). Lovell claims that land ownership among the Saxons was

communal until they arrived in England. Maitland disagrees. We respectfully side with Maitland.

On the subject of the medieval parliaments, and their decline in Europe, *see* Antonio Marongiu, *Medieval Parliaments: A Comparative Study* (1968), and A. R. Myers *Parliaments and Estates in Europe to 1789* (1975).

The Common Law is another limitless topic. One helpful introduction is Arthur R. Hogue, *Origins of the Common Law* (1966). A well-regarded reference is Theodore F. T. Plucknet, *A Concise History of the Common Law*, 5th ed. (1956). *Black's Law Dictionary*, 6th ed. (1990) contains numerous antiquated terms and is helpful when reading about the Common Law in earlier ages. On juries, see Patrick Devlin, *Trial by Jury* (1956). We cannot go into detail here, but Devlin shows the pure happenstance that led to the jury as we now understand it. On torture, see John H. Langbein, *Torture and the Law of Proof: Europe and England in the Ancien Régime* (1977).

On the contrast between the Common Law and the Roman-derived European Civil Law, as well as an excellent short summary of the Common Law from a foreign perspective, see René David and John E. C. Brierley, *Major Legal Systems of the World Today*, 2nd ed. (1978). These authors note that "the organizational framework" of English law is "totally different" from that the law of the "Romano-Germanic family" and that is only with "the greatest difficulty" that the Continental lawyer can understand the Common Law. Id. at 309–10. The George Orwell quote is from his essay "England, Your England."

On the operation, competency, and power of medieval English government, particularly after the Norman conquest, see Joseph Strayer's short and learned book, *On the Medieval Origins of the Modern States* (1970). Strayer is more state-centric in his focus than we are. The distinction between the "strength" and "scope" of the state is from Francis Fukuyama, *State Building: Governance and World Order in the 21st Century* (2004).

Domesday Book is covered in countless scholarly works. Maitland wrote a highly technical book on it, *Domesday Book and Beyond: Three Essays in the Early History of England* (1907). Maitland's comments on individual rather than collective ownership of property are from this book, as cited in Macfarlane's *Maitland*. The concept of frozen capital, and its liberation by clear legal title is from Hernando de Soto, *The Mystery of Capital: Why Capitalism Triumphs in the West and Fails Everywhere Else* (2000).

A discussion of the law of trusts may be found in Macfarlane's *Maitland*, including quotes from Maitland. The discussion of the law of trusts and the comparison to corporations is based on several of Maitland's works, including essays included in *Selected Essays*, H. D. Hazeltine et al., ed. (1936). On English opposition to primogeniture, *see* Joshua C. Tate, "Caregiving and the Case for Testamentary Reform" 42 *U.C. Davis Law Review* 129 (2008).

A forgotten masterpiece on the rise of religious tolerance is John Neville Figgis, *Political Thought from Gerson to Grotius: 1414–1625: Seven Studies* (1907). This book is dense and so learned that many of the references will inevitably be lost on the reader. But it is very much worth hacking-through, and it has some beautiful passages. Figgis was a friend of Lord Acton, and shared with him the unfathomable level of erudition possessed by several Victorian-era scholars, including Stubbs, Maitland, and Freeman.

Peter Ackroyd's *The Life of Thomas More* (1998) provides an almost tactile portrait of the late middle ages in England, as well as a vivid depiction of the man.

The books attributing American freedom and prosperity solely or mainly to Protestantism are a shoreless sea. Although often overstated, the contribution of Protestantism to America is beyond question, and is well described in, *inter alia*, Evans's *The Theme is Freedom*. Evans is good on the Medieval Constitutionalism embodied in the beliefs and practices of the English Protestant settlers of North America. The Second Vatican Council's Declaration on Religious Freedom is available online.

On the Royal Navy, see N. A. M. Rodger, *The Safeguard of the Sea: A Naval History of Britain, Volume 1, 660–1649* (1997) and *The Command of the Ocean: a Naval History of Britain, Volume 2, 1649–1815* (2004), with a third volume forthcoming. A very good shorter treatment is Arthur Herman, *To Rule the Waves: How the British Navy Shaped the Modern World* (2005).

## AMERICA 1.0

An excellent source for the transfer of English political and legal institutions to North America is Evans, *The Theme is Freedom*. On the transfer of English economic practices and institutions, see Jonathan R. T. Hughes,

*American Economic History*, 3d ed. (1990). This book, although packaged as a college textbook, is a masterful and clearly told tale of the rise of America. The book is now in its eighth edition, and inexpensive copies of earlier editions are available online. An excellent short summary of English influences is Hughes's essay "A World Elsewhere: The Importance of Starting English," in F.M.L. Thompson, ed., *Landowners, Capitalists and Entrepreneurs: Essays for Sir John Habakkuk* (1994).

Two old textbooks set forth the transfer of English institutions to America: S.E. Forman, *Essentials in Civil Government: A Text-Book for Use in Schools*, rev. ed. (1915), and John Fiske, *Civil Government in the United States Considered with Some Reference to its Origins* (1890). These books are clear and well-written and depict the American understanding of the origins, limits, and role of government power at the time. Both are highly recommended.

The quotations from Montesquieu and Tocqueville are from the respective books included in Alan Macfarlane's *Modern World* series, and the quote from Macfarlane is from his *Tocqueville*.

We draw on Fischer, *Albion's Seed*, for the four waves of settlement. Regarding the Scots Borderers, see George MacDonald Fraser's colorful depiction in *The Steel Bonnets: The Story of the Anglo-Scottish Border Reivers* (1971). The tale continues on this side of the Atlantic in James Webb, *Born Fighting: How the Scots-Irish Shaped America* (2005). A classic picture of backwoods America is Horace Kephart, *Our Southern Highlanders: A Narrative of Adventure In the Southern Appalachians and a Study of Life Among the Mountaineers* (1913).

On William Penn and the founding of Pennsylvania, *see* Jonathan R.T. Hughes, *The Vital Few: The Entrepreneur and American Economic Progress*, expanded ed. (1986). The quote about the Yankee farmer is from Hughes, *American Economic History*.

The discussion of New York is from the blog post by Lexington Green, "Four Centuries of Holland on the Hudson," September 12, 2005, http://chicagoboyz.net/archives/3489.html. The quote is from David Hackett Fischer, *Liberty and Freedom: A Visual History of America's Founding Ideas* (2004). A brilliant capsule history of the economy of New York City is Edward I. Gleazser, "Urban Colossus: Why Is New York America's Largest City?," FRB New York – *Economic Policy Review*, 2005, v11(2, Dec.), 7–24.

The quote from Daniel Hulsebosch is from his *Constituting Empire: New York and the Transformation of Constitutionalism in the Atlantic World, 1664–1830* (2009). The quote regarding the new principle that colonies were to be treated as equals is from Samuel Eliot Morison, Henry Steele Commager, William Edward Leuchtenburg, *The Growth of the American Republic*, 6th ed. (1969).

On an earlier generation's view of the English roots of the US Constitution in England, see C. Ellis Stevens, *Sources of the Constitution of the United States, Considered in Relation to Colonial and English History* (1894) and Hannis Taylor, *The Origin and Growth of the English Constitution, an Historical Treatise, In Which Is Drawn Out, By The Light Of The Most Recent Researches, The Gradual Development Of The English Constitutional System, And The Growth Out Of That System Of The Federal Republic Of The United States, in Two Volumes* (1899). On James Kent, see Carl F. Strychin, "The Commentaries of Chancellor James Kent and the Development of American Law," *The American Journal of Legal History*, Vol. 37, No. 4 (Oct., 1993), pp. 440–463. On the early practice of American law from the time of the first settlements, see Charles Warren, *A History of the American Bar* (1911).

The British Proclamation of 1763 can be found in Martin Ridge and Ray Allen Billington, eds., *America's Frontier Story: A Documentary History of Westward Expansion*, Reprint ed. (1980), p. 161.

On the Northwest Ordinance, *see* Jonathan R. T. Hughes, "The Northwest Ordinance in Historical Perspective," in David C. Klingman and Richard K. Vedder, ed., *Essays on the Economy of the Old Northwest* (1975), as well as Hughes' *American Economic History*, and "A World Elsewhere."

On the origin of Anglo-American gun rights, *see* Joyce Lee Malcolm, *To Keep and Bear Arms: The Origins of an Anglo-American Right* (1996). On the decline of gun rights in England, *see* Joyce Lee Malcolm, *Guns and Violence: The English Experience* (2004).

On the Yankee Diaspora, the best book we have found is *The Expansion of New England: The Spread Of New England Settlement And Institutions To The Mississippi River, 1620–1865* (1909). *See also* Stewart H. Holbrook, *The Yankee Exodus: An Account of Migration from New England* (1950).

On wheat agriculture, *see* Hugill, *World Trade*. On transportation of grain from the Midwest, and on the settlement of both North and South, and the wheat and cotton economies, see Hughes, *American Economic*

*History*, and Cronon's *Nature's Metropolis*. The authors also consulted D.W. Meinig, *The Shaping of America: A Geographical Perspective on 500 Years of History, Volume 1, Atlantic America, 1492–1800* (1986), and *Continental America, 1800–1867* (1992). The maps in the Meinig books are particularly good. On Eli Whitney, *see* Hughes, *The Vital Few*.

The *Somerset* case of 1773 ending slavery in England was ruled on by Lord Mansfield, a very influential judge who made many other important rulings in several other areas of law. In *Somerset* the court granted a writ of habeas corpus on behalf of a slave held by his owner in England. Lord Mansfield attempted to rule on a narrow basis, without establishing a clear rule with regard to the legality of slavery. Nonetheless, *Somerset* was taken by anti-slavery activists to mean that there could be no slavery in England. Because there was no written, published report of the opinion issued by Mansfield, the myth was able to overtake the more prosaic reality, and *Somerset* came to be understood as outlawing slavery in England. This complex situation is detailed in James Oldham's excellent book *The English Common Law in the Age of Mansfield* (2004).

On the Southern slave economy, *see* Hughes, *American Economic History* and Hugill, *World Trade*. On the politics of slavery, *see* William W. Freehling, *The Road to Disunion, Vol. I, Secessionists at Bay: 1776–154* (1991) and *Vol. II Secessionists Triumphant, 1854–1861* (2007). The Frederick Douglass July 4, 1852 speech is available on the Internet. The Langston Hughes quote is from his poem "Let America be America Again," in Arnold Rampersad, ed., *The Collected Poems of Langston Hughes* (1995).

On the closing of the frontier, the classic text is Frederick Jackson Turner, "The Significance of the Frontier in American History," included in Ray Allen Billington, ed., *Frontier and Section: Selected Essays of Frederick Jackson Turner* (1961). Turner is invoked as the proponent of the "frontier thesis," which asserts that settlement of the frontier as the predominant factor in American life. Turner's successors in turn rejected the deep roots of American culture, via England, in the Teutonic past. These later scholars referred disparagingly to any reference to these roots as the "germ theory," and claim that this germ theory was rebutted, using phrases like "laughed out of the room." But no actual rebuttal seems to have occurred, because since it is true, it cannot be rebutted. As is often the case, reading what the writer actually wrote shows a different picture from later, vulgar simplifications. Turner wrote:

> In the settlement of America we have to observe how European
> life entered the continent, and how America modified and devel-
> oped that life and reacted on Europe. Our early history is the study
> of European germs developing in an American environment. Too
> exclusive attention has been paid by institutional students to the
> Germanic origins, too little to the American factors.

Notably, Turner does not dispute the existence of "European germs" and
"Germanic origins" but says that too little attention has been paid to
American factors. In our day, the once unquestioned existence of these
Germanic/Teutonic-English origins has been almost forgotten. The balance Turner sought to restore has been entirely lost, though in the "opposite direction." Turner was correct about the need for balance, and later
historians are wrong to omit a major part of the story.

Further, Turner's claim that the settlement of the West involved
repeated returns to primitive conditions is not accurate. The original
trailblazers did live in primitive conditions. But as William Cronon shows
in *Nature's Metropolis*, people did not move West to operate subsistence
farms, but to participate in a larger economy, and they speculated in land
at least as much as they settled on it to stay. Further, they did not lose all
contact with their relatives, business associates, or financiers in the East.
Turner, by romanticizing the frontier, and seeking an American nation-
alist explanation for our collective character, overemphasized one part of
what actually happened.

A superb article on the transition from family farms to mechanized
agriculture, including the role of the federal government, is James C.
Malin, "Mobility and History: Reflections on the Agricultural Policies of
the United States in Relation to a Mechanized World," *Agricultural History* 17 (October 1943): 182.

An interesting study of a key feature of the America 1.0 economy, animal muscle power, is Phil Stong, *Horses and Americans* (1939). The death
of a way of life means the loss of an enormous amount of sophisticated
knowledge that cannot be recovered or appreciated by later generations.
Stong points out that America was for many years, and as late as 1939,
the horse-breeding and horse-selling powerhouse of the world, an aspect
of American economic might entirely forgotten today. He also makes a
compelling but incorrect argument for the future importance of horses in

both peace and war, which shows how hard it is to predict the economic future, but especially how wrong it is to expect a continuation of past practices to last forever.

Laura Ingalls Wilder's *Little House* books are children's classics. However, for the adult reader, they provide a vivid picture of frontier family life and work. The books are, among other things, an economic history of America as it was actually lived.

A remarkable example of the ongoing nostalgia for the themes and images of America 1.0 is the commercial for the Dodge Ram pickup truck that aired during Superbowl XLVII. The commercial featured a speech by Paul Harvey from 1971 entitled "So God Made A Farmer," with images of rural American life. This commercial captures the ongoing belief that the America of family farms and rural life is, in some inexplicable way, the "real America."

## AMERICA 2.0

First published in 1942, Thomas C. Cochran and William Miller, *The Age of Enterprise: A Social History of Industrial America*, rev. ed. (1961) is a very good book on the transformation of the industrial American economy and the peak years of America 2.0. *See also* Hughes, *American Economic History* on this period. *See* Hugill, *World Trade,* on transportation in this era. The authors also consulted D.W. Meinig, *The Shaping of America: A Geographical Perspective on 500 Years of History, Volume 3, Transcontinental America* (1998). On Eli Whitney and Andrew Carnegie, *see* Hughes, *The Vital Few.* We also referred to Robert H. Weibe, *The Search for Order, 1877–1920* (1967). On big business using regulation to preserve their monopoly power and profits, *see* Gabriel Kolko, *The Triumph of Conservatism: A Reinterpretation of American History, 1900–1916* (1977). A good overall history of the American economy is John Steele Gordon, *An Empire of Wealth: The Epic History of American Economic Power* (2004). Remarkably, Gordon only has one sentence on the Northwest Ordinance. Nonetheless, on the history of America 2.0, Gordon is very good. The leading role of Yankees in the rise of American science and technology prior to the Civil War is described in Dirk J. Struik, *Yankee Science in the Making* (1948).

On the *General Regulations for the Army* and its influence of business practices in the United States *see* Charles F. O'Connell, "The Corps of Engineers and the Rise of Modern Management," in Merritt Roe Smith, ed. *Military Enterprise and Technological Change: Perspectives on the American Experience* (1987). The role of government armories as the initial innovators in machine production and interchangeable parts is probed in detail in Otto Mayr and Otto C. Post, *Yankee Enterprise: The Rise of the American System Manufacturers* (1981), particularly the chapter "Military Entrepreneurship" by Merritt Roe Smith.

A well-illustrated history of early industrial America, the roots of America 2.0, is Brook Hindle and Steven Lubar, *Engines of Change: The American Industrial Revolution, 1790–1860* (1986). On manufacturing in this era, *see* David A. Hounshell's classic, *From the American System to Mass Production, 1800–1932: The Development of Manufacturing Technology in the United States* (1985). An excelleint supplement to Hounshell is Philip Scranton, *Endless Novelty: Specialty Production and American Industrialization, 1865–1925* (1997). Scranton shows the immense variety of business enterprises existing in this era, many of which were meant to satisfy customer desires for fashion or novelty. On the Chicago water reclamation and drainage system, *see* Joseph Gies, *Wonders of the Modern World* (1967).

The first major wave of immigration to the United States was from Ireland. On the Irish in American politics, *see* Steven P. Erie *Rainbow's End: Irish-American and the Dilemmas of Urban Machine Politics, 1840–1985* (1988). On the challenge of assimilating the first Irish immigrants in New York, *see* William J. Stern, "How Dagger John Saved New York's Irish," *City Journal* (Spring 1997).

A classic on urban conditions among the urban poor of this era is Jane Addams, *Twenty Years at Hull House* (1912).

On industry seeking federal regulation, *see* Richard Sylla, "The Progressive Era and the Political Economy of Big Government," *Critical Review*, Vol. 5, No. 4 (1992).

On the steel industry, *see* Hughes, *The Vital Few*, the chapter on Andrew Carnegie. On the steel industry and the US Navy, *see* Benjamin Franklin Cooling, *Gray Steel and Blue Water Navy: The Formative Years of America's Military-Industrial Complex, 1881–1917* (1979).

On labor unrest, *see* Louis Adamic and Jon Bekken, *Dymamite: The Story of Class Violence in America* (1931). On the labor movement, *see*

Melvyn Dubofsky, *We Shall Be All: A History of the Industrial Workers of the World* (2000).

On the formation of a new middle class, *see* Robert H. Weibe, *Self-Rule: A Cultural History of American Democracy* (1995). The creation of the America 2.0 workforce and the rise of a new kind of middle class are described in Olivier Zunz, *Making America Corporate, 1870–1920* (1990).

On the centralizing effects of the First World War, *see* Robert Higgs, *Crisis and Leviathan: Critical Episodes in the Growth of American Government* (1989). The impact of the First World War on the United States is detailed in David M. Kennedy, *Over Here: The First World War and American Society* (1980). Kennedy's Chapter 2, "The Political Economy of War: The Home Front," shows elite dissatisfaction with the "irrationality" of the free market economy. The Wilson Administration's attempt to control the war economy from Washington was a failure. Franklin D. Roosevelt was Wilson's Assistant Secretary of the Navy, and the Navy Department's de facto operational chief. FDR learned from the failure of Wilson's overly centralized, government-centric approach to war production. His own war administration took a far more cooperative and effective approach and enlisted the cooperation of big business for the war rather than fighting against it.

Hughes chapter in *The Vital Few* on Henry Ford is very good on the rise of the auto industry, as is Hounshell's chapter on the assembly line in *American System to Mass Production*. Two excellent books providing an insider's view of the rise of the auto industry are Walter P. Chrysler, *The Life of an American Workman* (1937) and Alfred P. Sloan, *My Years with General Motors* (1964). Detroit was the Silicon Valley of the era 1900–40. The discussion in Hugill, *World Trade,* of the auto industry is also illuminating, with many fascinating technical details.

On the underappreciated subject of rapid technological advance during the Great Depression, *see* Alexander J. Field "The Most Technologically Progressive Decade of the Century," *American Economic Review*, September 2003. We believe that much of our current economic malaise and persistent high unemployment is a result of similar factors. Whole categories of jobs are going away and never coming back, just as happened in the 1930s.

## THE GREAT U-TURN

A key work in our thinking about the establishment of America 2.0 and the Great U-Turn is Michael Barone, "Constitutionalism and Democracy," unpublished presentation to the Jack Miller Center Summer Institute, University of Virginia, Charlotteville, Virginia, June 23, 2010. For the politics of the era, *see* Barone's *Our Country.* Barone's essay "Can Big Government Be Rolled Back" (2012) shows the efforts to resist the expansion of the 2.0 state from 1928 to 2012. The lesson is that any such effort requires a clearly articulated program and persistence in pushing the program to enactment. The fortuitous presence of committed and knowledgeable leaders is also required, as Barone recounts it.

On the rise of the Republican Party in the South, primarily as a modernizing and suburban party, *see* Gerard Alexander, "The Myth of Racist Republicans," *The Claremont Revies of Books*, Spring 2004.

On the regulatory state, *see* Thomas K. McCraw, *Prophets of Regulation: Charles Francis Adams; Louis D. Brandeis; James M. Landis; Alfred E. Kahn* (1986). McGraw shows the Progressive beginnings of the regulatory machinery under Adams, an attempt to push toward a competitive model rather than regulated monopoly embodied in the career of Justice Brandeis, the New Deal era and later exemplified in the life of Landis, and successful deregulation of trucking and airlines led by Kahn, at the direction of Jimmy Carter. Hughes, *The Vital Few*, contains chapters on "regulatory entrepreneurship" as embodied in the career of Mary Switzer, who was instrumental in establishing a Federal role in vocational rehabilitation and served as commissioner of the Vocational Rehabilitation Agency, and Marriner Eccles, who was was a key figure in setting up the FDIC.

For a romantic picture of the rise of the labor movement, and a gritty and anecdotal depiction of its decline and fall, told from ground level by a labor lawyer in Chicago, *see* Thomas P. Geoghegan's classic, *Which Side Are You On?: Trying to Be For Labor When It's Flat On Its Back* (1991).

For the growth of the regulatory state in response to the Depression and the Second World War, *see* Higgs, *Crisis and Leviathan.* For a stirring visual portrait of industrial America at the height of its warmaking power, *see* Joshua Stoff, *Picture History of World War II American Aircraft Production* (1993). For photographs capturing something of the of the US shipbuilding effort, *see* Nicholas A. Veronico, *World War II Shipyards by the*

*Bay* (2007). A contemporary book that gives a good feel for both the scale and scope of the American war effort is John Anderson Miller, *Men and Volts at War: The Story of General Electric in World War II* (1948). The authors were only able to glance at Arthur Herman, *Freedom's Forge: How American Business Produced Victory in World War II* (2012).

To get a feel for mobilizing the United States government for World War II, nothing beats the dry pages of *The United States at War: Development and Administration of the War Program by the Federal Government* (1946). The lead author was Pendleton Herring who was the architect of the National Security Act of 1947, which created the government machinery which waged the Cold War to a successful conclusion. A good book on the management of the war by its senior commanders, and the civilian managers who built the war machine, is Eric Larrabee, *Commander in Chief: Franklin Delano Roosevelt, His Lieutenants, and Their War* (1988).

On the imminent collapse of the "Special Interest State that has shaped American life for 70 Years," *see* James V. DeLong, The Coming of the Fourth American Republic, *The American: The Online Magazine of the American Enterprise Institute*, April 21, 2009. DeLong says fourth, we say third, but who's counting? We agree that the current model is falling apart.

Mancur Olson's two most famous works show how the downward spiral into a parasitic regulatory state begins, *The Logic of Collective Action: Public Goods and the Theory of Groups* (1965), and where it ends up, *The Rise and Decline of Nations: Economic Growth, Stagflation and Social Rigidities* (1982), *see also* Jonathan Rauch, *Demosclerosis: The Silent Killer of American Government* (1994), David Cay Johnston, *Free Lunch: How the Richest Wealthiest Americans Enrich Themselves at Government Expense (And Stick You with the Bill)* (2007), Charlotte Twight, *America's Emerging Fascist Economy* (1975), and *Dependent on DC: The Rise of Federal Control over the Lives of Ordinary Americans* (2002). John Samples, *The Struggle to Limit Government: A Modern Political History* (2010) depicts the creation of the New Deal order and its progeny, the incomplete Reagan counterattack, and the Bush-Clinton reestablishment of a corporatist regime.

An excellent picture of the rise and decline of the American Big City, a 2.0 phenomenon that peaked in 1950 is Peter D. Lineman and Witold Rybczynski, "How to Save Our Shrinking Cities," *The Public Interest*, Spring 1999. It is a bracing dose of realistic anti-romanticism about American urban life.

## DOMESTIC POLICY

For an "Austrian" view of the impossibility of the United States overcoming its debt burdens ("Government bonds at today's levels represent a pool of malinvestment unequalled in global history"), *see* Martin Hutchinson, "Drowning in Malinvestment," *Asia Times*, September 19, 2012.

An excellent, recent book on the arbitrary, burdensome, and destructive federal regulatory machine is Iain Murray, *Stealing you Blind: How Government Fat Cats are Getting Rich Off of You* (2011). The title makes the book sound like a rant, but it is much more than that, making its case with both numbers and anecdotes. It also serves as a good overview of what a serious derregulatory platform must address.

On overly broad prosecutorial discretion, *see* Glenn Harlan Reynolds, "Ham Sandwich Nation: Due Process When Everything is a Crime, (January 20, 2013). Available at SSRN: http://ssrn.com/abstract=2203713 or http://dx.doi.org/10.2139/ssrn.2203713.

A "trial balloon" for treating domestic political dissent as proto-terrorism is the study published by the Combating Terrorism Center (CTC) at the United States Military Academy, entitled "Challengers from the Sidelines: Understanding America's Violent Far-Right," January 15, 2013. Mark Safranski provides a critique and analysis in his post "The Controversial CTC Report," http://chicagoboyz.net/archives/34585.html.

The term CLAD manufacturing, meaning customized, localized, additive, distributed was originated by the commenter "Mrs. Davis" on the ChicagoBoyzblog.http://chicagoboyz.net/archives/34381.html#comment-429404.

The reference to "Exit" and "Voice" is derived from Albert O. Hirschman, *Exit, Voice and Loyalty* (1970).

On Canadians and Americans moving back and forth across the border, *see* Marcus Lee Hansen, *Mingling of the Canadian and American Peoples: Volume I, Historical* (1940).

Our discussion of educational reform has been influenced by Glenn Harlan Reynolds's posts on his Instapundit blog, http://pjmedia.com/instapundit/, and his *The Higher Education Bubble* (2012) and *The K–12 Implosion* (2013).

Jay Winik's *April 1865: The Month That Saved America* (2006) begins with a survey of secession plots and threats that threatened to split

America into multiple nations from the time of the Revolution to the eve of the Civil War. Most Americans will be unfamiliar with precisely how rampant secessionism has been in American history.

## FOREIGN AND DEFENSE POLICY

Robert Kagan's *Dangerous Nation: America's Place in the World from its Earliest Days to the Dawn of the 20th Century* (2007) is a useful summary of the degree to which foreign policy and foreign military threats have shaped American consciousness and political choices from the planning to the present day. "Splendid isolation" was an unrealized ideal, not a description of reality. Walter Russell Mead's *Special Providence* is also good on the framework of American foreign policy over the country's entire history. Mead identifies four "schools" of American foreign policy, which partially overlap with Fischer's four cultural zones described in *Albion's Seed*.

There is a discussion of a "network commonwealth" in Bennett's *Anglosphere Challenge. See also* Bennett's post, "A Concert of Civilizations," explorersfoundation.org/glyphery/311.htmal, December 21, 2005.

Geoffrey Perrett's *A Country Made By War, From the Revolution to Vietnam – the Story of America's Rise to Power* (1990) is a reminder of how much of American life has been shaped by war.

On the role of the maritime power in a global system, *see* Clark G. Reynolds, "The British Strategic Inheritance in American Naval Policy, 1775–1975," in Benjamin W. Larrabee, ed., *The Atlantic World of Robert G. Albion* (1975), "'Thalassocracy' as a Historical Force," and "Reconsidering American Strategic History and Doctrines," in *History and the Sea: Essays on Maritime Strategies by Clark G. Reynolds* (1989).

On an American strategy based on "command of the commons," *see* Barry R. Posen, "Command of the Commons: The Military Foundations of US Hegemony," *International Security*, Vol. 28, No. 1 (Summer, 2003).

Jack S. Levy and William R. Thompson, "Balancing on Land and at Sea: Do States Ally against the Leading Global Power?", *International Security*, Vol. 35, No. 1 (Summer 2010) demonstrate that a maritime hegemon does not provoke a balancing alliance of other powers. This supports the argument for limiting land engagement in Eurasia in the absence of a hegemonic challenger.

The work of demographer Gunnar Heinsohn suggests that only a community with a "youth bulge" of young men can wage a sustained conflict. Low birth-rate countries are "demographically demobilized." The United States lacks the demographic capacity for sustained land combat. *See,* for example, "Youth Bulges, Violence and Development," slides for presentation dated April 2, 2008, available on the Internet.

# Acknowledgments

We would like to gratefully acknowledge the generous support of The Explorers Foundation, without which this book would not have happened.

Additionally, we would like to acknowledge previous assistance from the Anglosphere Institute and funding from the U.S. Margaret Thatcher Foundation for the research leading to the writing of this book.

Finally, we would like to thank our wives, families, friends, and associates who encouraged and assisted in many ways, including but not limited to Leif Smith and Pat Wagner for the large amount of editorial advice and review, Jonathan Gewirtz, Mark Safranski, Peter St-Andre, and Helen Szamuely for the ongoing discussion of the book's topics, James McCormick for his incisive editorial assistance, Madhu Dahiya and Nate Lauterbach for helpful comments on the manuscript, to Pascal Tripier-Constantin for his knowledge of French anthropology and for helping us understand various things written in French, to John O'Sullivan as a tireless advocate for the book, to Glenn Reynolds for graciously agreeing to write the Foreword, and to Brian Micklethwaite for pointing us to the family systems theories of Emmanuel Todd in the first place.

Finally, a special thanks to Roger Kimball for his openness to the idea of the book and his patience during the writing of it.

# Index

3-D printing, 204, 213

401(k) accounts, expropriation of, 191

abolitionists, 122, 132–133, 146
abortifacients, 8
abortion clinics, 7
abortions, 57; political conflict over, 7–8;
  surgical, 8
Absolute Nuclear Family (ANF): as
  basis of American culture, 169, 207;
  children in, 150–151; cultural assumptions, 171; development of, in reaction
  to imposing primogeniture, 79; existence of, 76; features of, 52; mobility
  of, 151; transportation across Atlantic,
  128–129; type of, 121. *See also* Nuclear
  families
acclamation, selection of ruler, 87
Ackroyd, Peter, 113
Acton, Lord John Emerich Edward,
  86–87, 88
Adams, John, 122
additive manufacturing: contributions
  to medicine, 213; in housing construction, 8–9, 12; keeping material wants
  cheap, 3; limitations of, 18; machines
  for, 4, 204–205; in undercutting sales
  taxes, 12
adopted children, genetic backgrounds
  of, 26
Afghanistan: intervention of, 218; limits
  of transformation in, 263;
  nation-building in, 184; Taliban in,

239, 252–253; warfare in, 87, 250, 262
African Americans: academic progress
  of children, 17; assess of, to economy,
  17; black majority states and, 17; Exodusters and, 229; music of, 127; rights
  of, 226; slavery and, 129–133
agrarian America, transition to industrial America, 187
agriculture, industrializing American,
  148–149
air conditioning, development of, 176–
  177
air transportation, expansion of, 176
Alamo, 215
*Albion's Seed* (Fischer), 150
alcoholism, 203
Algeria, France's colonial wars in, 155
Alinsky, Saul, 133
allodial lands, 108
Al-Qaeda, 184
Alzheimer's disease, treatment for, 213
America: back and forth movement
  between Canada and, 228; bias
  toward decentralization in, 236;
  capacity for reinvention, 235; continuity and change in, xv–xxi; continuity
  of regional cultures in, 52–53; domestic front in, xi; expropriation of
  domestic creditors by internal inflation, 190–191; future of, 1–22; hope
  for, xv; impact on the rest of the
  world, 24; individualist culture in, 1;
  institutional "iterations" of, xx; legal
  system in, as factor in assimilation, 54;

Central Treaty Organization (CENTO), 245
Chancellor's courts of equity, 110
Chapter 11 bankruptcy, 233
Charles I, King of England, 102
Chesapeake Bay: settlers of, 123–124; transportation along, 151
Chicago: boom of downtown, 11; development of, xvii; reverse of river in, 160
Chicago Drainage Canal, 160
"Chicago way," 36
children: in Absolute Nuclear Family, 150–151; academic progress of black, 17; Americanization of immigrants, 54; formation of households by adult, 28; genetic background of adopted, 26; number of, in American nuclear, 188; parents provision of financial assistance to, 27–28; parents strict equality in treatment of, 28–29
Chile, return to democracy, 243
China, 238; aging of, 216; Communism in, 248, 250–251; entry into world marketplace, 242–243; as foreign threat, xi; manufacturing in, 243; as member of Shanghai Cooperation Organization (SCO), 259; military in, 250–251; move toward political liberalization and, 251–252; nationalistic claims against Japan, 14; new manufacturing techniques in, 14; policy changes in, 14; political and economic arrangements in, 24; population growth of, 14; premodern culture in, 246; transparency and trust problems of, 195
Chinese immigrants, exclusion of, 158
Christianity, xxiii
chronological narrative, 83
Churchill, Winston, 179
circumstantial evidence, 95
cities: development of suburbs, 160; for-eign visitors to, 158–159; governance of large, as challenge, xvii; growth of, 163–164; living conditions in, 158–159; public health services in, 160; rapid rise of huge, xvii; sanitation departments in, 165; size of, 163. See also specific by name
citizens: involvement, in law enforcement, 10; relations between government and, 10
civil defense, during Cold War, 274–275
civil disputes, Common Law and, 91–94
Civil Law, 51
civil peace, 138
civil rights, 125; guarantees of, 225–227; struggle over, 70
Civil Rights Act (1964), 129, 226, 228–229
civil society, 111; English creation of, 84–85; revival of, 41, 112; strengthening of, 112
Civil War (1861–1865): Abolitionist movement leading to, 122; army rifles in, 153; build-up to, 145; bureaucracy in, 153–154; cost-benefit term of, 146; draft in, 89, 152, 159; emergence of new railroad companies after, 154–155; end of, and land sales, 147–148; expansion of federal power in, 167; growing wealth following, 159–160; Industrial America and end of, 150; industry at time of, 152; productivity rate using slave labor and, 145; replacement of soldiers in, 153; result of, 147; Southerners after, 139; western penetration of Confederate troops in, 237. See also Confederacy
Civil War Amendments, 226
Clinton, William Jefferson "Bill," 183–184, 244
closed union shop, 165
coal miners, strikes by, 164
co-determination, German policy of, 33

**America 3.0** *has been set in Kingfisher, a family of types designed by Jeremy Tankard. Frustrated by the paucity of truly well-drawn fonts for book work, Tankard set out to create a series of types that would be suitable for a wide range of text settings. Informed by a number of elegant historical precedents – the highly regarded Doves type, Monotype Barbou, and Ehrhardt among them – yet beholden to no one type in particular, Kingfisher attains a balance of formality, detail, and color that is sometimes lacking in types derived or hybridized from historical forms. The italic, designed intentionally as a complement to the roman, has much in common with earlier explorations in sloped romans like the Perpetua and Joanna italics, yet moderates the awkward elements that mar types like Van Krimpen's Romulus italic. The resulting types, modern, crisp, and handsome, are ideal for the composition of text matter at a variety of sizes, and comfortable for extended reading.* * *The display type is FF Meta, a family of types created by the renowned (and prolific) German designer, Erik Spiekermann.*

DESIGN & COMPOSITION BY CARL W. SCARBROUGH